The Gothic in Children's Literature

HAUNTING THE BORDERS

EDITED BY

ANNA JACKSON, KAREN COATS,
AND RODERICK McGILLIS

Routledge
Taylor & Francis Group
New York   London

Routledge
Taylor & Francis Group
270 Madison Avenue
New York, NY 10016

Routledge
Taylor & Francis Group
2 Park Square
Milton Park, Abingdon
Oxon OX14 4RN

© 2008 by Taylor & Francis Group, LLC
Routledge is an imprint of Taylor & Francis Group, an Informa business

Printed in the United States of America on acid-free paper
10 9 8 7 6 5 4 3 2 1

International Standard Book Number-13: 978-0-415-96036-6 (Hardcover)

Library of Congress Cataloging-in-Publication Data

The gothic in children's literature : haunting the borders / edited by Anna Jackson,
 Karen Coats, and Roderick McGillis.
  p. cm. -- (Children's literature and culture ; 43)
 Includes bibliographical references and index.
 ISBN 978-0-415-96036-6 (hardback : alk. paper)
 1. Children's stories, English--History and criticism. 2. Children's stories,
Commonwealth (English)--History and criticism. 3. Horror tales, English--History
and criticism. 4. Horror in literature. 5. Gothic revival (Literature)--Great Britain.
6. Gothic revival (Literature)--English-speaking countries. I. Jackson, Anna, 1967- II.
Coats, Karen, 1963- III. McGillis, Roderick.

PR830.C513G67 2007
823'.08729099282--dc22   2006101148

Visit the Taylor & Francis Web site at
http://www.taylorandfrancis.com

and the Routledge Web site at
http://www.routledge.com

The Gothic in Children's Literature

Children's Literature and Culture

JACK ZIPES, SERIES EDITOR

CONTENTS

SERIES EDITOR'S FOREWORD

Dedicated to furthering original research in children's literature and culture, the Children's Literature and Culture series includes monographs on individual authors and illustrators, historical examinations of different periods, literary analyses of genres, and comparative studies on literature and the mass media. The series is international in scope and is intended to encourage innovative research in children's literature with a focus on interdisciplinary methodology.

Children's literature and culture are understood in the broadest sense of the term children to encompass the period of childhood up through adolescence. Owing to the fact that the notion of childhood has changed so much since the origination of children's literature, this Routledge series is particularly concerned with transformations in children's culture and how they have affected the representation and socialization of children. While the emphasis of the series is on children's literature, all types of studies that deal with children's radio, film, television, and art are included in an endeavor to grasp the aesthetics and values of children's culture. Not only have there been momentous changes in children's culture in the last fifty years, but there have been radical shifts in the scholarship that deals with these changes. In this regard, the goal of the Children's Literature and Culture series is to enhance research in this field and, at the same time, point to new directions that bring together the best scholarly work throughout the world.

Jack Zipes

INTRODUCTION

Walk into any children's bookstore and you will note a decidedly Gothic flavor to many of the titles on display. From creepy picture books to Harry Potter to Lemony Snicket to the Spiderwick Chronicles to countless vampire series for young adult readers, fear or the pretence of fear has become a dominant mode of enjoyment in literature for young people.

The essays in this volume represent a critical response to this publishing trend in children's literature. They seek to understand its history, to thematize its expressions, and to theorize its presence and importance in children's literature.

While adult Gothic has received much critical attention, and the popularity of Gothic narratives at the turn of the millennium has been analysed in studies such as Mark Edmundson's *Nightmare on Main Street*, surprisingly little critical attention has been paid so far to Gothic children's literature. Yet in children's literature today, the Gothic is mainstream.

This movement toward children's Gothic is an extraordinary development, given that, as Dale Townshend argues in *The Haunted Nursery*, children's literature emerged as a genre largely in reaction to the popularity of the adult Gothic romance. What could be more unsuitable for child readers than Gothic romances like *The Castle of Otranto*, *The Monk*, or *The Italian*, with their focus on the perverse and the forbidden, on adult sexuality and religious doubts and heresies? Instead, the eighteenth-century child reader was directed towards educational and improving texts, such as Mary Wollstonecraft's *Original Stories from Real Life: with Conversations Calculated to Regulate the Affections and*

1

Form the Mind to Truth and Goodness. Children were expected to covet books that seasoned sound instruction with the tame delights that came from light whimsy rather than the more piquant pleasures of a good shiver.

It is difficult to see the appeal today. Children today would be more likely to enjoy the chapbook romances children used to read before a literature specifically created for children was developed, stories such as "Jack the Giant Killer," "Robin Hood," "Children in the Wood," or "Whuppity Storie." Indeed it is the stories that Enlightenment philosophers warned children against reading, such as the stories of Raw Head and Bloody Bones, that are likely to be the ones that children today would pick up first. Of course, the mere fact that Locke and others were so concerned about the prevalence of these grisly tales indicates that the children of the eighteenth century were no less likely to prefer these stories. Children, it seems, have always had a predilection for what we now categorize as the Gothic, for ghosts and goblins, hauntings and horrors, fear and the pretence of fear. As Townshend argues, this appetite was fed by their nursemaids, in part because fear effectively secures docile behaviour, and in part because the nursemaids themselves enjoyed the titillations of a good horror story. Perhaps the really strange development of the eighteenth century was the transformation of the Gothic narrative into an adult genre, when it had really belonged to children's literature all along.

Nonetheless, transformed it was, and the Gothic was soundly suppressed in children's literature in favour of morally uplifting texts that suited the desires of adults to construct an innocent child that could be trained up into a rational adult of Enlightened values. While there might always have been stories children particularly liked to read, it is usual today to recognise the marketing of books for children in the eighteenth century, usually dated back to the publication of John Newbery's *A Little Pretty Pocket Book* in 1744, as the beginnings of children's literature as a genre. This view of the modern origins of children's literature fits with an understanding that the eighteenth century saw the shift in thinking about childhood that made such literature seem necessary, with Locke and Rousseau among the first to thematize the different needs and psychology of children and make recommendations based on these beliefs. Despite their pronouncements and recommendations, however, we would do well to remember what Shavit terms the "literary polysystem" (1986: ix) in which children's literature from the beginning has existed in two forms: the acceptable and the unacceptable, or the literary and the popular. The Gothic has had a place for much of this time in the popular. It forms part of what Wordsworth called "gross and violent stimulants." It is not polite or decorous or even sophisticated in that high culture way, nor does it serve the publicly sanctioned aims of education that have always been considered an important role of children's literature.

While our understanding of childhood today can still, to some extent, be understood as inflected by Enlightenment and Romantic ideas of childhood, children's literature has changed so dramatically since the eighteenth century it is arguably a different genre altogether. Children's literature today, as a distinct genre distinguished not only by its intended audience but by stylistic and formal features, might be better dated back to the Golden Age of children's literature in the Victorian period. *Alice's Adventures in Wonderland*, originally published in 1865, arguably represents the first children's book that children today still recognise as children's literature and do in fact continue to read. Curiously, Alice disappears down a hole into a world which seems to invite exactly the same kind of psychoanalytic reading that the Gothic genre as a whole insistently calls for. All the same, *Alice in Wonderland* is not a Gothic text. Instead, the logic that is so displaced in this world, the morals and manners that are overturned, belong to the didactic texts that had been designed to take the Gothic story's place. When the genre of didactic narrative is turned back on itself, and indeed turned upside down and inside out, the result is not a return to the Gothic stories children used to read before children's literature was invented, but the beginning of a new children's literature tradition, the tradition to which all subsequent children's literature belongs. Just as the first Gothic novel, *The Castle of Otranto*, was already a pastiche and self-consciously parodic send-up of the genre that it itself established, modern children's literature too arguably begins with a pastiche of its own generic conventions. Both the Gothic and children's literature begin as genres haunted by both the future and the past.

However much the pedagogues of the day sought to expunge the Gothic from the literary imagination of children's books, it continued to seep in. The nineteenth century, for instance, saw the Gothic for young readers surface in books influenced by *Jane Eyre*. The most obvious example is Burnett's *The Secret Garden* with its haunted house and grounds. L. M. Montgomery also plays with Gothic conventions in her Emily series and some of her stand-alone novels and short stories; indeed, there are many examples of Gothic influence along the byways of writing for the young particularly by women in the latter half of the nineteenth century. Mary Molesworth, for example, domesticates this tradition, and L. T. Meade transforms the school into a haunted place.

By the late twentieth and early twenty-first centuries, the books children are reading are, as the essayists in this volume demonstrate, haunted once again by the Gothic. As Nadia Crandall and Julie Cross argue in their chapters, many contemporary texts for children are resolutely Gothic in form and substance; they invoke and parody specifically Victorian settings. Crandall locates Gothic contexts and subtexts as the controlling motifs in cyberfiction, demonstrating the similarities between the labyrinthine structures of Gothic castles and computer games, and revealing the common thematics of double consciousness, metafiction, and moral disintegration that plague both nineteenth century narratives and ultra-contemporary speculative fictions. Cross focuses her attention on the varieties of humour at play in child Gothic, from the exaggerated grotesqueries of the villains to the subtle play of parody that has been at the heart of Gothic since its inception. While few young readers can be versed in the Victorian melodrama that these texts parody, Cross argues that they nevertheless know the codes well through their familiarity with other pop-Gothic texts, including comic book narratives, television series, and films. She argues further that, rather than going over the heads of their readership, comic Gothic's use of irony and parody continues to stretch children's literary competencies.

Part of the reason for the persistence of the Gothic across centuries of children's literature must be due to the ease with which the typical Gothic chronotope can be allegorized as the mind. Though askew from the point of view of an historical present, Gothic tales often offer a sort of free-floating setting. The Gothic chronotope is often a place, very often a house, haunted by a past that remains present. As a child grows, more and more experiences, good and bad, displace into memory, forming the intricate passages where bits of his or her past get lost, only to re-emerge at unexpected times. The child's mind becomes a crowded, sometimes frustratingly inaccessible place at the same time as his or her body morphs in uncomfortable ways. As Anna Jackson and Anna Smith argue in their essays, Gothic motifs of the uncanny are particularly apt for the metaphorical exploration of the vicissitudes of adolescent identity. The uncanny emerges in the adolescent novels they explore to both highlight change and trigger it. It becomes a complex metaphor for the transition the characters undergo with respect to their place in their families and their family history. But, as Smith notes, the Gothic also offers fertile ground to explore beyond the conventions of the family to the adolescent's place in larger social and cultural constellations of identity. The results can affirm psychological models of development or they can open those models of development up to scrutiny and critique, as is evidenced in Alice Mill's reading of Garth Nix's *Seventh Tower* series. The female adolescent in particular, as explored by June Cummins, undergoes what might be referred to as "Gothic moments" in an otherwise rational life. Key moments of feminine transition—menarche, marriage, childbirth, etc., marked as they are by blood, submission, loss of a firm sense of one's former identity, and loss of control—are potentially moments that are best represented with Gothic motifs. That is, they are moments when symbols of dark labyrinthine tunnels, monstrous trolls, ghosts, wayward fluids, murder, etc. are the best symbols we have for the bodily and social changes wrought by menstruation and the possibilities it closes and opens for women's subjectivity. Contemporary heroines in otherwise non-Gothic texts do not devolve into drippy Gothic heroines after their moment, but that is part of the persistence of the Gothic through cultural change. That is, in the time when the Gothic was emerging as an important genre, medical science was just starting to replace the mystery of the female body with scientific facts; hysteria was the dominant response to sexual confusion and abuse; cultural codes were still writing marriage as a loss of power and autonomous identity for women; and pregnancy and childbirth were just downright dangerous, messy, and awful; so the losses these women suffered were more or less entrees into a more or less permanent Gothic subjectivity. In modernity, all of that has been re-scripted, but despite frontier pragmatism, the transparency of today's medically understood body, the replacement of hysteria by depression, and the new approach to having it all in the revised feminist pop culture fairy tales, there are still those fear-enshrouded moments where the archaic body reasserts itself—those moments when our new scripts fail us in the face of the mute mystery of embodiment. We are quick to regain our footing these days, though, and to respond more often than not with the laughter that mitigates Gothic horror, but the Gothic landscapes and conventions remain familiar to us because they are, to some extent, inside us.

While Gothic conventions are readily familiar to child readers who find mental analogues in their formulaic landscapes and often humorous approach to psychic horrors, children are kept interested through the constant changes made to the conventions, the new twists and surprises that are always introduced. While the chapbook romances children were reading before (and during and beyond) the eighteenth century are remarkable from today's perspective partly for how very little the stories and even the renditions of them change over time, Gothic conventions and motifs are remarkable for how rapidly and consistently they change, in form and in significance. Its landscapes and conventions change in response to cultural shifts in the fears, values, and technologies that inscribe themselves into our subjectivities. This makes it a genre, as a number of critics have commented, particularly responsive to its historical moment and cultural location.

Rose Lovell-Smith's essay on the Gothic beach in New Zealand literature discusses the importance of history in determining the significance of local landscape. The haunted history of the beach, she argues, makes it possible for the beach to take the place of Europe's ruined castles or America's haunted houses as a Gothic site in New Zealand literature. This shift in the location of the Gothic is then responsible for another whole set of changes to, and antipodean reversals of, Gothic conventions: trapdoors lead upward, not downward, houses extend into the landscape rather than open up with inner chambers, the family is not withdrawn and suspicious of strangers but dangerously free with its hospitality, the common motif of incestuous inbreeding is reversed with the family secret having to do with adultery—sexual relations inappropriately external to the family. And the cultural relocation of the Gothic genre Lovell-Smith argues is what enables Mahy to transform a genre in which "the realm of the Gothic house is the realm of the patriarch," so that the Gothic house in Mahy's *The Tricksters* is ultimately identified with, and as the possession of, the central character Harry, one of Mahy's many astonishingly powerful young heroines.

The three novels that Karen Sands-O'Connor looks at similarly relocate the Gothic away from the traditional European setting in a ruined past, and give it a colonial setting. The difference is that these novels are all written from a British perspective. Sands-O'Connor suggests that the Gothic conventions in these novels reflect cultural anxieties that remain unresolved, and that this lack of resolution is reflected in a failure on the part of these texts to satisfactorily resolve the narratives, with the best option presented to the child characters, she argues, being "to retreat, leaving destruction in their wake." Offering "little escape for these children from the hauntings of history," these novels, she argues, fail to offer the sorts of resolution offered by "traditional Gothic novels." Perhaps because the Gothic conventions are not sufficiently transformed and appropriated by a new, local tradition, the Gothic in these novels can only serve to indicate historical fault-lines and failures, but in doing so brings those fault-lines and failures in to the narratives themselves.

Children's and young adult texts have become veritable playgrounds for revising and expanding the Gothic chronotope. Indeed the children's book itself becomes a new location for the Gothic, with its intricate architecture of intertextuality and labyrinthine reference, as Rebecca-Anne Do Rozario cleverly points out. Children's Gothic thus innovates in ways other than setting and family sexual dynamics. While traditional Gothic narratives introduced the ambiguously attractive character of the hero-villain, the moral lines have always been clearly drawn. That is, the Gothic maintains that evil is undeniably evil, no matter how attractive it may be, and its corruption must be as forcefully and completely expelled as possible. Nowhere is there any suggestion that evil might simply be misunderstood, or forgivable, or in any way assimilable to everyday life as a positive force. Nor is there a suggestion that the victims of the Gothic hero-villain are in any way complicit in their fate. Though no one essay in this collection takes on the challenge of articulating an ethics of children's Gothic, several show ways in which the Gothic is managed within the texts they discuss, and in so doing reveal a range of ethical responses. One would expect that in the most traditional scenario of children's Gothic, the child characters would mimic their female counterparts in adult Gothic as the innocent, unwitting victims of an external malevolence. Their rescuers would also come from outside their ranks, and the narrative arc would produce a climactic encounter between the forces of evil and the forces of good whose denouement would include the sound expulsion of the evil that threatened them. Indeed this is the way some children's Gothic plays out, even when it has its tongue in its cheek. Most children's authors, however, such as Roald Dahl and Lemony Snicket, while preserving the child's innocence and the utter externality of the evil that threatens, innovate by giving the child some clever weapon with which to fight their attackers. James' Giant Peach, Matilda's psychic energies, and Sunny Baudelaire's efficacious bite, for instance, enable the children to put up a good fight and sometimes even roundly defeat their enemies.

Recent children's Gothic, however, reflects our culture's changing attitude toward the innocence of children, as well as what seems to be a cultural shift in our willingness to unilaterally assign blame. When ten-year-olds kill two-year-olds for kicks, when children take weapons to school and rain down death on their classmates, when they post sexy pictures of themselves on myspace.com, when they enthusiastically join in their culture's jihad, we have to revise our sense of what they know and who they are. Sure we blame the adults who shamelessly exploit them, but we also begin to experience a sense of unease about the degree to which they are complicit in their own exploitation. In keeping with a more general trend to complicate victim/abuser status, we begin, in a strange way, to dignify the child by granting him or her complex motivations that are not the results of a bland innocence. Perhaps they are not blank slates after all, or, if they are, all the protection in the world can't keep them from the tangled web of what we once located as a teratology, but might have to revise into a more nuanced understanding of what it means to be human. Laurie N. Taylor argues that these ambiguities of childhood innocence, children's need for protection, their ability to be resilient and competent in the face of adult corruption, and the relocation of the monstrous find a ready home in Goth comics, which directly challenge traditional paradigms of a neglectful and often oppressive patriarchal adult culture.

The ethical innovations of some recent children's Gothic, then, seem to hinge on children assuming at least some responsibility for the irruption of the Gothic in their worlds, and/or actively working to find a way to either ameliorate or assimilate it. Rather than seeing the Gothic as an anomalous intrusion into their lives from some external and alien force, the children in many contemporary Gothic novels court their dark side, and own it as an aspect of the self. They don't nurse any illusion that they are innocent victims in the drama in which they find themselves. Mahy's Harry, for instance, realizes that the evil and dangerous Trickster brothers are as much her creation as the gentle, good brother, and that anger and fear are useful tools in crafting a life worth living. This is a very different response to haunting than that proposed in the texts Sands-O'Connor analyzes; rather than retreat from the uncomfortable knowledge she has gained, Harry acknowledges her responsibility for bringing the evil into the world and asserts her agency in the face of it. A similar stance is taken in the texts by Neil Gaiman that Karen Coats examines. In each text, the child is in some way implicated in the appearance of the evil in her world—it is not a purely external foe. Knowing that, the characters turn to face the evil for which they are partly responsible, and work to expel it from their world. How unlike their innocent Gothic foremothers, whose stock response was flight, and whose only hope lay in rescue.

The inrushing of the Gothic into children's culture, then, speaks among other things to our social order's sense of unease with the knowingness of children and the ambiguity of victimization; were it a purely reactionary or conservative trend, however, it would respond with calls for ease or social stability, with the simple if violent expulsion of evil and the restoration of the status quo. On the other hand, by allowing for the return of the repressed, children's Gothic just might be a site for recalculation, reassessment of how things are, and hence even the disestablishment, dismantling, or at least a questioning of the status quo. The most radical texts in recent literature seek not to expulse or contain the Gothic, but rather to make a viable space for it in the topology of the human. The main character in M. T. Anderson's *Thirsty*, which Rod McGillis treats in his chapter, can't join in his culture's hatred of the monstrous, for he has discovered it within himself; either to kill himself or to accept his fate would be reactionary, whereas to find a way between those two alternatives will change his culture. Finding this middle ground is the imperative that informs the new ethics of children's Gothic.

Where, then, do we find ourselves with respect to contemporary children's Gothic? It is a genre that presents us with structural consistencies that accommodate historical change, innovations and appropriations that suit it to new anxieties, and an ethics that boldly challenges our cherished beliefs about childhood. Perhaps it is time to assess children's Gothic on its own terms, as a pure form destined for a decidedly knowing audience, who hears its parody and excess as a call to know ever more about what really haunts us. A closer look at what might be called a pure irruption of the Gothic into children's literature might help us locate its cultural and personal importance for contemporary child readers. Consider the following poem:

THE GHOUL

The gruesome ghoul, the grisly ghoul,

without the slightest noise

waits patiently beside the school

to feast on girls and boys.

He lunges fiercely through the air

as they come out to play,

then grabs a couple by the hair

and drags them far away.

He cracks their bones and snaps their backs

and squeezes out their lungs,

he chews their thumbs like candy snacks

and pulls apart their tongues.

He slices their stomachs and bites their hearts

and tears their flesh to shreds,

he swallows their toes like toasted tarts

and gobbles down their heads.

Fingers, elbows, hands and knees

and arms and legs and feet—

he eats them with delight and ease,

for every part's a treat.

And when the gruesome, grisly ghoul

has nothing left to chew,

he hurries to another school

and waits . . . perhaps for you.

(Jack Prelutsky 1976)

"The Ghoul" is one poem in a collection of Gothic poems in Jack Prelutsky's *Nightmares: Poems to Trouble Your Sleep* (illus. Arnold Lobel). This book contains a dozen poems that deal with a haunted house, a vampire, a werewolf, an ogre, a witch, a troll, a bogeyman, and other creatures that terrify. The audience for "The Ghoul" and the other poems is undoubtedly children of primary school age, say 6 to 12 years of age. In other words, both Prelutsky and his publisher assume that a poem such as "The Ghoul" will appeal to a young readership, and that it contains something purposeful for that audience. And indeed, the poem does offer an accomplished example of form, nicely capturing the familiar 4/3 beat lines of nursery rhyme, using monosyllables and two syllable words carefully, shaping alliterative lines, and rounding the poem structurally to echo the beginning in the ending. Extended paratactic sentences give the impression of anaphora—seven of the 24 lines begin with "he," and another eight begin with "and." In effect, the poem is a long list of items the ghoul will find tasty: bones, back, lungs, thumbs, tongues, stomachs, hearts, flesh, toes, heads, fingers, elbows, hands, knees, arms, legs, and feet. Seventeen items for the ghoul to chew, and then he's off to find another meal. Clearly, this poem is not intended to traumatize its young readers, but it does offer a brutal vision of little children eaten outside their school. Just as clearly, this poem indicates the connection between children and the Gothic. It takes the second most familiar place for many children— school—and posits a malevolent creature waiting just outside the doors to snag unwary children on their way outside. To put this another way, we might note that school in this poem is an uncanny place. That which is familiar now has a haunting presence. As in familiar Gothic narratives, the innocent are victims of insensitive violence. They are prey to a Gothic villain of monstrous proportions.

And without a doubt, this poem is dramatic in its delight in the ghoul's cannibalism. Whatever dreams this ghoul comes from, he haunts the schoolyard the way the bogeyman might haunt a dark wood. He is a presence that disturbs with the very sense that he is somehow real, even as we know he is a fiction. He is real because he represents something—just what this something might be is the mystery. What does he represent? Why is he lurking about the school? Where has he come from? And from what dread hand has he taken his existence? And what dread heart can withstand his presence? The ghoul is a Gothic monster because he frightens and because he transforms the familiar into the strange and threatening. The school and its yard become castle and forest of traditional Gothic, and the ghoul is the fearsome figure who just might be as close to us as our own family. The haunting here might remind us that schools can, indeed, be dangerous places.

But what makes this poem and its Gothic posturing appealing and purposeful? The appeal, of course, rests in the safe distance of reader from text. The reader or listener can experience a frisson, the pleasure of a good shiver, confident that he or she does not live in the world the poem evokes. Everyone likes a good shiver because it shakes us free of security while leaving our security intact. The appeal is the appeal of danger, beckoning us to be just a bit more daring, a bit more wild than our normal lives might allow for. The Gothic world of "The Ghoul" gives us a space for safe fear. We can safely indulge our instinct for death. "The Ghoul," too, is funny, as the Gothic often is. Typically, it achieves its humour through excess; it presents a vision ridiculous in its extremes. Just as the labyrinthine corridors, dark forests, rampant escapades of Gothic deliver location and action beyond the familiar and the contained, so too does this short poem deliver a content that spills over its 24 lines. The Gothic releases forces usually repressed; mere anarchy is loosed and contained at the same time. In Gothic, we have the return of the repressed. Our enjoyment is visceral: the cracking of bones and the snapping of backs. Parts of the body are delicious morsels, tasty tarts, and candy snacks. The appeal of the Gothic has something to do with unrestraint, transgression, and the overturning of normalcy. In "The Ghoul," the creature is a cannibal; he breaks a taboo as surely as the famous Gothic villains break various taboos. Here the delicacy, innocence, and even sanctity of little children are vulnerable to the worst abuse imaginable, and the poem ends with a turn directly to the reader. The reader too may be next. The force of this turn is not dissimilar to the force of the "jump" at the end of a jump tale. The appeal is directly *to* the reader.

Now, part of the poem's success has to do with its form and language. It moves along nicely, tripping off the tongue as easily as the ghoul might chew on a thumb or pull apart a tongue. In some way, the Gothic always relies on sound, even if this is the sound of silence, the silence that forces us to guess, to imagine, and to worry. Something waits, and waits patiently, without the slightest noise. The alliteration and the openness of the accents accentuate the silence. The only sounds this poem offers are the sounds of a body crunched and wrenched apart. Form carries the force of the Gothic horror while at the same time it deflects this force. For example, in a literary move familiar since Homer, the poem delivers a figure just when we might be overwhelmed with the horrific nature of what we are reading. In the midst of a stanza describing cracking bones, snapping backs, and squeezing lungs, we read that the ghoul chews thumbs like candy snacks, and in the next stanza while the ghoul slices stomachs, bites hearts, and shreds flesh, we read that he swallows toes like toasted tarts. The similes shift register; we might recall a story such as "Hansel and Gretel," in which two children find a cottage of candy and gingerbread and also a cannibalistic witch who intends to eat them as one of her treats. The connection between children and sweets seems appropriate, even perhaps natural. Remember what little girls are made of—sugar and spice and everything nice. Children are sweet things. Suddenly, we might notice how this poem challenges the implications of our association of children and candy. Perhaps this poem surveys territory more recently travelled by James Kincaid.

Once we establish the appeal of the poem, we might reasonably see the purpose the poem might serve. If the Gothic has any direct connection to children's literature and its history, then this is most likely to the cautionary tale, as Dale Townshend's survey of late eighteenth-century children's literature and the Gothic suggests. Whereas the appeal of the poem may be psychoanalytic, the purpose is social. Little children beware; dangers lurk in the large world, right outside your school. The poem ultimately serves to caution children against strangers; it serves to remind them of the dangers they may encounter right in their own familiar spaces. The narrator ends the poem with a direct warning. Why this warning is socially important is because it warns readers to be vigilant, to stay close to home, to remain with their friends, to avoid straying even a short way. The Gothic has this effect. It warns of the dangers mysteriously close to even the most familiar places. It reminds us that the world is not safe. It challenges the pastoral myths of childhood, replacing these with myths of darkness drawing down, creatures in the forests of the night. Reading a poem such as "The Ghoul," we might be reminded of the potential for Gothic fear and darkness in just about every story we have. For example, think of Sarah Moon's version of "Little Red Riding Hood" (2002) in which the wolf drives a large sleek black automobile, Red Riding Hood travels wet noirish city streets, and grandma's house is a sleazy hotel room. The empty bed and dishevelled sheets that confront us in the final picture of this book are a challenge. They challenge us to look boldly into this world's underbelly, to know that the underworld is not simply a metaphor, to take the hauntedness of our lives as an opportunity for strength—the strength to dream strong dreams, to capture the energy of the Gothic villain and put it to positive use. The Gothic is a paranoid mode, but only if we succumb to its fears, fears exacerbated by the violent eruptions of and against children that have so dominated the media's imagination in recent decades.

We might succumb to fear when we read "The Ghoul"; however, the parodic force of the poem works to undermine fear. The poem is overcharged, its language exaggerated to the point of humour. It might make you squirm. Arnold Lobel's illustration situates the ghoul on top of the monkey bars. He stares down at the school from the bars that are almost as high as the school itself. Three small faces peer anxiously from a window. The texture of this illustration invokes the work of Edward Gorey, and like Gorey's work, this illustration is wry. Its humour is sophisticated. The monkey bars are just inches away from the school's front steps. The compression works both to render the picture unreal and also to evoke the Gothic's Freudian work of condensation. The focus in the illustration is on eye contact between the children and the monster. He is the center of their attention and they are of his. This monster has something fascinating about him with his concentrated stare, his pointy ears, long chin, bald head, sharp nose, and devilish eyes. The ghoul is very much the Gothic villain.

Gothic villains, from Victor Frankenstein and Montrose to Count Olaf and Chet the Celestial Being, attract us because they are flamboyant and irrepressible. Their desire refuses to be contained. They are audacious, living with sublimity as a common occurrence of the everyday. They are, in that psychoanalytical sense, both ourselves and our "other." We have been thinking through a Blakean language that might see the Gothic villain as, potentially, either the Prolific or the Devourer. This figure might turn destructive and chaotic or it might offer energy for creative and constructive action. In other words, the Gothic may either deliver subversive possibility or demand the safety of conformity. In either case, it presents us with a fantasy of desire, and desire, we know, is out of reach. We can never fully conform and remain active and engaged in life unless we become automatons, and we can never fully subvert the social order without destroying our own foundation. The Gothic is a form that examines our fear of desire. In children's fiction, it often takes the form of a fantasy, as in the fantasy of the lurking ghoul. As Slavoj Žižek (2002) asserts, fantasy teaches us how to desire, and perhaps this is true of Gothic fantasies. Reading "The Ghoul" just might result in a readjustment in our desire for escape from the confines of the educational institution.

REFERENCES

Edmundson, M. (1997). *Nightmare on Main Street: Angels, Sadomasochism and the Culture of Gothic.* Cambridge, MA; London: Harvard University Press.

Moon, S. (2002). *Little Red Riding Hood.* Mankato, MN: Creative Editions.

Prelutsky, J. (1976). *Nightmares: Poems to Trouble Your Sleep.* A. Lobel (Illus.). New York: Greenwillow.

Shavit, Z. (1986). *Poetics of Children's Literature.* Athens: University of Georgia Press.

Žižek, Slavoj. (2002). *Welcome to the Desert of the Real.* London; New York: Verso.

1

THE HAUNTED NURSERY: 1764–1830

Dale Townshend

Nothing, in my opinion, can be more reprehensible than the too common practice in nurses and servants, of alarming the tender minds of children with the idle tales of hobgoblins, haunted houses, &c. the effects of which are to impress them with that timidity, which is afterwards removed with the greatest difficulty, even when advanced in life, and with minds naturally superior to such little things. Sporting with the passions is always a dangerous project, for by such imprudence the mind may be so deranged as to be incapable of ever acting again with regularity and composure. [. . .] Many from the sudden impulse of terror, have, from such wanton frolics, lost their lives; whilst others again have had their intellects so much impaired, as to be rendered miserable, and altogether disqualified for the occupations of life ever after. (Dr. Churchill, *Genuine Guide to Health*, as cited by James Plumptre in a footnote to *The Truth of the Popular Notion of Apparitions, or Ghosts, Considered by the Light of Scripture: A Sermon* [1818])

It is late 1764. *The London Chronicle or, Universal Evening Post* for December 27–29 announces the publication of a book for children entitled *The History of Little Goody Two-Shoes* by a certain Mr. Newbery. As the history of children's literature so frequently rehearses, writer, publisher, and book merchant John Newbery had opened up the market for children's fiction twenty years earlier with the publication of *A Little*

Pretty Pocket Book. But late 1764 demands attention in another respect: Horace Walpole's *The Castle of Otranto* was published in a modest edition of 500 copies on Christmas Eve of that year. For all their temporal coincidence, the differences between these two texts are salient, and not only in terms of the ages of their respective intended readerships: while Walpole had succeeded in introducing to the world of narrative fiction what the second edition of *Otranto* would term a "Gothic" taste for the supernatural (Clery 1995), Newbery subjected the apparition in *Goody Two-Shoes* to a spectacular act of exorcism.

In the inset tale, an orphaned Margery, the eponymous Goody Two-Shoes herself, attends the funeral of Lady Ducklington in the Parish Church. Long after midnight on the day of the service, the parishioners are awoken by a chilling sound of the bell inexplicably tolling in the church steeple. Unsurprisingly, their susceptible imaginations conjure up thoughts of the spectral return of the recently buried woman, for "all thought it was Lady *Ducklington's* Ghost dancing among the Bell-ropes" (Newbery 1977: 48). But of an instance of supernatural haunting, Mr. Long, the Rector, remains unconvinced, and returning to the darkened church to confirm his scepticism, he throws open its doors to reveal no ghost but the figure of Goody Two-Shoes herself. Having fallen asleep on the pew during the funeral service, she had accidentally been locked in the church, remaining there for much of the night until it occurred to her to ring the church-bells in order to alert the parishioners to her whereabouts.

Although such a version of the "explained supernatural" would not be out of place in Ann Radcliffe, *Goody Two-Shoes* takes off in a direction quite different from that of the emergent Gothic tradition in refusing, from the outset, to countenance the ghost as anything other than the figment of a foolish, irrational mind. The second section of the book undertakes a similar dismissal of superstition when the now married heroine stands fallaciously accused of witchcraft: "Mercy upon me!," the narrative voice cries out, "People stuff Children's Heads with Stories of Ghosts, Faries, Witches, and such Nonsense when they are young, and so they continue Fools all their Days" (1977: 119); "After this, my dear Children," the narrator continues, "I hope you will not believe any foolish Stories that ignorant, weak, or designing People may tell you about *Ghosts*; for the Tales of Ghosts, Witches, and Fairies, are the Frolicks of a distempered Brain. No wise Man ever saw either of them" (1765: 56). The same month in late 1764 which saw, with *Otranto*, the hard-earned admission of the ghost to the pages of popular adult romance, the spectre—or, more accurately, the mere ghost of a ghost—was expelled from the realms of respectable literature for children.

Newbery's endeavor here was informed by at least two things. First, *Goody Two-Shoes* self-consciously signals its aims to counteract the perceived effects of a particular brand of storytelling for children, pitting the virtues of print culture over the antediluvian trappings of orality in the process. At least since the early modern period, British culture had consistently associated ghosts and children with the oral tradition in storytelling, and this primarily through that most maligned and misunderstood of cultural personae: the Old Wife. Although, as Mary Chamberlain (1981) has argued, the Old Wife had originally dispensed such crucial services to her society as advice concerning pregnancy, childbirth and the administering of herbal remedies and cures, the rise of science during the early modern period served severely to de-legitimize the modes of knowledge in which she traditionally dealt. This denigration of feminine forms of knowledge fused seamlessly with a growing cultural prejudice against the belief in the existence of ghosts (Nashe 1594). Re-enacting the scientific devaluation of her medical practices, the Old Wife's orally transmitted tales of supernatural activity would become a particular object of cultural derision in Shakespeare's *Macbeth*, *The Winter's Tale*, and *The Tempest*. Lady Macbeth, for instance, dismisses her husband's horrified, somewhat feminized reactions to the appearance of Banquo's ghost as analogous to the ridiculous effects of an old woman's story of ghouls told to impressionable child-listeners at a fireside: "O, these flaws and starts / (Impostors to true fear) would well become / A woman's story at a winter's fire, / Authoris'd by her grandam" (III.iv.164–167).[1] Indeed, so pervasive had these associations between women, orality, and ghost stories become that, in 1595, George Peele would produce and publish *The Old Wife's Tale*, a short dramatic entertainment in which Madge, the eponymous old wife herself, resolves to "drive away the time with an old wife's winter's tale" (1595: 89–90). What follows is a dramatised story replete with atmospherically suggestive thunder and lightning, spirit possession, a disembodied head that rises from a well, and the unburied corpse of one Jack which issues forth a ghost.

The female storyteller recurs in contexts of closer temporal proximity to the rise of the Gothic aesthetic too, and in the *Spectator* on March 14, 1711, Joseph Addison invoked the scenario of the Old Wife, the fireside, and the child-listener as a means of launching a familiar Enlightenment critique of superstition.

> I remember last Winter there were several young Girls of the Neighbourhood sitting about the Fire with my Landlady's Daughters, and telling Stories of Spirits and Apparitions. [. . .] pretending

to read a Book that I took out of my Pocket, [I] heard several dreadful Stories of Ghosts as pale as Ashes that had stood at the Feet of a Bed, or walked over a Church-yard by Moon-light. (Clery & Miles 2000: 14–15)

Strictly speaking, of course, there is nothing inherently "Gothic" about these and other such cultural representations of the Old Wife and her dealings in terrifying tales for children, and we might only approach the back-dating of what appears to us now to be their characteristically "Gothic" concerns with scenes of horror and terror, ghosts and ghouls, death and haunting with extreme caution. As Alfred E. Longueil has pointed out, only in the late 1790s did "Gothic" assume some of the senses in which we most frequently employ it today, that is, as "a mere synonym for that grotesque, ghastly, and violently superhuman" strain in fiction (1923: 459). Even so, this oral tradition of supernatural story-telling is central to the history of the Gothic in children's literature because it assists in the reconstruction of the historical context in which the devoutly anti-oral, anti-supernatural impulses of a book like *Little Goody Two-Shoes* could play themselves out.

The philosophical underpinnings of Newbery's fiction are no less salient, for in asserting that children, having been exposed to tales of spectral activity in their youth, were likely to "continue Fools all their Days," *Goody Two Shoes* disclosed its affinities with the education theories of John Locke as outlined in *Some Thoughts Concerning Education* (1693).

The first Step to get this noble, and manly steadiness, is, what I have above mentioned, carefully to keep Children from frights of all kinds; when they are young. Let not any fearful Apprehensions be talked into them, nor terrible Objects surprize them. This often so shatters, and discomposes the Spirits; that they never recover it again; but during their whole Life, upon the first suggestion, or appearance of any terrifying Idea, are scatter'd and confounded [. . .]. (1693: 176)

As it turns out, Locke's account of the permanent and irreversible effects of fear would enjoy a particularly extended cultural afterlife, and almost one hundred years later, the same reservations would be expressed by the radical Catharine Macaulay in her *Letters on Education* (1790). Here too, the tales of the haunted nursery are said to leave their indelible traces upon even the least craven of grown men: "Many men…have confessed to me … that they could not go through a church yard in the dusk of the evening, without feeling the full weight of the stories of the nursery" (1790: 72).

Setting in place another image that would recur throughout the educational tracts of the next century, Locke anxiously sketched a scenario in which nursemaids and other servant-girls terrify into subjection the children placed in their care through horrific tales "of *Raw-Head* and *Bloody Bones*, and such other Names, as carry with them the Idea's [*sic*] of some thing terrible and hurtful, which they have reason to be afraid of, when alone, especially in the dark" (Locke 1693: 196). As Locke's characteristic concern with acts of writing and inscription phrases it, the servant girl's tales of horror imprint upon the tabula rasa of infancy a series of unfortunate yet indelible inscriptions. Conceptualized here as a faulty mechanism of discipline, the ghost is likely to engender in the child nothing more than an irrational fear of the dark, the haunted child being as far removed from the Lockean ideal of the rational Enlightened gentleman as conceivably possible. Not even Ann Radcliffe's politics of radical dissent would sufficiently dislocate the Lockean links between ghosts, superstition, and female members of the lower orders in her Gothic romances of the 1790s. In *The Mysteries of Udolpho*, for instance, the bourgeois heroine Emily St Aubert continuously disavows her own foolish predisposition towards superstition by projecting it onto her servant girl, Annette (Radcliffe 1794: 301).

Given that Locke's *Some Thoughts Concerning Education* predated Newbery and the formal rise of children's literature by approximately fifty years, the philosopher's critique of fear-inducing tales for children is aimed largely at the chapbook or penny history, a particular form of street literature that succeeded the black-letter broadside ballads of earlier periods. A mere glance at some popular titles reveals the extent to which these fictions served Enlightenment culture as the primary repository of the maligned tales of the older, unapologetically supernatural oral tradition in storytelling: *The Witch of the Woodlands*, *The History of Dr John Faustus*, *The Portsmouth Ghost*, *The Guildford Ghost*, and so on (Ashton 1992). Wordsworth's musings on chapbook illustrations in "The Excursion" (1814) provide further insight into this fictional form's almost characteristic leaning towards the horrific, the dreadful and the ghostly.

Profuse in garniture of wooden cuts

Strange and uncouth; dire faces, figures dire,

Sharp-knee'd, sharp-elbowed, and lean-ankled too,

With long and ghostly shanks – forms which once seen

Could never be forgotten! (Book I, ii, 181–44)

Again, though not Gothic in the strictest sense of the term—chapbook renditions of the supernatural, after all, lacked as an aesthetic base the *frisson* of terror imported into the Gothic through the discourse of the sublime—they nonetheless served as host to the spectre, the phantom or the apparition, one of the Gothic's most definitive elements. And despite the fact that such esteemed men of letters as Boswell, Johnson, Carlyle, Goethe, Lamb, Wordsworth, and Coleridge would all document their voracious appetite for chapbooks as children (Neuburg 1968), there is much to suggest that these flimsy fictions, together with oral tales of the supernatural, constituted an unofficial vein in children's literature of the period.

Although Andrew O'Malley (2003: 17) has usefully described the "residue" of the chapbook that persists in respectable forms of children's literature of the late eighteenth century, we might remember the frequency with which this residue became, like the ghost in *Goody Two-Shoes*, the object of a concerted expulsion. One such chapbook, *An Account of Some Imaginary Apparitions, the Effects of Fear or Fraud*, printed and sold in Dunbar, Scotland, in 1792, went so far as to include as an epigraph an anonymously penned sonnet which powerfully encapsulates the Locke-inspired resistance to the "Gothic" elements of the chapbook during the 1790s.

> Would you your tender offspring rear
>
> With minds well-form'd, devoid of fear,
>
> Ne'er let the nurse with idle tale
>
> Of Ghost their infant ears assail,
>
> Or Bug-a-boo! Or Chimney Sweep!
>
> To Terrify them into Sleep.
>
> Thus, when matur'd by rip'ning age,
>
> And brought up *n* [*sic*] the world's great stage,
>
> No midnight horrors vex the Soul
>
> Of howling dog, or hooting owl!
>
> But on they move with manly tread,
>
> Across the mansions of the dead;
>
> Or pass the ruin'd tower, where
>
> Tradition says Goblins appear. (1792: n.p.)

A distinctive pattern within eighteenth-century children's literature is beginning to reveal itself: Locke urged the reading of certain morally uplifting tracts over others of a more gruesome nature; Newbery published *Goody Two-Shoes* partly in order to counteract the effects of orally transmitted ghost stories for children; certain writers of chapbooks, such as Hannah More in her *Cheap Repository Tracts*, sought to retrieve the form from the abuses it had suffered at the hands of popular horror (More 1795–1797). Each gesture of what we would in today's critical terms identify as the "Gothic" occasions, if only negatively through the process of Kristevan abjection, was followed by the production of more respectable, culturally approved forms of literature for children. Simply put, culturally approved forms of children's literature become everything that the Gothic is not. In a ceaseless dialectic of action and reaction, the ghost is vigorously stamped out of children's literature in the same decades that witnessed the consolidation of not only the Gothic aesthetic, but a firm sense of what constituted the middle-class child, his education, and his books too.

The pattern repeats itself in clearer, more startling terms when we consider the work of three eighteenth-century women writers—Mary Wollstonecraft, Anna Laetitia Barbauld, and Maria Edgeworth—each of whom took up the pen partly in order to combat what they took to be certain worrying trends in contemporary children's fiction. In each instance, Gothic would be written out of respectable literature for children even while each writer would deem it appropriate at other points in her career to put Gothic convention to considered, distinctly adult use. Mary Wollstonecraft's *Thoughts on the Education of Daughters* (1787) had expressed its affiliations with the educational practices of Locke from the outset, railing against a childish penchant for fanciful tales of the supernatural in no uncertain terms: "They [children] are mostly fond of stories, and proper ones would improve them even while they are amused. Instead of these, their heads are filled with improbable tales, and superstitious accounts of invisible beings, which breed strange prejudices and vain fears in their minds" (10). Consequently, when Wollstonecraft turns to the writing of children's fiction in her *Original Stories from Real Life: With Conversations Calculated to Regulate the Affections and Form the Mind to Truth and Goodness* (1788), she advocates the use of Reason as a firm corrective to those superstitious faults which "ought never to have taken root in the infant mind" in the first place (359).

While these stories might occasionally be said to entertain a form of muted Gothic potential—some, more than others, include scenes of absent maternity, crumbling battlements, ruined dwellings, and horrid descriptions of French modes of imprisonment—they qualify as Gothic only in a very limited sense. Strictly speaking, they are not Gothic at all, for perhaps most tellingly, the collection is utterly devoid of a ghost: the closest Wollstonecraft's child reader gets to the spectre is in the tale of the assassin who is "haunted," and not in any supernatural sense, but merely by the mental recall of his victim's physical image (427). But when Wollstonecraft later in her career writes for young adults, Gothic conventions seem to serve her well. Having included in her anthology of appropriate reading matter for young women *The Female Reader* (1789) some of the darker moments of graveyard verse as well as John Aikin's seminal Gothic tale *Sir Bertrand, a Fragment*, Wollstonecraft would later, with the publication of *The Wrongs of Woman: or, Maria* in 1798, confidently enlist such distinctly Gothic conventions as rape, insanity, incarceration, and live burial in her exploration of the contemporary condition of women.

A similar tendency is identifiable within Anna Laetitia Barbauld's oeuvre. Although Barbauld's works for children prolifically span the period 1778–1796, her *Hymns in Prose for Children* (1781) is the best known today. In claiming that "The peculiar design of this publication is, to impress devotional feelings as early as possible on the infant mind" (Preface, v), Barbauld discloses her affinities with Locke's conceptualization of the child as tabula rasa, an impressionable wax-like surface upon which certain experiences, both positive and negative, leave their mark. Somewhat predictably, then, Gothic fear and suspense, horror and terror do not present themselves to Barbauld as plausible aesthetic alternatives, for as the writer's Lockean frame of reference had spelled out, a child, once terrified, was likely to remain irrationally susceptible to fear throughout later life. But when Barbauld writes for adults, terror is relocated from the margins of her children's fiction to assume centre stage. Though herself no writer of Gothic romance—*Sir Bertrand* constitutes an almost certain case of authorial misattribution—her essay "On the Pleasure Derived from Objects of Terror" (1773) rendered Anna Laetitia a key figure in the discourse of Gothic sublimity that runs from Edmund Burke, through James Beattie, to Ann Radcliffe and beyond. More significantly, though, Barbauld's essay turns upon a telling distinction between mature and immature, adult- and child-like experiences of sublime enjoyment: while the young might be yoked with "pale and mute attention to the frightful stories of apparitions" only through the mechanism of curiosity, it is only the imagination of the adult reader that is capable of taking its full, sublime pleasures in the enjoyment of the marvelous, the novel, and the new (Norton 2000: 283). The Gothic imagination, in these terms, becomes the sole prerogative of the adult reader.

The same may be said of Maria Edgeworth: although, in a canny transgression of paternal authority, Maria had given expression to the darker, Gothic sides to her imagination in *Castle Rackrent: An Hibernian Tale* (1800), there is nothing in, say, *The Parent's Assistant* (1796), a collection of children's stories co-written with her father Richard Lovell, that convincingly answers to either horror, terror, or Gothic supernaturalism. Like Wollstonecraft, the closest Edgeworth's representation of dead mothers, tyrannous landlords, witch-like women, and the ruined castles ever gets to the Gothic is through a form of muted, never-to-be-realized potential. Even more telling is the fact that *The Parent's Assistant* is utterly devoid of a ghost, for as the Preface assures the parent reader, "care has been taken to avoid inflaming the imagination." Instead, these stories read today like the bourgeois ideological apparatuses that they are, particularly in the emphasis they bring to bear upon industry, the dangers of an over-familiarity with servants, and the abuses to which the older, aristocratic model of entitlement lent itself.[2]

In all three writers, Gothic is excluded from children's fiction, but unproblematically engaged in the works and aesthetic essays they wrote specifically for adults. As Clara Reeve, the author of the seminal supernatural fiction *The Old English Baron* (1778), put it in *The Progress of Romance* (1785), only certain books might be "put into the hands of children with safety, and also with advantage" (101). Consequently, her list of recommended reading for children comprises the resolutely anti-supernatural impulses of writers such as Newbery, Marshal, Mrs. Barbauld, and Mrs. Trimmer, alongside the sobering precepts of juvenile history, geography, and morality (102–103).[3] Writers of Gothic romance for adults could not bring the same conventions to bear when contemplating the case of literature for children.

And yet, what seems to us now to be a perplexing case of literary double standards really serves as indisputable evidence of the shift that was occurring, in the work of Rousseau, Blake, Wordsworth, and others, in the conceptualization of childhood from the end of the eighteenth century onward: the absence of Gothic from children's literature of the period reflects childhood's recently discovered discursive and ontological peculiarity. Childhood, of course, is not without a complex discursive history of its own. As Philippe Ariès has famously and somewhat controversially argued, medieval European culture lacked a sense of childhood as a separate and distinct phase of human existence.[4] More recent studies of the history of childhood repeatedly stress that modern conceptualizations of the child locate their origins only in so recent a past as the Romantic movement of the late eighteenth century.[5]

Under the broad cultural influence of writers such as Rousseau, Blake and Wordsworth, childhood, though once a time barely distinguishable from adolescence and even adulthood, had by the beginning of the nineteenth century generally come to be perceived as a unique and distinctive phase in human existence. As Rousseau put it in *Emile, or On Education* (1762), "Nature wants children to be children before being men. [. . .] Childhood has its ways of seeing, thinking, and feeling which are proper to it" (90). The child, it was clear, could under no circumstances be fed on the rich Gothic diet of the adult reader—in Macaulay's terms, the writer, the aesthetician, and the educationalist alike ought to be particularly clear about "the difference in point of taste between the child and the adult" (1790: 51).

When, in 1798, Maria Edgeworth and Richard Lovell put forward their Locke- and Rousseau-informed views on child-rearing in *Practical Education*, their removal of Gothic from the fiction they wrote for children was given careful rationalization. If, for the Edgeworths as for others, the Associationist paradigm meant that even books of the most spotless moral intent could conceivably serve as the first chain in a metonymic slide into destruction, the sublime, the full experience of which relied on the reader's powers of unlimited associations, presented the writer of children's books with a particular difficulty.[6] Terror, too, was for the Edgeworths an inappropriate mode for children, for if, as father and daughter reasoned, the child was indeed that Rousseauean entity of original innocence, the terror-based catharsis of negative emotion was rendered entirely redundant. Consequently, it is not long before they turn their attention in *Practical Education* to the sublime terrors of the orally transmitted ghost story: "The early associations which we perhaps have formed of terror, with the ideas of apparitions, and winding sheets, and sable shrowds, should be unknown to children" (Vol. I, 140–141).

Unsurprisingly, the Edgeworths express their admiration for at least one prudent mother who scrupulously policed, and then removed with a sharp pair of scissors every offending word, line, or passage from a book prior to making it available for the perusal of her young children (Vol. II, 87). Of all such offending scenes, it was the Gothic that presented the most urgent case, and citing *verbatim* Akenside's celebration of the ghostly imagination in his poem ("Hence, finally by night / The village-matron, round the blazing hearth, / Suspends the infant-audience with her tales" *et cetera*), the Edgeworths opine that "we hear [here] only of the pleasures of the imagination, we do not recollect how dearly these pleasures must be purchased by their votaries" (Vol. I, 141). Literary expurgation, then, presents itself as the only possible alternative, for "No prudent mother," they insist, "will ever imitate this eloquent village matron, nor will she permit any beldame in the nursery to conjure up these sublime shapes, and to quell the hearts of her children with these grateful terrors" (Vol. I, 142). Exorcism of the ghost, though, depends for the Edgeworths upon a far more complex process than it did for Newbery in *Goody Two-Shoes*, and citing the examples of Perreault's Blue Beard and the story of the Hobgoblin in Berquin's *Children's Friend*, they advocate the bathetic conversion of horror into the liberating effects of humorous laughter (Vol. II, 94).

To this disqualification of the Gothic for children, Sarah Trimmer would lend her support. Trimmer's place in the history of children's literature in Britain cannot be over-emphasised, for in her attempts at confronting, sorting and taming the somewhat monstrous proliferation of books for children ever since Newbery's endeavours in the 1740s, her regular reviews of children's literature constituted much of the official Christian line on education and child-rearing in the first few decades of the nineteenth century. As the self-appointed "Guardian of Education" to Georgian culture, Trimmer ran her regular journal of that name between 1802 and 1806. Although she strongly disapproved of the Edgeworths' Rousseauean leanings, Trimmer would reiterate many of the reservations they had expressed with what was, by now, the distinctly "Gothic" elements in contemporary children's fiction. In her review of *Youthful Recreations; containing the Amusements of a Day*, for instance, her distaste for the Gothic mode is clear: "In one particular only we find ourselves at a loss to form a decided judgment. – We mean in respect to the account which is introduced of a supposed *haunted house*. To our apprehension it is advisable to omit from children's books every thing that has a tendency to excite or revive the idea of *ghosts*" (Vol. I, 267). The ghost, however, is nothing that a physical act of excision cannot cure, and in sympathy with the advice offered by the Edgeworths, Trimmer proposes that "a pair of scissars [sic] will easily rectify this error [. . .] without spoiling the book, as the story can be spared" (Vol. I, 267).

When it comes to ghosts, Trimmer is equally humorless, and not even Newbery's expulsion of the mere spectre of a spectre in *Goody Two-Shoes* was executed to her complete satisfaction. As her later review of the story put it, "We have also a very great objection to the Story of Lady Ducklington's Ghost (though extremely well told, and as well applied) for reasons we have repeatedly given" (Vol. I, 431). Within the context of Trimmer's frequently articulated repugnance to Gothic in *The Guardian of Education*, those reasons hardly needed spelling out. Once again, textual expurgation was the route to literary redemption.

Needless to say, Trimmer's own foray into children's fiction in, say, her *Fabulous Histories: Designs for the Instruction of Children, Respecting Their Treatment of Animals* (1786), leaves no space for the delights of ghostly superstition.

As the maligned objects of these and other reviews attest, there were, of course, a number of marked exceptions to this official censuring of the Gothic in children's literature of the late eighteenth and early nineteenth centuries. The Preface to Marshall's *The Wisdom of Crop the Conjuror*, for instance, flew flagrantly in the face of contemporary educational theories by insisting that the effects of ghastly fictions upon the child's mind were neither permanent nor irrevocable, but likely to be outgrown with the onset of maturity: "that which seems more injurious (the representing of hobgoblins, monsters, &c.) is as soon confuted as the other, (not ill-meant) but ill-judged opinion" (quoted in O'Malley 2003: 32).

Another such instance is Horace Walpole's own *Hieroglyphic Tales*, the collection of short narrative pieces posthumously published in *The Works of Horatio Walpole, Earl of Orford* (1798) which has hitherto barely featured in critical discussions of either "adult" versions of the Gothic or of children's literature of the period. At least two of the six stories in Walpole's collection were written, possibly as early as 1757, for a nine-year-old child by the name of Miss Caroline Campbell, the eldest daughter of Lord William Campbell who lived with her aunt the Countess of Ailesbury. Horror drips darkly from Walpole's pen, and what follows is an unsettling blend of fairytale and Gothic fictional elements, a hybrid form not unlike the famous blending in *Otranto* of the ancient romance and the modern novel. Ever-faithful to the anti-Catholic sentiments of the Gothic, one of the stories in *Hieroglyphic Tales* concerns an Archbishop who, having mistaken it for a brandied peach, cannibalizes a human fetus preserved in a jar, and who later, having been promoted to the office of Pope, bears a son through an incestuous relationship with his own sister. When Walpole writes Gothic for children, he does so in terms that would make Monk Lewis blush.

More disturbing, though, is the Evangelical tradition in children's writing epitomised by Isaac Watts's *Divine Songs, Attempted in Easy Language for the Use of Children* (1715), a form of religious writing for young readers in which excruciating scenes of horror and terror, often more graphic than those utilised in self-consciously Gothic fictions, received frequent—though not entirely uncontested—utilisation. Although Watts, following Locke, had later criticised horror and terror as appropriate modes for children in his educational tract *The Improvement of the Mind* (1782), his *Divine Songs* sternly delivered a form of hell and brimfire theology informed by a sense of the child's innate wickedness. Indeed, Watts's identification with the tradition of religious dissent implied, in part, his subscription to what Colin Heywood (2001: 33) and others have referred to as an Augustinian conceptualization of childhood: the child as heir to the doctrine of Original Sin, or childhood as the utterly depraved receptacle to the transgressions of countless former generations. Already, the Gothic overtones to Augustinian theology are striking: as the bogus editor of *Otranto* put it, Walpole's tale was based upon the moral that "the sins of the fathers are visited on their children to the third and fourth generation" (Walpole 1764: 41). In Isaac Watts, consequently, the Gospel of Mark's divine injunction to "Suffer the little children" becomes disturbingly literal. Infant mortality, in fact, is celebrated in Watts's *Songs* far more frequently than life, and within the context of repeatedly recurring images of graves, shade, darkness, hell fire, torture, punishment, and eternal damnation, the resurrection of the Christ figures more as a vampiric return of the undead than any triumphant vanquishing of sin: "Behold him rising from the grave; / Behold him raised on high: / He pleads his merit there to save / Transgression doom'd to die" (Song III). If the ghost was to be admitted to children's literature at all, it had to be Holy in origin, intention and effect, for following Locke (1693: 246), Watts had been keen in his educational tracts to discriminate between positive and negative manifestations of supernatural activity.

Mrs. Sherwood's *Fairchild Family* in three parts (1818–1847), too, enlisted Augustinian conceptualisations of childhood in the work of Evangelical moralising, making use of Gothic conventions as poignant as those of a Lewis or a Maturin in the process. In one famous episode, the three young Fairchild children are made to sit beneath a gibbet containing the putrefying corpse of a fratricide in order to underline the father's lesson concerning the importance of amicable sibling relations. Gothic horror as poignant as that evoked in the description of the rotting corpse of Agnes's baby in *The Monk* is employed as a technique of moral instruction. Indeed, so close did these moral writers stray to the Gothic mode that subsequent editions of *The Fairchild Family*, in what appears to be an application of Edgeworthian advice, elided this particular scene, replacing it with a rewritten ending and an altogether less punitive morality. Sarah Trimmer too, in characteristic fashion, would protest against the manifold "horrors" depicted in much religious children's literature of her day, citing an extract about a mischievous boy whose buried corpse was worried by birds from Mr. Pratt's *Pity's Gift* (1802: 305–306) as the epitome of misguided fictional convention. While British culture officially barred the Gothic from literature for children, the Evangelical tradition had employed tropes and techniques remarkably Gothic in nature in the production of tracts and fictions for the young.[7]

In the final decades of the eighteenth century, though, the anti-Gothic sentiments expressed by the Edgeworths, Sarah Trimmer, and Catharine Macaulay would be interrogated, resisted, and thoroughly revised. Although Rousseau was no champion of the childhood reading—Rousseauean educational ideals involve more the child's muscular, sensuous engagement with the natural world than any disciplined appreciation of the printed word—the philosopher's emphasis in *Emile* upon childhood as the "sleep of reason" unwittingly did much work in the Gothic's favor. And while Locke had cautioned against the effects of the child's exposure to the nursemaid's ghostly tales, Rousseau had advocated the child's gradual and deliberate exposure to all objects of fear. Rousseau undertakes a strategic inversion of Locke's argument in order to claim that it is parental *failure* to expose the infant to objects of terror that renders the individual fearful throughout later adult life. The program of systematic desensitization that ensues pertains for Rousseau no less to the gradual exposure of the child to threatening creatures of the natural world than it does to his fear of the dark, an irrational terror which, for Locke, was largely instilled in him through the harrowing tales of the haunted nursery. Rousseau's point in *Emile* (1762) is the very opposite.

> Accustomed to having a good footing in darkness, practiced at handling with ease all surrounding bodies, his feet and hands will lead him without difficulty in the deepest darkness. His imagination, full of the nocturnal games of his youth, will be loath to turn to frightening objects. If he believes he hears bursts of laughter, instead of belonging to sprites they will be those of his old comrades. If an assemblage appears, it will not be for him the witches' sabbath but his governor's room. The night, recalling to him only gay ideas, will never be frightening for him. Instead of fearing it, he will like it. (137)

With the educational impact of Rousseau, the door of the haunted nursery had been prized open on rusty hinges.

To these philosophical murmurings, British Romantic writers, essayists, and poets would be quick to respond. Wordsworth's defense of imaginative, even ghostly stories for children in book five of *The Prelude* (1799–1805) is well known. In the 1850 version of the poem, Wordsworth would at once disclose his voracious appetite for chapbooks as a child, while nostalgically recalling a lost era of reading in which the energy of the imagination was given unlimited, somewhat magical reign: "Oh! give us once again the wishing cap / Of Fortunatus, and the invisible coat / Of Jack the Giant-killer, Robin Hood, / And Sabra in the forest with St. George!" (Book V, 341–344). Although Alan Richardson has argued that these lines mask Wordsworth's inherently conservative aim to nurture the minds of children upon fanciful tales of innocuous political content (1994: 123), they also serve as testament to the definite shift in educational priorities occasioned by the rise of high poetic Romanticism. Indeed, echoing Rousseau, Wordsworth argued that his youthful unrestrained wanderings in the dark forests of romance had enabled him to withstand the potentially annihilating effects of horror when confronted with the corpse of the drowned man on the shores of Esthwaite's lake (Book V, 448–455).

As Summerfield (1984: 200) has argued, William Godwin provides a defense of the unfettered, ghostly imagination under the nom de plume of William Scolfield. While railing against the Gothic trash of the circulating libraries in his stinging review of *The Monk* in the *Critical Review* (1797), or later in that damming footnote in *Biographia Literaria* (1817), Coleridge would variously document his support for imaginative, even sublime forms of fictional entertainment for children across his letters and public lectures. In a lecture delivered at Bristol in 1795, for instance, Coleridge criticized the heavy, unimaginative moralizing of a children's writer such as Maria Edgeworth, and promoted, like Wordsworth, the highly imaginative forays of popular chapbooks and romances. Clearly, the earlier terms established in the work of Wollstonecraft, Barbauld and Edgeworth have been fundamentally reversed: with Romanticism, the Gothic is abjected from the poetic realm of high art, but hastily reconfigured, even in the work of the Romantic poets themselves, as the stuff of juvenilia.[8]

Always the sure sign of intense imaginative engagement, Gothic curiously becomes with Romanticism an appropriate mode for children while being denounced as a dangerous and aesthetically inferior form for adults. Wordsworth, in the 1802 Preface to *Lyrical Ballads*, is perhaps the best example of this paradox: while celebrating the ghastly reading matter of his own boyhood, he also inveighs against the "thirst after outrageous stimulation" occasioned by "frantic novels, sickly and stupid German tragedies, and deluges of idle and extravagant stories in verse" written in the Gothic mode (cited in Wu 1998: 359).

Shelley had similarly expressed his childish self's passionate invocation of the ghost, in all the ecstasies of terror, during his celebration of the powers of the sublime and the beautiful in the "Hymn to Intellectual Beauty" (1816): "While yet a boy I sought for ghosts, and sped / Through many a listening chamber, cave and ruin / And starlight wood, with fearful steps pursuing / Hopes of high talk with the departed dead" (V, 49–52). The haunted boyhood, in fact, becomes a central preoccupa- tion in the work of Coleridge, Wordsworth, Byron, Shelley, Scott, and others, but unlike the negative connotations it had received in Locke, the haunted child serves the Romantics as the epitome of imaginative engagement, the nostalgic recollection of the young poet's heightened sensitivity to both the natural and supernatural worlds.

Arguing against Locke's sense of the child as tabula rasa negli- gently inscribed upon by the servant girl's ghostly tales, Charles Lamb in his 1821 essay, "Witches, and Other Night Fears," would assert the Romantic notion of the child as a labyrinth of spectral terror even at its pre-linguistic origins. If the child is always, already haunted, it is of little or no consequence whether he is exposed to the tales of the haunted nursery or not. Rather, and as Lamb argues, all that these books might provide is a particular focus for the child's innate reserve of terror: "It is not book, or picture, or the stories of foolish servants, which create these terrors in children. They can at most but give them a direction" (Vol. II, 68). In this sense, the effects of ghostly tales are more positive than negative, and as in Wordsworth and Coleridge, and later Mary Shelley, Lamb turns the intense imaginative engagement of his own haunted childhood into the object of extreme Romantic nostalgia (Vol. II, 67). Contrasting his experience as a six-year-old child of a panto- mime entitled *Lun's Ghost* with his later, adult experience of the same piece, he mourns the loss of his intense, somewhat enchanted responses to the dramatic procession of "grotesque Gothic heads" (Vol II, 99).

The views advanced by Lamb in 1821 had already informed the sib- lings' collaborative literary endeavors for children as early as *Tales from Shakespear* [sic] of 1807. With Mary producing renditions of comedies such as *The Tempest* and *A Midsummer Night's Dream*, Charles's atten- tions were devoted to the more masculine challenges of tragedy: *King Lear, Macbeth* and *Hamlet*. When taken as a whole, the collection proves to be a radical intervention into the field of children's fiction: within a context characterized by the extreme censuring of supernatural fiction for the young, *Tales from Shakespear* [sic] succeeded in introducing to children's literature the two strands of Gothic that had been delineated by Nathan Drake in his *Literary Hours; Or Sketches Critical, Narra- tive, and Poetical* (1804): the fairies, sprites, witches, and goblins of the so-called "sportive Gothic," and the ghostly hauntings and spectral visitations of the "terrible Gothic" (Kliger 1952: 235–236). Seemingly, the Lambs well understood that, if the ghost was to be admitted to the pages of children's literature, this could only be achieved through the employment of Shakespeare as its medium. In Lamb's version of

Hamlet, Horatio and the soldiers' account of the spectre's appearance upon the castle's battlements is said to be "too consistent and agreeing with itself to disbelieve" (Vol. III, 173), and far from banishing, as Newbery had done, their accounts as the stuff of superstitious nonsense, the young prince engages the ghost of his murdered father in the most spine-chilling of encounters. Supernatural terror is the aesthetic response that Lamb most wishes to elicit: "The terror which the sight of the ghost had left upon the senses of Hamlet, he being weak and dispirited before, almost unhinged his mind, and drove him beside his reason" (Vol. III, 175).

A similar sense applies to *The Family Shakespeare*, the selection of Shakespeare plays intended for "young readers" and their parents and expurgated by the siblings Harriet and Thomas Bowdler in 1807 (Preface, vii). The Preface to the anonymous first edition of 1807 recalls the language of expurgation or even literal defacement employed by Trimmer and the Edgeworths: while some original passages are described as being "wholly omitted," others are "rendered unexceptionable by a very little alteration" (vi). However, what makes this edition so different from the work of contemporary expurgators is the Bowdlers' refusal to subject Shakespeare's supernaturalism to any process of revision, elision, or excision; as in the Lambs' *Tales*, *The Family Shakespeare* radically conserves the role and provenance of Ariel in *The Tempest*, the fairies in *A Midsummer Night's Dream*, Caesar's spirit in *Julius Caesar*, the witches and the ghost of Banquo in *Macbeth*, and the spectre of the old King in *Hamlet*.

Drake's "sportive" and the "terrible" Gothic come into their own across selected aspects of the Shakespearean oeuvre. Here, too, it is the armor-like protection afforded by the emergent myth of Bardology that protects the ghost from any likely act of expurgation. The Preface to *The Family Shakespeare* even makes an oblique attempt at justifying its bold inclusion of the spectre in a work specifically intended for young readers by invoking the authority of Elizabeth Montagu, the "author of that elegant essay, in which SHAKESPEARE is vindicated from the illiberal attacks of VOLTAIRE" (Preface, vi). This constitutes more than just a respectful acknowledgment of the famous blue-stocking and Thomas Bowdler's long-time friend, for in her well-known essay "On the Praeternatural Beings" (1769), Montagu had argued, against the tide of cultural prejudice, for the centrality of the supernatural to Shakespeare, "our Gothic bard": "Ghosts, fairies, goblins, elves, were as propitious, were as assistant to Shakespear [*sic*], and gave as much of the sublime, and of the marvellous, to his fictions, as nymphs, satyrs, fawns, and even triple Geryon, to the works of ancient bards" (Clery & Miles 2000: 34).

Tales from Shakespear [sic] was an immediate success; responses to *The Family Shakespeare* were far more mixed and guarded: while one admirer regarded such a "*castrated* version" of Shakespeare's plays as desirable, others felt that the "mutilations" effected upon the Bard were both inappropriate and unnecessary (Perrin 1970: 75). A review of the first edition in *The Christian Observer* of 1808 felt that the expurgation was not thorough enough—a sentiment echoed amidst great equivocation and ambivalence by the Reverend James Plumptre in his *Four Discourses on Subjects Relating to the Amusement of the Stage* (1809). James Plumptre's own views, expressed later in one of his published sermons, *The Truth of the Popular Notion of Apparitions, or Ghosts, Considered by the Light of Scripture* (1818), provide insight into why several contemporaries, including Plumptre himself, curiously regarded Bowdlers' Shakespeare as insufficiently bowdlerized. Somewhat predictably, Plumptre's attempts at refuting the popular belief in ghosts in this sermon turns to the case of Shakespeare, and the vogue that the Bard is enjoying currently in British culture. Conceding, on the one hand, that "There is much less belief in Apparitions, in this enlightened age and country, than when our great dramatic poet (Shakespeare) wrote," he also regretfully observes that "yet I cannot but think, that much of the belief which at present prevails, is owing to his representations which still keep possession of the stage" (1818: 14). Plumptre's attention turns directly to the case of children, and he rehearses the Lockean terms of the debate: "Much of this belief [in ghosts] too is kept up by the ignorance and superstition of those who are appointed to the care of children; and a belief in the fearful tales of the nursery is with much difficulty, if at all, to be rooted out in the minds of most by reason and revelation in their riper years" (1818: 14–15). It would seem that, with regards to the Gothic in children's literature, old habits die hard.

Despite the climate of attenuated but ongoing resistance to ghost stories for children in the first two decades of the nineteenth century, Eleanor Sleath published *Glenowen, Or The Fairy Palace* in 1815. This highly imaginative fiction for children vacillates deftly between Gothic in its lighter and darker, sportive and terrible manifestations; suggestions of ghosts and hauntings effortlessly combine with a celebration of the fanciful powers of the unfettered imagination. The point to be made, though, is that, with Sleath, the earlier tendency in Wollstonecraft, Barbauld, and Edgeworth to reserve the Gothic exclusively for adult readers is no longer in operation: as the writer of three-volume Gothic romances such as *The Orphan of the Rhine* (1798), the Gothic mode informs those aspects of Sleath's oeuvre intended for adult and child reader alike. Still, the Gothic in children's literature would long remain the object of extreme cultural concern.

At the instigation of Lord Brougham, the Society for the Diffusion of Useful Knowledge was founded in London in 1826, an institution which sought to control the reading habits of the working classes through mediating between publishers, writers, and readers themselves. While commissioning works deemed "useful" by the growing utilitarian spirit of the age (encyclopedia, maps, agricultural information, and so forth), the Secretary Thomas Coates, in his opening address to the other members of the committee on 28 May 1829, made it quite clear that the eradication of the Gothic in children's literature constituted one of the Society's most important aims: "The tales of horror so constantly taught," Coates emphasized, "belong to a worse class—their bad effects upon individual happiness and character can hardly be exaggerated. To remedy this serious evil, and greatly to multiply the few good and wholesome books now in use for children—amongst which Mrs. Barbauld's, Dr. Aikins and especially Miss Edgeworth's occupy the first rank—is one of the objects to which the attention of the Committee is directed" (1829: 37). In seeking to revive the fictional tradition of Barbauld, Aikins, and Edgeworth, the Society's anti-Gothic imperatives are clear.[9]

In the *Edinburgh Review* for January–May 1828, too, an anonymous reviewer quoted the Society's objectives regarding Gothic tales for children, deeming them to be "the soundest doctrines, clearly and strongly stated" (1829: 129). But the Society collapsed in 1848, and if this was not enough to signal its ultimate failure, a pantomime version of *Otranto* entitled *Harlequin and the Giant Helmet* had opened on 26 December 1840 at the Theatre Royal, Convent Garden, to the delight of child and adult audiences alike. Though the script for the piece was never printed, what does survive is Gilbert Abbott A'Beckett's cognate drama *The Castle of Otranto: A Romantic Extravaganza*, a theatrical adaptation of Walpole's fiction that was first performed in April 1848, the same year of the Society's dissolution. Dancing on the grave of the Society for the Diffusion of Useful Knowledge, the pantomime softened the Walpolean blows of incestuous horror and supernatural terror through the humor-inducing effects of rhyming doggerel verse. A mere 80 minutes in duration, this theatrical piece was eminently suited to a young audience. Hereafter, though, the restless spirit of the haunted nursery would have to lie silently in wait for later and so occasional a writer of ghostly stories for children as Charles Dickens for the renewal of its dark energies and the reinvigoration of its powers and effects.

ENDNOTES

1. See Mary Ellen Lamb's article entitled "Engendering the Narrative Act: Old Wives' Tales in *The Winter's Tale, Macbeth,* and *The Tempest*" (1998).

2. For a sustained reading of the middle-class affiliations of much late eighteenth-century children's literature, see Andrew O'Malley's argument in *The Making of the Modern Child* (2003).

3. If Reeve's list of recommended reading for children in *The Progress of Romance* (1785) implies a stark divide between pure entertainment and heavy moralising, it is important to remember that, as Alan Richardson has argued in "Wordsworth, Fairy Tales, and the Politics of Children's Reading" (1991), the distinction between delight and instruction, entertainment and moral didacticism is hardly absolute in children's literature of the late eighteenth and early nineteenth centuries. For a similar argument, see Mitzi Myers's essay "Romancing the Moral Tale: Maria Edgeworth and the Problems of Pedagogy" (1991).

4. For a critique of Ariès's account of the absence of childhood in medieval culture, see Shulamith Shahar's argument in *Childhood in the Middle Ages* (1990).

5. See, for example, Hugh Cunningham's argument in *Children and Childhood in Western Society Since 1500* (1995), Colin Heywood's *A History of Childhood: Children and Childhood in the West from Medieval to Modern Times* (2001), and Lawrence Stone's *The Family, Sex and Marriage in England, 1500–1800* (1977).

6. For an account of Associationist thought and its relations to the Gothic aesthetic, see Robert Miles's chapter "The Hygienic Self: Gender in the Gothic" in *Gothic Writing 1750–1820: A Genealogy* (1993). For an account of how these anxieties would play themselves out in the critical reception of Gothic romance during the 1790s, see Samuel Taylor Coleridge's response to Lewis's *The Monk* in Clery and Miles' *Gothic Documents: A Sourcebook, 1700–1820* (2000), pages 185–189.

7. See, in this regard, Patricia Demers's account of the Gothic in Mrs. Sherwood's *The Monk of Cimiès* in "Mrs. Sherwood and Hesba Stretton: The Letter and Spirit of Evangelical Writing of and for Children" (1991).

8. See Michael Gamer's account of the relationship between the Gothic and the juvenilia of the Romantic poets in *Romanticism and the Gothic: Genre, Reception, and Canon Formation* (2000).

9. See the relevant sections on children's literature and the Society in Monica C. Grobel's unpublished doctoral thesis, *The Society for the Diffusion of Useful Knowledge, 1826–1846, and its Relation to Adult Education in the First Half of the Nineteenth Century* (1932).

REFERENCES

A'Beckett, G. A. (1848). *The Castle of Otranto: A Romantic Extravaganza, in One Act, as Performed at the Theatre Royal, Haymarket*. London: National Acting Drama Office.

Akenside, M. [1795] (2000). *The Pleasures of the Imagination*. J. Wordsworth (Intro.). *Revolution and Romanticism, 1789–1834*. Washington, DC: Woodstock.

An Account of Some Imaginary Apparitions, the Effects of Fear and Fraud. Various authors. Dunbar: n.p. [1792?].

Ariès, P. (1996). *Centuries of Childhood*. Robert Baldick (Trans.). Adam Phillips (Intro.). London: Pimlico.

Ashton, J., (Ed.). (1992). *Chapbooks of the Eighteenth Century*. London: Skoob.

Barbauld, A. L. [1781] (1977). *Hymns in Prose for Children*. Classics of Children's Literature. New York: Garland.

Chamberlain, M. (1981). *The Old Wives' Tales: Their History, Remedies and Spells*. London: Virago.

Clery, E. J. (1995). *The Rise of Supernatural Fiction, 1762–1800*. Cambridge: Cambridge University Press.

Clery, E. J. & Miles, R. (Eds.). (2000). *Gothic Documents: A Sourcebook, 1700–1820*. Manchester: Manchester University Press.

Coleridge, S. T. (1960). *Shakespearean Criticism* (2 vols.). Thomas Middleton Raysor (Ed.). London: Dent.

Cunningham, H. (1995). *Children and Childhood in Western Society Since 1500*. London; New York: Longman.

Demers, P. (1991). Mrs. Sherwood and Hesba Stretton: The letter and spirit of evangelical writing of and for children. In James Holt McGavran, Jr., (Ed.), *Romanticism and Children's Literature in Nineteenth-Century England* (pp. 129–149). Athens; London: University of Georgia Press.

Drake, N. (1804). *Literary Hours: Or Sketches Critical, Narrative, and Poetical*. 3rd Ed. London: Printed for T. Cadell and W. Davies.

Edgeworth, M. [1796] (2003). *The Parent's Assistant; Moral Tales for Young People*. Elizabeth Eger and Clíona Ó Gallchoir (Eds.). London: Pickering and Chatto.

Edgeworth, M. & Lovell, R. [1801] (1996). *Practical Education* (3 vols.). Jonathan Wordsworth (Intro.). *Revolution and Romanticism, 1789–1834*. Poole: Woodstock Books.

Gamer, M. (2000). *Romanticism and the Gothic: Genre, Reception, and Canon Formation*. Cambridge: Cambridge University Press.

Grobel, M. C. (1932). *The Society for the Diffusion of Useful Knowledge, 1826–1846, and its Relation to Adult Education in the First Half of the Nineteenth Century* (4 vols.). Dissertation; London University.

Heywood, C. (2001). *A History of Childhood: Children and Childhood in the West from Medieval to Modern Times*. Cambridge: Polity.

Kliger, S. [1952] (1972). *The Goths in England: A Study in Seventeenth and Eighteenth Century Thought*. New York: Octagon.

Kristeva, J. (1982). *Powers of Horror: An Essay on Abjection*. Leon S. Roudiez (Trans.). New York: Columbia University Press.

Lamb, C. & Lamb, M. (1903). *The Works of Charles and Mary Lamb* (6 vols.). E. V. Lucas (Ed.). London: Methuen & Co.

Lamb, M. E. (1998). Engendering the narrative act: Old wives' tales in *The Winter's Tale, Macbeth*, and *The Tempest*. *Criticism* 40, 529–553.

Locke, J. [1693] (1989). *Some Thoughts Concerning Education*. J. W. Yolton & J. S. Yolton (Eds.). Oxford: Clarendon.

Longueil, A. E. (1923). The word 'gothic' in eighteenth-century criticism. *Modern Language Notes* 38, 453–460.

Macaulay, C. [1790] (1994). *Letters on Education*. J. Wordsworth (Intro.). *Revolution and Romanticism, 1789–1834*. Oxford: Woodstock.

Miles, R. (1993). *Gothic Writing 1750–1820: A Genealogy*. London: Routledge.

More, H. (1977). *Cheap Repository Tracts 1795–1797*. Classics of Children's Literature. New York: Garland.

Myers, M. (1991). Romancing the moral tale: Maria Edgeworth and the problematics of pedagogy. In J. H. McGavran, Jr. (Ed.), *Romanticism and Children's Literature in Nineteenth-Century England* (pp. 96–127). Athens; London: University of Georgia Press.

Nashe, T. (1594). *The Terrors of the Night: Or, A Discourse of Apparitions*. London: n.p.

Neuburg, V. E. (1968). *The Penny Histories: A Study of Chapbooks for Young Readers over Two Centuries*. London: Oxford University Press.

Newbery, J. [1744] (1966). *A Little Pretty Pocket-Book*. M. F. Thwaite (Intro.). Juvenile Library. London: Oxford University Press.

———. [1765] (1977). *The History of Little Goody Two-Shoes*. B. Alderson (Preface). Classics in Children's Literature. New York: Garland.

Norton, R. (Ed.). (2000). *Gothic Readings: The First Wave, 1764–1840*. London: Leicester University Press.

O'Malley, A. (2003). *The Making of the Modern Child: Children's Literature and Childhood in the Late Eighteenth Century*. London; New York: Routledge.

Peele, G. [1595] (1996). *The Old Wife's Tale*. Charles Whitworth (Ed.). New Mermaids. New York: Norton.

Perrin, N. (1970). *Dr Bowdler's Legacy: A History of Expurgated Books in England and America*. London: Macmillan.

Plumptre, J. (1818). *The Truth of the Popular Notion of Apparitions, or Ghosts, Considered by the Light of Scripture: A Sermon*. Cambridge: James Hodson.

Radcliffe, A. [1794] (1966). *The Mysteries of Udolpho*. B. Dobrée (Ed. & Intro.), F. Garber (Notes). The World's Classics. Oxford: Oxford University Press.

Reeve, C. [1785] (1930). *The Progress of Romance And The History of Charoba, Queen of Aegypt.* New York: The Facsimile Text Society.

Richardson, A. (1991). Wordsworth, fairy tales, and the politics of children's reading. In James Holt McGavran, Jr. (Ed.), *Romanticism and Children's Literature in Nineteenth-Century England* (pp. 34–53). Athens; London: University of Georgia Press.

_____. (1994). *Literature, Education, and Romanticism: Reading as Social Practice, 1780–1832.* Cambridge: Cambridge University Press.

Rousseau, J.-J. [1762] (1979). *Emile, or On Education.* A. Bloom (Trans. & Intro.). London: Penguin.

Shahar, S. (1990). *Childhood in the Middle Ages.* Chaya Galai (Trans.). London; New York: Routledge.

Shakespeare, W. (1953). *Macbeth.* K. Muir (Ed.). The Arden Edition of the Works of William Shakespeare. London: Methuen.

_____. (1807). *The Family Shakespeare.* Expurgated by T. Bowdler & H. Bowdler. London: J. Hatchard.

Shelley, P. B. (1977). *Shelley's Poetry and Prose: Authoritative Texts, Criticism.* D. H. Reiman & S. B. Powers. New York: Norton.

Sherwood, Mrs. [1818–1847] (1913). *The Fairchild Family.* Lady Strachey (Ed.). London: Adam and Charles Black.

Sleath, E. (1815). *Glenowen, Or The Fairy Palace: A Tale.* London: Black and Co.

Society for the Diffusion of Useful Knowledge. (1829). *Reports and Prospectus, 1829.* London: George Taylor.

Stone, L. (1977). *The Family, Sex and Marriage in England, 1500–1800.* Harmondsworth: Penguin.

Summerfield, G. (1984). *Fantasy and Reason: Children's Literature in the Eighteenth Century.* London: Methuen and Co.

Trimmer, S. [1802–1806] (2002). *The Guardian of Education: A Periodical Work* (5 vols.). *1802–1806.* M. Grenby (Ed.). Bristol: Thoemmes.

Watts, I. (n.d.) *Twenty-Eight Divine Songs, for the Use of Children.* Edinburgh: Oliver & Boyd.

Walpole, H. [1764] (1968). *The Castle of Otranto, Three Gothic Novels* (pp. 37–148). P. Fairclough (Ed.), M. Praz (Intro.). Harmondsworth: Penguin.

_____. [1798] (1999). *The Works of Horace Walpole, Earl of Orford* (5 vols.). M. Berry (Ed.), P. Sabor (Intro.). London: Pickering and Chatto.

Wollstonecraft, M. [1787] (1989). *Thoughts on the Education of Daughters: With Reflections on Female Conduct, in The More Important Duties of Life.* In J. Todd & M. Butler (Eds.). *The Works of Mary Wollstonecraft, Volume IV* (pp. 3–49). London: William Pickering.

_____. [1788] (1989). *Original Stories from Real Life; With Conversations, Calculated to Regulate the Affections, and Form the Mind to Truth and Goodness.* In J. Todd & M. Butler (Eds.). *The Works of Mary Wollstonecraft, Volume IV* (pp. 353–450). London: William Pickering.

———. [1789] (1989). *The Female Reader: Or Miscellaneous Pieces, in Prose and Verse: Selected from the Best Writers, and Disposed under Proper Heads: for the Improvement of Young Women.* In J. Todd & M. Butler (Eds.). *The Works of Mary Wollstonecraft, Volume IV* (pp. 53–350). London: William Pickering.

Wordsworth, W. [1799–1805] (1979). *The Prelude, 1799, 1805, 1850: Authoritative Texts, Context and Reception, Recent Critical Essays.* J. Wordsworth, M. H. Abrams, & S. Gill (Eds.). New York: Norton.

Wu, D. (Ed.). (1998). *Romanticism: An Anthology with CD-ROM*, 2nd ed. Oxford: Blackwell.

2

CYBERFICTION AND THE GOTHIC NOVEL

Nadia Crandall

On first consideration, cyberfiction and the Gothic novel appear to have little in common. The Gothic novel, generally agreed to have originated with *The Castle of Otranto* (1764), reached its late apogee in the closing decades of the nineteenth century with R. L. Stevenson's *Strange Case of Dr. Jekyll and Mr. Hyde* (1886) and Bram Stoker's *Dracula* (1897). By contrast, cyberfiction found its earliest expression a century later in the cyberpunk stories of Philip K. Dick and his successors. Cyberfiction for children, moreover, is so recent a form that it is only just emerging as a coherent genre.

The plots of cyberpunk, and its related genre steampunk, are often set not simply in the future, but in an alternative world where technological advances have followed an unexpected trajectory. In cyberpunk, the technologies are generally cybernetic in character, whereas steampunk variants tend to employ the technologies of the time in which they are set. Often these are quasi-Victorian settings, featuring steam and clockwork technologies used in the service of a dystopian narrative. Indeed, most cyberpunk and steampunk fiction concerns itself with the interface between humans and their machines, their "punk" character manifesting itself in the social breakdowns caused by the alienation its writers imagine are inherent in that interface.

Cyberfiction texts also operate at the intersection of humans and machines, though they sometimes lack the dystopian agenda. In cyberfiction, the protagonists engage with virtual reality through computer games, the Internet, or other forms of interactive cyberspace, as well as with their real-world environments. In part because of the genre's imaginative origins in Victorian fictions such as Mary Shelley's *Frankenstein* and the works of Jules Verne and H. G. Wells, and in part because this digital universe is new and intangible, writers have looked to the past to find a paradigm which will enable them to create an accessible world for their readers. One such paradigm, so widely used that many cybertexts might be considered as an expression of the Gothic, is that of the nineteenth-century Gothic novel.

Ronald Paulson (2004: 271) points out that the Gothic has been most powerful as a literary form in times of moral and political uncertainty, and that the "decadent" or late Gothic emerged partly as a response to anxiety over rapid social changes at a time when controversies over religion, moral values, and education dominated the discourse of the day. Scientific advances, too, were changing the world in fundamental ways. The telegraph, telephone, typewriter, phonograph, bicycle, motor car, and electric light bulb all received patents between 1850 and 1900. One preeminent new field of knowledge was psychology, which prior to the latter half of the Victorian era was effectively uncharted. It rapidly gained formal recognition, however, with the first psychological library established in 1879, and the founding of the American Psychological Association in 1892, and became a dominant factor in fin de siecle anomie, calling into question assumptions about identity, the construction of reality, and the nature of human relationships. For the science of psychology threatened people in the very places they felt safest: in themselves, in their homes, and in their family and social relationships.

These sources of unrest and uncertainty are mirrored in our contemporary lives. Indeed, the zeitgeist of the late Victorian period bears striking similarities to our own. Rapid technological change is evidenced by the fact that cellular telephones, video games, DVDs, and the World Wide Web were all invented during the last decades of the twentieth century. And our twenty-first century construction of cyberspace offers direct parallels to the nineteenth century construction of psychology. In little more than a decade, digital technology has become omnipresent in our lives and is hailed as both boon and peril. It challenges the integrity of personality because of the ease with which fictional identities can be created. When people can move at will between multiple identities and multiple worlds, they face the troubling problem of which "reality" is real. And because cyberspace bypasses the physical signals which allow us to assess the trustworthiness of our interlocutor, human relationships are called into doubt.

These close parallels have led authors of cyberfiction to apply Gothic tropes directly to their work. In struggling with questions similar to those of late nineteenth-century writers, they have created fictional worlds which, while superficially disparate, are in fact startlingly similar. In their treatment of psychic landscape, the divided consciousness, and the moral framework which informs them, contemporary writers have drawn directly from late Victorian models. Furthermore, the metafictive conventions which permeate the nineteenth-century Gothic have been reinvented for contemporary child readers.

To illustrate my argument, I use two iconic Victorian texts, *The Strange Case of Dr. Jekyll and Mr. Hyde* (1886) and *Dracula* (1897). These have captured the popular imagination to such an extent that they are now accessible to children through books, comic strips, and screen adaptations. My contemporary texts are *Cybermaman* (Jardin 1996), a picture book which was published simultaneously in the United States and France, and *Shadow of the Minotaur* (Gibbons 2000) and *Ultraviolet* (2001) published in the United Kingdom. These texts are representative of a broad body of work for children that has emerged in the past two decades and is generally thought to have originated with Gillian Rubinstein's *Space Demons* (1987). Subsequently, children's authors such as Jay Ashton, Terence Blacker, Malorie Blackman, Pat Cadigan, Gillian Cross, Maggie Furey, Philip Gross, Tim Kennemore, Conor Kostick, Terry Pratchett, and Chloe Rayban have worked in this arena.

In *Cybermaman*, three children mourn their dead mother. They enlist the help of Mr. Zeig, a scientist, to venture inside a computer in search of lost data files containing her images. There, they rescue her from the clutches of the cyber pirate, Mr. Jones. *Shadow of the Minotaur*, set in small-town England, concerns Phoenix, a disaffected teenager. He turns away from difficulties in the real world to immerse himself in a deadly computer game where he has to defeat the Minotaur. *Ultraviolet* is set in a dystopian future, and explores the moral and physical decay of a world in which video games have largely replaced reality. Each of these texts, Gothic and cyberfiction alike, takes place at least partially in an alternative reality which I will refer to as dream-space. Transgressive and liberating, dream-space is always set in opposition to conventional constructs of the real world.

THE LANDSCAPE OF THE PSYCHE

Neither cyberspace nor the human psyche has any physical dimension. Yet Gothic novels are extremely visual and use a metaphorical shorthand, readily apprehended by the reader, to represent psychological terrain. Stevenson, for example, draws explicit parallels between the alleyways of Victorian London and the hidden pathways of the mind. This is his description of the entrance to Jekyll's old consulting room: "nothing but a door on the lower story and a blind forehead of discoloured wall on the upper; and bore in every feature the marks of prolonged and sordid negligence" (Stevenson 1886: 8). Count Dracula's castle also symbolises the psyche. The rooms open to Jonathan Harker represent the conscious, ordered functions of the mind. Although they are safe, they are also unbearably restrictive. Beyond them lies a maze of corridors and locked doors, which Harker feels compelled to explore. It is here that he encounters the nightmares which represent the untrammelled energy of the unconscious.

Harker's experience can be readily transposed into the conventions of a computer game. While he stays in the rooms assigned to him by the Count he is safe, but he cannot progress. Once he begins to explore, he encounters either dead ends or life-threatening challenges in the shape of female vampires, wolves, and precipitous cliffs. Tools that might help him in his quest are either arbitrarily removed or prove useless. Instead, he must search for the one true talisman, the key to the castle.

Gothic and quasi-Gothic structures are omnipresent not only in computer games, but also in cyberfiction. Even where there is no castle, there will be a maze, a labyrinth of corridors, a military barracks, or a network of sewers or railways which serve the same psychological and narrative purpose. Here too, they represent the complexities of the mind in thinly veiled metaphors. In *Ultraviolet*, maze-like tunnels link each home to the central nexus of Condorcet, just as the neural networks of the brain are linked through synapses. Like Dracula's castle, they seem to breed terrors: "Inside the black spider the long, ribbed tunnels have a life of their own. Conversations and door closures wafted on the air conditioning produce strange quacks and clashes, whispers, booms, sudden shouts, howls and prophesies" (Howarth 2001: 2). The maze in *Minotaur* is even more threatening. Dark and foul smelling, it is strewn with gobbets of human flesh.

One quality shared by these structures is that although the artefacts and furnishings toward which the author directs the readers' gaze seem richly described, they are in fact quite insubstantial. Punter (1996: 189) points out that the Gothic mansion or castle is always without an overall plan, no matter how solid the details might appear. Indeed, Harker's experience of Dracula's castle is that, try as he might, he cannot find a way to reach the exterior. A computer game works in the same way. Cyber landscapes have no perceptible boundaries.

A second essential quality of these spaces is that they heighten real-life experience. Good and evil, triumph and despair, are magnified in the Minotaur's maze just as they are magnified in the subconscious, in dreams and nightmares. Adams, the small-town bully, becomes a demon. Phoenix, the hesitant newcomer, turns into a hero. The Minotaur grows so powerful that it threatens to escape from the computer game and into the real world.

Finally, there is always an element of antiquity in both Gothic landscapes and cyberspace. Dracula's castle in Transylvania is a mediaeval building. Dracula himself is centuries old. Like all vampires, he suffers the curse of immortality. Yet the story is set firmly in the closing years of the nineteenth century and contains innumerable references to new technologies that were transforming the Victorian world. Jonathan Harker brings Kodak photographs with him to Transylvania. Mina Harker keeps a typewritten journal. Dr. Seward records his diary on a phonograph. This juxtaposition of ancient and modern extends further. The revolvers carried by Van Helsing and his friends are impotent against vampires. Instead, they defeat Dracula with a collection of simple items, such as garlic, a crucifix, and a sharpened wooden stake. Similar juxtapositions are explored in *Minotaur*. The computer technology of the *Legendeer* is "experimental" and cutting edge, yet Phoenix's voyage of self-discovery leads him into the past. From the recent past, through his dead Uncle Andreas, he gains a better understanding of his role as the Legendeer. From the dream-space of the game, the ancient mythological past, Phoenix gathers confidence and power. His most potent weapons are primitive ones, the sickle and the sword. Often, as with Medea, he outwits his enemies without any use of arms.

In *Cybermaman*, a text for younger children, the virtual-transporters on which Lily, Felix and Cesar travel into cyberspace are so cutting edge that they haven't yet been fully tested. Yet the children's voyage leads them back to the past as a way to retrieve the memories of their dead mother. And their most potent weapons against the cyber pirate who has kidnapped her are good, old-fashioned ones: courage, hope, and love, together with a proper disregard for the arbitrary rules of adults.

In the opening spread, Monsieur Plume sits in his study (Illustration 1). His name in French means feather or quill pen or fountain pen, and he's a Latin teacher. He is clearly caught up in the past, both the ancient past with his Latin books, and the recent past in mourning for his wife Lucy. The psychological space he inhabits is represented by the Eiffel Tower, a landmark Victorian building. Later, when Lily, Felix, and Cesar shrink into minute digitised information packets for their journey through cyberspace, the hub where they embark is described as a vast, anxious space rather like the Gare de Lyon, also a Victorian

Toute la famille
Plume mangeait deux fois
par jour, du bout des lèvres,
des plats qui n'étaient plus d'**Elle** ;
même le poulet-frites du mercredi avait
le goût terrible de son absence.

César, l'aîné, faisait croire aux siens
qu'il s'était consolé avec **son ordinateur**,
celui que sa mère lui avait offert, à l'époque
où le poulet-frites était encore une fête. Son
Ulysse II appartenait certes à une autre

Illustration 1.

structure, and their vehicle is the kind of rusty goods wagon that would have been familiar to any Victorian child. Moreover, the psychological intensification of dream-space is made explicit. When Lily calls for her mother, "an echo repeated her anguished cry, which bounced off the hard drive, making her feelings sound as if they had been amplified" (1996: 19).

All readers know the heft of a sturdy wooden stick and the smell of garlic. All know the thrill of outwitting an opponent. By making simple tools effective against supernatural threats, authors empower their audiences and allow them to identify more closely with fictional heroes. Archaic structures, the castle and the maze, are also highly accessible, part of the collective consciousness. Their familiarity permits ready acceptance as the locus of a work of fantasy. Yet their chronological distance allows the reader to confront the power of the dead past, and in triumphing, reassert their oneness with the living present.

THE DIVIDED CONSCIOUSNESS

One of the profound joys of fiction is that readers can experience worlds other than their own. Safe in an armchair they might, at the very same moment, be fleeing from hostile witches or confronting armoured bears. This experience of inhabiting two realities contemporaneously becomes even more explicit in cyberspace. Most computer games, for example, invite players to select or construct an avatar, an icon of themselves, to represent them in their virtual encounters.

The divided consciousness is not at all new. Its literary origins date back to the late eighteenth century when Jean Paul Richter invented the term *doppelganger* and Ernst Theodor Hoffman was exploring the idea of dualism. However, it has been expressed most memorably in *The Strange Case of Dr. Jekyll and Mr. Hyde*. This short story has become central to the canon of our cultural literacy. Dr. Jekyll, an apparently respectable scientist with a duplicitous secret life, seeks to separate the two parts of his nature. He learns to transform himself into Mr. Hyde, the expression of all that is evil in his character, and for some time alternates between his two manifestations. Ultimately, Hyde grows murderous, and Jekyll has no choice but to destroy them both. Yet, far from being repelled by the evil in his nature, Jekyll is exhilarated by it: "I was conscious of no repugnance, rather of a leap of welcome. This, too, was myself. It seemed natural and human" (Stevenson 1886: 51). Where Jekyll feels shackled by the conventions of his class and profession, Hyde enjoys the advantages of anonymity, and revels in his freedom.

It is unsurprising, therefore, that when writers of cyberfiction seek paradigms for the quandaries of their fictional characters, caught between real space and cyberspace, they look to the Victorian Gothic for guidance. In *Shadow of the Minotaur*, Phoenix, like Jekyll, is subject to the restrictions of a world in which he feels ill at ease. He longs to escape his warring parents and the brutal hierarchies of a new school. Constrained by his timidity, he dreams of heroism. Instead, he is bullied, even emasculated, by his classmate, Steve Adams: "Phoenix imagined himself crashing his fist into Adams' leering face, but that wasn't his style. He *read* about fights or engaged in them in his on-screen battles with the demons. That was the best sort of fighting, the kind you could stop at the touch of the off-button" (Gibbons 2000: 26). Inside the computer game, *Legendeer*, everything changes. Through his avatars, and ultimately in his own person, Phoenix must deploy all his physical and mental skills to survive. He relishes his new-found vigour. "Somehow, the game gave him a sense of himself, of what he might be. It scared him all right, but he still felt he could beat it. He could be a hero" (2000: 72). He learns to harness his latent physical power, in part, by celebrating the potency of the mythical creatures he encounters: "Pan was present in person, man from the waist up, goat from the waist down.... And the strangest thought came to Phoenix. *I'm home*" (2000: 33). The passage echoes Jekyll's "leap of welcome" when he first encounters himself as the simian Hyde (Stevenson 1886: 51).

This duality of experience, the constrained and the liberated, the visible and the hidden, allows writers to explore aspects of forbidden behaviour within dream-space. In the Victorian Gothic, for example, eroticism is a dominant theme. Indeed, as Punter points out, Dracula has extraordinary sexual magnetism (1996: 20). In a series of metaphors for intercourse, the vampire invades every sacred space: bedrooms, tombs, asylums, bodies, and the minds of his victims. Dracula's assaults on Mina Harker are all the more shocking because they parody sexual congress. They take place in her bed at night and Mina's white nightdress is stained with blood as if she has lost her virginity as well as her soul to Dracula. Similarly, in *Minotaur*, Phoenix is coming to terms with puberty, and this undeniably shapes the narrative. When he inhabits dream-space he can, like Jekyll, explore his sensuality in a way that is denied to him in his ordinary life. Phoenix's extended powers, his ability to fly in winged sandals, his prowess with the adamantine sickle, are metaphors for the delights of adolescence when a developing body and testosterone-fuelled strength offer a seemingly magical range of new experiences to young men.

Splitting and emancipating the self is central as well to *Cybermaman*. With Lucy Plume dead, everything seems amiss. There are no fresh flowers in the house, food doesn't taste the same, and like many children, Lily, Felix, and Cesar feel oppressed by the adults around them. Having been shown the virtual-transporters that might lead them to their mother's data files, they are forbidden to use them. But of course they must. Once inside the computer, the physical bodies they have abandoned begin to falter. Their pulses slow and their temperatures fall. By contrast, their virtual existence is liberating, the children strong, empowered, and free to follow the truth of their emotions. This dichotomy is evident when they are shown unconscious, blurred and prone in the real world, but vividly alive in cyberspace (Illustration 2).

Within dream-space, the common anchors of experience fragment. Perceptions of place, language, and time become distorted, often symbolizing the extent to which a character has shifted away from reality. In *Jekyll and Hyde*, for example, regularity of habit implies a balanced and rational

Illustration 2.

temperament. The converse is also true. Hyde is a creature of the night. His assignations and crimes occur almost without exception in darkness. As Jekyll is drawn deeper into the struggle with Hyde, his seclusion and erratic habits attract the concern of servants and friends. Ultimately he is unable to sleep at all for fear of waking as Hyde (Stevenson 1886: 60).

This trope, common in cyberfiction, correlates with our real-world experience of cyberspace in which time is fluid and reversible. The video can be rewound, the DVD played in scene increments, and the computer game started again and again at the same level in the same battle against the same enemy. And as Juliet Dusinberre points out in a different context, the distortion of time is often intimately connected with the dissolution of language (1987: 181–182). In *Ultraviolet,* the more that time is pulled out of shape, the more disruption there is in syntax and narrative order. Violet eschews regular meals and sleep in favour of gaming, to the point where she can no longer recognise the boundaries between fantasy and reality. Both her use of language and her ability to communicate with others are severely compromised.

In *Minotaur*, Phoenix notes early on that a good computer game "seemed to be able to pull time out of shape, mould it and remake it the way a potter does a vase on the wheel" (Gibbons 2000: 14). Indeed, *Legendeer* threatens the Graves family at first in an entirely quotidian way, through John's immoderate working hours. So engrossed is he, that he barely stops to eat or rest. Later, the true power of the Games-master becomes evident as time stops in the real world, with all the clocks halted at 7:30 and all motion suspended.

This convention is also central to *Cybermaman*, where the plot turns on the idea that virtual reality interrupts the course of time. The point surfaces early on with a series of references to Salvador Dali's dripping clock paintings. As Lily, Felix, and Cesar make their way through their online encyclopaedia, they encounter the clocks which are not only battered and misshapen, but also out of focus. In this text, however, the most important thing about time stopping is that people never grow old, and never die. Lucy Plume may be absent from the physical world, but she lives on in the virtual world, so that when Lily, Felix, and Cesar finally track her down, she is able to respond to their call. She emerges from her data-file and smiles at her children.

FISSURES IN THE MORAL FABRIC

Dream-space is not only transgressive, it is invasive. Where the moral imperfections of individuals allow, it extends outward into the real world. Thus Dracula gains a foothold in England only where there are fissures in the moral fabric. One early victim is Lucy, a frivolous young woman whose flirtatiousness attracts three marriage proposals in one day. Another victim, Renfield, is an inmate of a lunatic asylum. He indulges a horrifying habit of consuming live creatures. Beginning with flies and spiders, he graduates to birds and ultimately, under Dracula's tutelage, to the consumption of human blood.

This trope has been readily adopted in cyberfiction for children, where it conforms to an existing real-world debate about the dangers of virtual reality. Valerie Walkerdine's analysis posits a class distinction in the relative perceived dangers of public space and cyberspace (1998). For the closely supervised, middle-class child, cyberspace offers a safe environment in which social and intellectual pursuits can be fostered. By contrast, a poorly supervised, working class child is considered a member of the vulnerable-minded, proto-violent masses whose addiction to cyber interactions threatens a cohesive society. Indeed, one of the tensions in *Minotaur* is that Phoenix, an educated middle-class child, becomes caught up in a level of violence within his computer game which would be entirely unacceptable in the real world.

In *Ultraviolet,* a catastrophic imbalance in the external world is mirrored by the breakdown of a society in which people no longer interact with their neighbours, and in which none of the familiar routines of domestic life are observed. Yet Violet's father, Nick, helps perpetuate these calamities by refusing to address the moral questions raised by the work he does. Violet herself, by retreating into virtual reality, avoids resolving the issues that really trouble her: the divorce of her parents and her membership in an exploitative social elite. Social disintegration is abetted, even caused, by the moral failures of the protagonists.

In *Cybermaman,* every adult has moral flaws. Monsieur Plume is so absorbed in his grief that he can't respond to the needs of his children, and he allows Mr. Zeig to digitize all of his wife's photographs without retaining any originals. There is something shocking about the way her images are discarded. Even the page layout (Illustration 3) confirms that the world is awry. At its centre, Mr. Zeig appears upside-down, pinioned by the design for one of his contraptions, and hobbled morally as well, compromised by his single-minded pursuit of new knowledge.

All dream-spaces represent the forbidden. Indeed, transgression into dream-space often takes the form of seeking proscribed knowledge. Jekyll wants to reconstruct the human soul. Frankenstein hopes to resurrect the dead. Mad scientists are iconic symbols for transgression in the Victorian novel, and Mr. Zeig is their cyberfiction equivalent. A pioneer in early computers, he is also the inventor of virtual-transporters. It is he who is responsible for launching the children into cyberspace, and putting them in mortal peril.

Dream-space releases characters from moral imperatives. Behaviour which would be unacceptable in one context becomes functional in another, and has an addictive appeal. Stevenson is illuminating about this kind of addiction. Knowing how repugnant and dangerous Hyde is, Jekyll still cannot resist this manifestation of himself: "I began to be tortured with throes and longings, as of Hyde struggling after freedom" (Stevenson 1886: 56). In *Minotaur,* Phoenix's efforts to assimilate in the real world are balanced by his aggression within the game. In the town of Deicterion, he wounds with an adamantine sickle, revelling in the fight. "With the start of the attack, Phoenix's senses had been sharpened. He was hearing intensely and feeling every twitch of his muscles" (Gibbons 2000: 124). Like Jekyll, Phoenix feels infinitely more alive when he is released from the constraints of his conventional existence.

Illustration 3.

It is unsurprising, then, that characters prefer transgression to conformity. The attraction is so compelling that they often do so despite the evident dangers. When the Parallel Reality suit inflicts real wounds, when the game characters themselves warn him away, Phoenix returns again and again until he is ineluctably ensnared by the Gamesmaster.

Transgression in *Cybermaman* is explored not only through Mr. Zeig but also through the character of Mr. Jones, the cyber pirate. Mr. Jones has chosen a virtual existence because he is disappointed with life, depressed by the grubby suburb where he lives and weary of his unrewarding flirtations. In cyberspace, he resides in a palace, he eats whatever he wants, and if he's lonely, he visits an Internet chat room where no one is ever shy. In this moral vacuum, everything is his for the taking, and nothing has to be paid for. Without even realizing it, Mr. Jones has committed an egregious crime. He has stolen Lucy

Plume and kept her captive. Surrounded in his virtual world by the consumables he thinks will make him happy, Mr. Jones wears his hair twisted into the semblance of two small horns. He is cast unequivocally as a cyberspace devil, and the construction of evil, a sophisticated one, is that of a moral vacuum free from the constraints of society and conscience, a place without boundaries.

Animals are an important metaphor for the transgressive nature of dream-space. In both Gothic novels and cyberfiction, they represent the unfettered subconscious, the chaos a society tries to hold at bay but which is, in fact, intrinsic. Dracula has wolves and rats at his bidding. He displays the ferocity of a carnivore with his pointed teeth and sharpened fingernails, and the agility of a lizard as he climbs up and down the castle walls. As a bat, one of his most frightening manifestations, he beats relentlessly at the window of Lucy's bedroom, even causing it to break in his urgent desire for her blood. Similarly, in *Ultraviolet*, the presence of animals represents the disequilibrium of the external world. "A lot of things come indoors, now the world got simmered in a pan. Slugs and snails, bats and beetles, crane-flies, swifts, even jack-rabbits" (Howarth 2001: 43). These animal incursions reflect a narrative process whereby the dangers that invade a society through its own moral fissures ultimately have to be faced. As the dream-space becomes untenable, the protagonists must confront real-world problems, or face destruction.

If dream-space is transgressive, the thematic intent of these novels is highly conservative. Even where the texts use the kind of polyphonic narratives which I discuss in the next section, they propound an underlying monologic ideology (McCallum 1999). They exhibit nostalgia for a clear moral code and a sense that the past must inform the future. The English are helpless against Dracula until they enlist the elderly Van Helsing who, as a philosopher and teacher, is equipped with superior sagacity. In *Ultraviolet*, the protagonist yearns for a world where the rhythm of daily pleasures and obligations carry on secure and uninterrupted. She longs for the old, cherished cycle of the seasons where crops and animals thrive, and for a community in which the wisdom of the past, represented by Thoreau, is valued for something other than salvage. In *Cybermaman*, Mr. Zeig the scientist, who plays with the dangerous future, is curbed by Monsieur Plume the classicist, who is rooted in the safer past. And the story ends on a clear moral note. Together, Monsieur Plume and his children reconstruct their family life based on real-world virtues.

These moral frameworks allow readers to root their response in widely held and conventional beliefs, enabling them to navigate securely through the terrifying disturbances and irrationalities of dream-space.

METAFICTIVE NARRATIVES

New fictional territories often elicit a questioning of narrative forms. One notable characteristic of Victorian Gothic fiction is narrative fragmentation. The story of *Dracula*, for example, is told by more than a dozen voices through journal entries, letters, telegrams, newspaper cuttings, and a ship's log. Where truth is relative and no one voice is completely reliable, readers are forced to engage by playing with the text, piecing together the narrative for themselves (Grieve 1998). At the same time the weight of documentation adds a kind of credibility. Indeed, the more fantastic the story, the more at pains is the writer to establish a secure mooring for it. This kind of fragmentation has obvious resonances for writers of cyberfiction. In *Ultraviolet*, for example, the narrative is constructed from newspaper headlines, television broadcasts, blogs, songs, e-mails and game instructions. These different formats effectively create a non-linear narrative and an achronological sequence of events, paralleling the experience of navigating through hypertext, in which a reader jointly constructs an "idio-text" with the author, which may be different at each "reading" (Amaral 2000: 4–5).

Narrative fragmentation can occur visually as well. *Cybermaman* uses a wide variety of visual effects to tell its story. The opening spread (Illustration 1) has text laid out in what looks like an ordinary paragraph, but there are already some unconventional elements. The typeface is black on grey with several key words in different fonts. The image is intended to establish the real-life credentials of the story. We're asked to believe in the solidity of the bookshelves, in the confusion of papers. At the same time, the lighting and the minor depth distortion give a real sense of movement. It's as if a camera is panning in on the lonely figure of Monsieur Plume. Indeed, throughout the book, there is a rhythm of set-up shots, panning shots, and close-ups.

As we move through the story, text and images are augmented with backdrops of technical drawings, wiring designs, microchip circuitry, and computer code. The reader is gradually inveigled into trusting the reality of a virtual landscape, and before long, the landscapes themselves become pure fantasy. Later still, the text begins to change. It no longer looks like a paragraph from a book. Instead, with its multiple fonts and use of colour, it more closely resembles a Web page with hyperlinks.

Cybermaman, then, tells its story by drawing from a wide range of media (photography, film, painting, theatre, technical drawing, and Web design) both to establish the verisimilitude of the narrative and then to comment on the text itself.

Illustration 4.

As Lily, Felix, and Cesar continue their virtual journey, they cause all kinds of disruption. The hard drive is damaged, and the words in their on-line encyclopaedia begin to fragment so that they must scramble over a pile of broken letters in their search through the computer (Illustration 4). Clearly, the book implies that conventional text is being superseded as the sole, or even at times the main, vehicle for the narrative.

In both Gothic and cyberfiction, dream-space is initially constructed in opposition to real space, and characters pass from one to the other with conscious intent. However, the boundaries quickly become blurred, for without collision and resolution the narrative cycle cannot be completed. Ultimately, at the point where worlds collide, it becomes impossible to distinguish between them. Dracula disarms his victims by inducing a kind of torpor which makes them unable to discern reality from dream. As Jonathan Harker writes of his first encounter with vampires: "I suppose I must have fallen asleep; I hope so, but I fear, for all that followed was startlingly real—" (Stoker 1897: 55). *Ultraviolet* takes this confusion a step further for, ultimately, neither Violet nor the reader are able to distinguish between dream, reality, and game. Indeed, Violet's gaming calls into question the entire final third of the text. Thus apparent turning points in her moral education become ambiguous. It is unequivocally brave for Violet to search for someone lost in the desert. It is unequivocally humane to release frogs into the Undercliff where they have a chance of survival. Yet we learn much later that all these actions took place in virtual reality.

In *Cybermaman*, as far as Lily, Felix, and Cesar are concerned, the encounter with their virtual mother is real. The narrator says: "Certain moments in cyberspace are just like real life, and this one was more like it than any other" (Jardin 1996: 58), and he goes on to describe how the Plume family re-establishes a dialogue with Lucy through the computer keyboard. They still had a mother who, even if not real, really listened to them. So the boundaries between the virtual and physical worlds have disappeared, and the experiences in one are able to inform the other.

All these texts exhibit considerable elision between signifier and signified. In Gothic novels where threats are multiple, intangible, or protean, a clear deconstruction of meaning takes place. Vampires cannot be hunted down by conventional means because they change their physical form at will, from wolves to bats to miasmal mist. Evil is not readily challenged because on one level, it cannot be identified. The vampire is a universal threat, symbolizing the inchoate darkness that imperils every soul. This elision is perhaps most obvious in *Ultraviolet*, however, where characters have more than one identity and readers must decide for themselves where each belongs in the moral construct of Violet's world. Smiley is also Davis Nailey, the Adviser. He may be an activist or a spy, or both. Random Squires may be the nom de plume of Daley Jope, or he may be a public relations invention. Dolly Jope is also Mary Jope who may or may not have drowned.

Finally, these texts often end by questioning their own veracity. In *Dracula*, when Harker re-examines the papers that have so painstakingly documented his story, he places their reliability in doubt. "We could hardly ask anyone, even did we wish to, to accept these as proofs of so wild a story" (Stoker 1897: 516). *Ultraviolet* becomes self-referentially "the book of the game" that Violet herself created using Edition Eight of Questholme. With at least five different endings, some more satisfactory than others, some more credible than others, the book invites readers to select whichever they prefer.

This analysis has been concerned with cybertexts that are produced in conventional book form. However, fiction is being created in radical new formats. Publishers are already marketing through cell phones and Web sites, and the distribution of complete novels through these media will not be far behind. Many children find in video games an entirely new resource for their imaginations, and writers a new market for their creative output. With these alternative formats, will the Victorian Gothic novel continue to operate as a paradigm for cyberfiction?

Recent video games suggest that the Gothic landscape remains a rich resource. In *Lara Croft: Tomb Raider: Legend* (2006), Lara climbs and fights her way through a series of maze-like structures. The action in *Resident Evil 4* (2005) takes place in an isolated village, and the ancient castle that dominates it. These settings are a kind of generic Gothic. They have no substance, no borders, but they contain the same amplification of terror, the same inchoate evils that nineteenth-century readers encountered in Gothic texts.

As new forms of semi-immersive and immersive virtual reality are developed, the issue of the divided self can only become more pressing (Somers 1995: 202). It will be increasingly important for gamers to distinguish between the moral imperatives of their real lives and the transgressive freedoms of the dream-space they inhabit while gaming.

Finally, our construct of narrative is changing in response to new media. The democratisation of publishing has led writers to make broader use of metafictive conventions. Bloggers may be writing an account of their own lives and experiences, or they may be adopting entirely fictional personas. Narratives may be constructed not merely with multiple voices, but through the contributions of multiple authors. Indeed, they may be partially created by their readers through hyperlinks and interactive programming. Contemporary writers will continue to deconstruct and reinvent the process of storytelling as they attempt to encompass entirely new fields of knowledge and new ways of thinking about our humanity. The Victorian Gothic novel provides a pertinent and dynamic model for this kind of narrative experimentation.

REFERENCES

Primary Texts

Gibbons, A. [2000] (2003). *Shadow of the Minotaur*. London: Orion Children's Books.

Gibson, W. [1984] (2003). *Neuromancer*. New York: Ace Books.

Howarth, L. (2001). *Ultraviolet*. London: Puffin Books.

Jardin, A. (1996). *Cybermaman*. Paris: Editions Gallimard Jeunesse; New York: DK Publishing.

Rubinstein, G. (1988). *Space Demons*. New York: Omnibus/Puffin.

Shelley, M. [1818] (1994). *Frankenstein*. London: Puffin Books.

Stevenson, R. L. [1886] (2003). *The Strange Case of Dr. Jekyll and Mr. Hyde*. New York: Norton.

Stoker, B. [1897] (2003). *Dracula*. London: Collector's Library.

Walpole, H. [1764] (1968). *The Castle of Otranto, Three Gothic Novels* (pp. 37–148). P. Fairclough (Ed.), M. Praz (Intro.) Harmondsworth: Penguin.

Secondary Texts

Amaral, K. (2000). Hypertext and writing: An Overview of the hypertext medium. Accessible through the University of Massachusetts library site with password permission.

Dusinberre, J. (1987). *Alice to the Lighthouse: Children's Books and Radical Experiments in Art*. London: Macmillan.

Grieve, A. (1998). Metafictional play in children's fiction. *Papers 8*(3), 128–131.

McCallum, R. (1999). *Ideologies of Identity in Adolescent Fiction*. London: Garland.

Paulson, R. (2004). Gothic Fiction and the French Revolution. In F. Botting & D. Townshend (Eds.), *Gothic: Critical Concepts in Literary and Cultural Studies* (Vol. 1). London; New York: Routledge.

Punter, D. (1996). *The Literature of Terror: The Gothic Tradition*. London: Longman Group.

Somers, J. (1995). Stories in cyberspace. *Children's Literature in Education, 26*(4), 202.

Walkerdine, V. (1998). Children in cyberspace: A new frontier. In K. Lesnik-Oberstein (Ed.), *Children in Culture*. Houndmills: Routledge.

3

FRIGHTENING AND FUNNY: HUMOUR IN CHILDREN'S GOTHIC FICTION

Julie Cross

Within children's fiction, the comic Gothic can no longer be ignored, so prevalent has it become in the last 15 years or so. Indeed, the genre is gaining in popularity in these early years of the twenty-first century, arguably because of millennial anxieties adding to fin de siecle uncertainty, ambiguity and paradox (Edmundson 1997: 3). Many texts aimed at older junior readers (around ten years of age and above), most part of a series or which have sequels, now incorporate the mix of "horror," "humour," and the Gothic. Perhaps the best known is Lemony Snicket's *A Series of Unfortunate Events* (started in 1999), featuring the three Baudelaire orphans and their ghastly guardian, Count Olaf, who seeks continually to gain their inheritance by nefarious means. Of course, the comic Gothic is not altogether new, even for this age group of readers. Roald Dahl's *James and the Giant Peach* (1961) features cruel, child-hating guardians in the form of Aunt Sponge and Aunt Spiker, and dark, even black, humour, but it was not until the late 1980s and 1990s that the comic Gothic as a genre took off for junior readers.

Snicket's *A Series of Unfortunate Events* has, in a large way, contributed to the increase in popularity of the genre, spawning many imitators. This planned series of 13 has achieved huge sales and many critical plaudits, which generally acknowledge the complexity and sophistication of the self reflexivity and intertextuality of the darkly witty texts, which are full of narrative tricks. Indeed, according to the series' illustrator, Brett Holquist, "It is the sophisticated sense of humour that makes them what they are"[1]; and Gregory Maguire, in a review of the fifth book, *The Austere Academy* (2002), states that "the books are for knowing readers, because the author is better at verbal humour than slapstick."[2] The sophistication of these comic Gothic texts is, then, not in much doubt, but what is of note are the notions of developmentalism inherent in Maguire's comment, associating "knowing readers" (by which most people may presume he means older readers) with more advanced humorous forms than slapstick. These ideas about the texts' developmental suitability are also evident in the recommendations of American reviewers from, for example, *Booklist*, *The Horn Book* and *Kirkus Reviews*, who generally advocate these "sophisticated" texts for junior readers aged between 10 and 14 (see http://clcd.odyssi.com).

However, I argue that, maybe surprisingly, much of the humour in some comic Gothic texts for *younger* readers also relies on a sophisticated understanding of irony, parody, genre convention, and "higher" order cognitive forms of humour, such as the perception of, and ultimate enjoyment and even acceptance of, incongruity. Incongruity forms of humour, where a reader perceives a difference between their expectations and the "reality" (Morreall 1987: 6), are generally acknowledged to be within the cognitive, even "intellectual," domain of humour (compare Hazlitt 1885; Morreall 1983, 1987; Berger 1997). Henrietta Branford's *Dimanche Diller* trilogy, for instance, offers a paradigmatic example of the subtlety, sophistication and complexities of higher forms of humour, such as parody and irony, which rely on children's cognitive and interpretive abilities (concepts which are often associated with greater reader maturity and perception), in texts intended for the very youngest of independent readers; the first book, *Dimanche Diller* (1994), won the *Smarties* book prize in Britain in 1994 in the 6 to 8 years category. The unheeded complexities of such texts, and the opportunities they offer for sophisticated reader understanding, should not go unrecognised. Comic Gothic texts for younger readers should be acknowledged as containing more than the unsophisticated, farce-like humour, and gross, sometimes even scatological humour which I believe are generally associated with the comic Gothic for young readers, due mainly to the limiting of critical attention to the works of Roald Dahl, particularly his classic comic Gothic texts such as *The Witches* (1983) and *Matilda* (1988).

Although Branford's award-winning *Dimanche Diller* trilogy offers a master class in sophisticated humour within the child comic Gothic for the youngest reader, the texts do contain some aspects of the general assumptions about comic Gothic texts for children seen in criticism of Dahl's oeuvre. This criticism (see West 1990; Culley 1991; Petzold 1992) generally focuses upon the emotional, psychological, even "bibliotherapy" functions of the humour of the texts, which are largely (if they are recommended at all) seen as "developmentally appropriate" to their young readers' stage of emotional and cognitive development. However, this emotional and psychological dimension of the comic Gothic is not limited to considerations of children's fiction. Sage (1994: 190) points out the peculiarly close relationship between horror and humour even in serious Gothic novels, in which farcical laughter can often ensue. Horner and Zlosnik (2000; 2005) posit that humour in the Gothic is also often generally considered as hysterical laughter, which serves as "comic relief" from the fearful aspects. It should not, then, be surprising that much attention has been paid to the humorous elements that are believed to provide beneficial psychological functions by helping allay the fears and anxieties thrown up by the Gothic aspects. The use of humour can introduce and make palatable the elements of horror that Reynolds et al. (2001: 3) believes are now aimed at readers as young as six or seven, and these texts often deal with children's deepest and unspoken fears. Boodman (2002: 185) points out how "[b]ooks that deal with kids' deepest and often unspoken fears—of separation, abandonment, loneliness and death—can be therapeutic, far more so than tales that are relentlessly optimistic." According to "relief" theories of laughter (stemming from the works of Freud 1905 and 1927, and Spencer 1911), humour can serve to release excess emotion and/or nervous energy that is vented through laughter to beneficial effect.

A common humorous way of dealing with such fears is through grotesque caricatures. Culley (1991: 60) points out, with reference to Dahl's *James and the Giant Peach*, that cruel individuals who are made ridiculous through gross exaggeration and who possess no redeeming features seem unreal, almost comic-strip figures, and this provides comic distancing. He mentions James' Aunt Sponge and Aunt Spiker, who, along with their distorted physical descriptions—Aunt Sponge is "enormously fat and very short" and Aunt Spiker is "lean and tall and bony"—are explicitly described in the text as "selfish and lazy and cruel, …beating poor James for almost no reason at all" (1961: 7–8). Child psychologist Paul McGhee (1989) points out that young children are most comfortable with incongruous representations (which these grotesques certainly are) when they are sure of their fictionality, which is made evident by ludicrous proportions and behaviour. However, Dahl's world of grotesque caricatures can be too simplistic. Rees points out that "the trouble with Dahl's world is that it is black and white—two-dimensional and unreal…as is normal with Dahl, evil is evil and

good is good" (1988: 152), and there are strong elements of moral didacticism which may not be desirable.

Similar grotesque caricatures appear in Branford's trilogy; for
instance, Valburga Vilemile, Dimanche's ghastly, cruel guardian, is a
classic grotesque caricature of a Gothic villain. She is portrayed as an
unscrupulous, bogus aunt to the orphaned heiress, Dimanche Diller.
Typical of the "child-hater" figure of comic Gothic children's fiction
(from Dahl to Snicket), "Valburga hated children" (Branford 1994a: 43)
and Valburga herself tells Dimanche, "What children want is squashing
down! What children want is flattening out!" (46). Such an attitude is,
of course, reminiscent of Dahl's monstrous head teacher, Miss Trunch-
bull, in *Matilda*, who tells a class full of children, "I have never been
able to understand why small children are so disgusting. They are the
bane of my life. They are like insects. They should be got rid of as early
as possible" (1988: 153).

It does seem as if these over-the-top grotesques/caricatures are an
important source of early humour. Such exaggerated types do not
require subtlety, and they are so ridiculous that they can have the effect
of reducing tension through humour (Anderson & Apseloff 1989: 106).
They can even provide psychological management of the uncanny by
the comic as the caricature's threat or its disturbing quality is dimin-
ished through comic ridicule (Thompson 1982: 5–6).

However, in the *Dimanche Diller* books, caricatures are not always
so black and white and overly simplistic, and they can provide more
than just comic relief. In the second book, *Dimanche Diller in Danger*
(1994), readers discover a much more ambiguous character, Valburga's
big, hulking American nephew, Wolfie T. Volfango, whom she has
engaged to kidnap Dimanche while she, Valburga, serves out her prison
sentence for her wrong-doings in the first book. Again, Wolfie is a caricature—we hear he is big and strong, with his "great jaw" which "surged
forward in a rippling cliff of bone" (14). However, any readers' fear of
Wolfie is soon likely to diminish as his stupidity becomes apparent. As
early as page 10, when Valburga has summoned Wolfie from America
to visit her in prison to tell him of her plot to kidnap Dimanche, she
tells him her plan, "slowly and carefully."

"Repeat after me," she whispered, when she had finished.

"After me," Wolfie T. Volfango murmured obediently.

Valburga closed her eyes. "Idiot! Start again." (1994: 10)

This opportunity for children to have the satisfaction of laughing at
a "stupid" adult is a long-standing mainstay of children's fiction. It is

well established that children in middle childhood in particular enjoy the superiority and mastery aspect of seeing and laughing at the misunderstandings of naïve and stupid characters (see Levine 1980; Tucker 1981). Such humour is enjoyed not least because children of this age are only just past that stage of misapprehension themselves.

However, the character of Wolfie also involves the humour of incongruity, a more cognitive, higher type of humour. Such humour relies upon a child's perception of something unexpected, illogical or inappropriate in some way to their normal view, which strikes them as funny. In the text, Wolfie is described as being physically big, strong, and threatening, but he is soon seen to be stupid and even cowardly. After Dimanche has been kidnapped by Wolfie at his evil Aunt Valburga's request and Dimanche asks why he can't release her, he says it's because "I'm scared of my auntie" (34), and he later even admits he's frightened of thunder and lightning. In fact, Wolfie's ambiguity is soon even more evident, as he turns against his aunt Valburga and helps Dimanche, becoming a very good friend to her (64 onwards).

Another main focus of critical attention relating to Dahl and, through association, the comic Gothic for young readers, is the cruder, lower and more obvious forms of humour, including farce and slapstick revenge and even gross-out, scatological humour (see, in particular, Rees 1988), which are widely seen as appealing to younger children, in particular, because of the lack of sophistication and crudeness of the subject matter. Although Branford's texts do not contain the grotesque bodily realism and scatology of many of Dahl's texts, they do include some slapstick, physical humour, which may serve, as West says about Dahl's work, "to mitigate the aggressive elements of the story" (1990: 116), and which may have the psychological function, as Marshall mentions (1982, in Culley 1991: 67) of "satisfy[ing] a subconscious need," especially if children are in similar situations with an authoritative, maybe even cruel, parental figure.

The fear which may be generated by reading of Valburga's numerous horrendous plans to do away with Dimanche so that she can get her hands on the family wealth (such as giving her a bicycle with no brakes and hypnotising her into nearly drowning herself) may be counteracted somewhat by the use of "revenge" slapstick. We see this, for instance, in the second book, *Dimanche Diller in Danger*, when Dimanche's new friend, Wolfie, is pulling with all his might to free Dimanche and himself from a millstone, where they had been kept prisoner by his Aunt Valburga. The force of his actions makes him fall— "right on top of his Aunt Valburga!" (Branford 1994b: 84). However, although this may be seen as suitable revenge for Valburga's many wrong-doings, in keeping with the respect Branford has for the abilities of her young readers, this justice is not overdone, and has more in common with a sense of the more mature form of an "intuitive sense of justice satisfied" than younger children's greater appreciation of "over-retaliation" (Zillman & Bryant 1989, in McGhee 1989).

Young readers' laughter at Valburga's misfortunes could also be argued to be a form of "subversive" amusement, as children are often thought to enjoy the opportunity for revenge against a cruel, repressive adult. Slapstick, violent humour can act as an outlet for children's normally repressed feelings about adults. This form of aggressive superiority humour can serve as a time out for children, who, through such humorous literature, can be free from the constraints of society for a time. Of course, such literature invariably incorporates a return to normality (Stephens 1992: 121), but the child has had the (temporary) pleasure of seeing the weak overcoming the powerful. According to relief theorists, such harmless acting out of vengeful fantasies can release negative feelings against those in authority and acts as a psychological safety-valve, letting out that which is normally repressed. In fact, so well known is this function that Dahl, in his narration of *Matilda*, points out, after Matilda has exacted numerous slapstick practical jokes upon her awful parents (such as putting superglue inside her father's hat), how "Her safety-valve, the thing that prevented her from going round the bend, was the fun of devising and dishing out these splendid punishments" (1988: 43).

Adults often frown upon this aggressive, violent slapstick humour that children are believed to relish because they see it as "subversive." Hobson, Madden, and Prytherch state, in relation to Dahl, that "[t]he books are full of crude, rude humour, which causes raised adult eyebrows, but guarantees delighted [child] readers" (1992: 63), and many adults believe that this sort of humour undermines authority and panders to children's natural rebelliousness (Petzold 1992: 191). However, it can be argued that this is not actually so, and the humour acts as a generally socially sanctioned form of transgression, which is conservative and ultimately helps to maintain the status quo. Such humour, as well as possibly providing the aforementioned psychological benefits to the individual, can also act as a form of steam letting that helps maintain social control, contributing to the harmonious cooperation of individuals within society (see, for instance, Bakhtin and his theories of the carnivalesque, 1984; and Mulkay's thoughts on humour and social control, 1988).

The association of Dahl's comic Gothic texts with the aforementioned low, "childish" forms of developmental humour also throws up more disturbing, deeper, possibly subconscious ideas about children and childhood. All the critics seem, to various degrees, to concur with Dahl's beliefs about young children's "lack" of civilisation and his strong developmental views. In an interview, Dahl states:

> I generally write for children between the ages of seven and nine. At these ages, children are only semicivilised. They are in the process of being civilised. (Cited in West 1990: 116)

West, in his defence of the psychological "usefulness" of Dahl's texts, also attacks Rees' underestimation of children's abilities, but he belies his proclamations about recognising children's capabilities when he says that the books generally appeal more strongly to children than adults because "the books...are intended to appeal to the less civilised side of children's sense of humour" (West 1990: 116). In addition, Culley (1991: 63) cites Cameron (1981), who, in seeming to criticise Dahl's violence, actually critiques his audience: "being literarily unsophisticated, children can react only to...the level of pure story."

Such negative views about children are not unusual. According to Cunningham (1995: 2), it has been common "to imagine the history of humankind as equivalent to the life cycle of a human being," with a gradual ascent from savagery/childhood to civilisation/adulthood. Lurie talks of children as "savages," "uncivilised" and "pre-social"—she talks openly of children as "an unusual, partly savage tribe" (1990: ix). She sees childhood as a separate culture, rather like a primitive society, or rather, several primitive societies, one leading into the other, with the period from the age of about 6 to 12 years of age corresponding to "early civilisation" (194–195). Such recapitulation theories may represent the more extreme end of the tendency, in our society, to perceive of children as "human becomings," rather than as human beings (Lee 2001: 8). According to Lee, children's lives and activities in the present are envisaged, in the main, as "preparation for the future," with childhood being seen as a journey towards a final, complete destination. Of course, this also implies that adulthood is perceived as a finished state, but this is increasingly questioned, even within psychology itself (Buckingham 2000: 14).

Unhelpful, over-generalised beliefs about the essential differences between children and adults obviously extend to perceptions about humour preferences. Jalongo (1985) cites Dunn (1921), who believes that "humor as the child sees it and humor to the adult mind are not one and the same" (1985: 109) and Sadker, Pollack, and Miller state that children are able to see "few incongruities," and so their sense of humour is "somewhat different and more limited than adults" (1977, in Roberts 1997: 11). Children's authors such as Jane Yolen also often believe that children have "no taste" and what may be hilarious to an adult may often go over a child's head (1985, in Roberts 1997: 12). Betsy Byars (1993) also states that "the gap between what adults think is funny and what kids think is funny is considerable." Although it would be ridiculous to deny some notions of a biologically determined developmentalism, I believe it is also foolish to deny that maturity does come with experience, and children need to be given the chance to experience higher forms of humour and literary sophistication, as different children will obviously perceive and appreciate differing forms of humour at varying times.

In addition, Klause (1987), Lypp (1995), and Lee (2001) imply that most differences between adults and children are probably due to inexperience rather than inability, and it is important to bear in mind that "children may be more competent than they are typically credited with being" (Buckingham 2000: 197). It is obvious that adult beliefs about children can lead them to act in particular ways toward children, and this tends to produce the behaviour that confirms adult thinking. As Buckingham (2000) and Alderson (2000) argue, this is a self-fulfilling process, and it is surely the case that children will only be able to become more competent if they are treated as though they are. The inclusion and appreciation of the more complex, sophisticated aspects of comic Gothic texts for young readers, which recognise the cognitive aspects of humour, and not just the well-recognised emotional and psychological functions, acknowledge children's abilities as learners, treating them as active beings, which, as Lee puts it, is part of the "broad cultural movement for the liberation of individual potential" (2001: 77), which has no finite, complete end. The activity of the child reader's mind is key here. In comic Gothic texts such as Branford's, young, developing readers are encouraged not to be passive. They have to work at the text and draw their own conclusions, thinking for themselves, and hence the texts are more genuinely child centred than more simplistic, slapstick, gross-out fiction, which capitalises on "shock value" and which is commonly thought, by many commentators and some authors, to be truly "childish."

There is so much more to the genre of child comic Gothic that has been passed over in the critical clamour to look only at the developmental aspects of one author's works, although this is somewhat understandable given Dahl's huge level of popularity.[3] However, analysis of Branford's trilogy reveals a much lesser tendency to patronise child readers and, indeed, reveals authorial respect for, and faith in, young children's cognitive abilities. Some of the forms of humour included in the texts, particularly the parody of melodrama and the use of irony, may also be useful for setting and strengthening the schemas for playfully ambiguous readings of comic Gothic fiction in the future for developing readers. These children who, as Margaret Meek points out (1988), are at such an important stage for the laying down of reading patterns and schemas, may, mostly unconsciously, intuit the "lessons" imparted by the use of such humorous forms, to beneficial effect.

These lessons include the benefits of active reader participation in meaning-making and an enjoyment and appreciation of the increased ambiguity which may result from the use of more sophisticated and complex forms of humour, alongside the acknowledged lower forms of humour, such as farce and slapstick (typical of Dahl's work). These additional contradictions (emanating from the combination of both high and low forms of humour in one text) add to the paradoxes and ambiguities which are readily acknowledged in the Gothic, and which I believe are even more evident in the comic Gothic. "Frightening and funny at the same time" is how reader Sam Grant describes the second in Branford's trilogy about the intrepid orphan, *Dimanche Diller in Danger*. This citation on the back jacket of the book highlights the notion of ambiguity; an ambiguity which Botting points out has long been recognised in the Gothic, as the formulae sometimes produces laughter as abundantly as emotions of terror or horror (1996: 168), and its absurdity in particular is eminently susceptible to parody and self-parody. The *comic* Gothic increases the genre's acknowledged ambiguity, instability, and boundary crossing,[4] because of its juxtaposition of the incongruous—fear-inspiring characters and terrible situations which may cause reader anxiety, but which are often also seen to be humorous and comically incongruous.

The acceptance of, and even appreciation of, this ambiguity may be of benefit to developing readers, as many commentators point out how contemporary life is becoming more and more uncertain, full of anxieties and complexity. For example, Lee, in his book *Childhood and Society: Growing Up in an Age of Uncertainty* (2001), highlights the rapidly changing world, where even adult life, with changing work patterns and the breakdown of traditional family units, is less stable that it used to be. Theorists from many disciplines reveal how adults cannot predict what they have to prepare children for; therefore what is needed is the development of a "flexible" person rather than a formulaic thinker (John 2003: 21). Learning to embrace ambiguity in literature may, ultimately, aid children in the creation of life skills, providing them with the tools to participate as active social agents, capable of cognitive and conceptual understanding. As Simons states about the positives of revelling in the paradox and ambiguity of postmodernity, "to live with ambiguity [to challenge certainty, to creatively encounter] is to arrive, eventually, at 'seeing anew'" (in Bassey 1999: 36), and rather than viewing ambiguity negatively in terms of confusing uncertainty, the advantages and plurality it offers for young readers can, and should, be embraced.

Indeed, this lack of ambiguity in Dahl's work (which has come to epitomise the child comic Gothic) is often critiqued. Petzold, discussing Dahl's *Matilda*, comments on how one of the complaints about Dahl's writing is that it is "too simple…missing the opportunity to teach them [children] something about the complexities of real life" (1992: 191), because of the implied author's moral certitude and "black and white" mentality. Similar criticisms of simplicity cannot be levelled at Branford's *Dimanche Diller* trilogy. These texts offer the cognitive pleasures of complex and sophisticated forms of humour which are more reliant on children's abilities and perception of incongruities than their emotions, and I believe that by including these, Branford acknowledges young children's literary competencies. According to Brodzinsky and Rightmyer (1980), children enjoy resolving more challenging forms of humour. They point out that their research shows that children with varying cognitive abilities tend to prefer humour which is moderately challenging (295).[5]

Of course, these higher forms of humour are subtle and run the risk of going undetected, yet they also acknowledge children's abilities and competencies. Potential difficulties for young readers include the following: In the case of irony, there is a combination of conflicting messages within one single "code." The young reader has to perceive the contrast between the written statement and any other implied meaning; something other than that which is literally said (Rose 1993: 87). According to Cart (1995: 30), such "understated" humour is at the opposite end of the humour continuum, as far away from crude slapstick as it is possible to be, and irony is particularly vulnerable to misunderstanding. Kümmerling-Meibauer (1999: 158) notes three potentially problematic stages children need to go through to be able to comprehend irony. First, they need to be able to tell falsehood from truth (in order to avoid taking ironic utterances literally). Second, they need to be able to infer another's beliefs (to avoid viewing the irony as a mistake); and third, child readers have to be able to infer another's intentions, so as not to confuse irony with intent to deceive. Mistakes in correctly accessing the irony can be made at any, or all, of these stages.

The parody included in these texts can also be problematic for young readers. I define parody in relation to such works as the humorous, exaggerated imitation of a literary genre and style, that of Gothic melodrama. Parody, like the Gothic itself, is known for its inherent ambivalence, as it is, by its very nature, a combination of two codes, one from the original text and one from the new parodic text (Rose 1993: 51).

The subtle, humorous forms of parody and irony are often inter-linked, and this is especially true of these texts; therefore I examine both in one passage from *Dimanche Diller in Danger.* In addition, irony, in particular, is notoriously difficult to demonstrate out of con-text; therefore I reproduce the whole of a letter from Valburga, who is languishing in prison, to her American nephew, Wolfie, which comes at the very beginning of the second book. Comments upon the types of irony will be made throughout the letter, and it must be remembered that irony as a concept gets it effects from below the surface, saying much more than it seems to be saying (Muecke 1969), so that readers need to be able to recognise the contrasts between the literal meaning and an implied unspoken meaning.

> Dear Wolfie
>
> I want you to pay me a visit in Olde England. Travel broadens the mind, Wolfie, and if yours is anything like your mother's it will need all the help that it can get.

This is, of course, a barbed jab aimed at Wolfie, who may, or may not, "get" the derogatory intent, as he is depicted as none too bright. Readers may notice that such insults are not the usual way a fond Aunty would start a letter to her "dear" nephew.

> I myself will not be free to show you round, owing to a grave mis-carriage of justice.

As well as the use of understatement here (Valburga cannot "show him round" as she is, in fact, in prison), there is evidence of an unreliable narrator/character, which is often associated with irony (see Booth 1974; Olsen 2003) due to the suspicion of deceit. As this sort of irony is at narrative level, it can be harder to grasp, but child readers of the previous book are likely to be well aware that Valburga more than deserved her punishment, so it is certainly not a "grave miscarriage of justice."

> Luckily, my old friend Gussie Godiva [Valburga's some-time assis-tant in her heinous plans] will. She runs the Post Office at Hilton in the Hollow, which is a lovely spot, and just the place for you to start your holiday.

> While you are there, Wolfie, I very much hope that you will meet a child called Dimanche Diller. Dimanche is an orphan, Wolfie, and you know you should be extra kind to orphans, don't you?

Again, judging by what is already known about Valburga's wickedness, child readers are likely to get this everyday, deliberate irony at the end of this passage. This overt, "stable" irony (Booth's term, 1974), whereby an utterance is actually the explicit opposite of that which is meant, may be easier for children to perceive as it is at word level. They are more likely to realise that being "kind to orphans" is the last thing on Valburga's mind—quite the opposite, in fact.

> If you take Dimanche on a little outing, her rich aunt will be most grateful to you, when you bring her back. And so will I.

> Do what I ask, Wolfie, and when I come out—which will be in approximately 1,725 days—I will repay your kindness.

Readers may now be getting the drift that Valburga is going to pay Wolfie to carry out her fiendish kidnapping plans whilst she is in prison.

> Your loving aunt Valburga.

> PS If you come to England and look for Dimanche, I will pay for your ticket on the plane.

> PPS Plus expenses.

> PPPS Plus a salary. A big one, Wolfie.

> (All quotations from Branford, 1994b: 7–9)

These postscripts re-emphasise the message that this is a job that Wolfie will be well paid for, just in case, he—or the reader—has missed that intent.

Most of the humorous irony, which is revealed by reading between the lines of the letter, picking up the veiled hints and appreciating the understatement, should not be lost on young readers, who will most likely be familiar with Valburga's evil machinations from the first book. This sort of indirect irony requires certain levels of reader sophistication and reconstructive abilities to be able to access or get the humour, and most of the irony is obviously much more than its usual simple definition of explicitly stating the opposite of what is meant (Roberts 1997: 76). Much of this irony involves awareness of language as well as knowledge about the world, and the young reader can be seen as a conscious agent who has to interpret the intended meaning.

Valburga's letter also includes another key aspect of a higher form of humour. This concerns parody, specifically the parody of melodrama, which is itself strongly associated with the Gothic.[6] Melodrama is associated with sensationalism, and was a popular form of entertainment in the nineteenth century, and so is generally considered a lowly form. In melodrama, the (often persecuted) good are always rewarded and the wicked villains (normally overtly evil) are punished (Peck & Coyle 1993: 98). The central interest often hinges on a secret, as it does in this trilogy, as Valburga is revealed not to be Dimanche's real aunt but merely an opportunist impostor.

A key aspect—an important, prominent melodramatic narrative device that is parodied here—is the technique of prolepsis, or foreshadowing, which is related to the concept of dramatic irony, in which the reader has the satisfaction of knowing more than the characters. Rather than the more usual technique of analepsis (the use of flashbacks in the narrative), prolepsis uses flash forwards, and hints at, or even tells of, what is to come.[7] Obviously, such a technique is concerned not with *what* will happen, but *how*, and this is related to the pleasures of the humour of expectation and comic anticipation. While some humour theorists point out the vital importance of surprise in humour (for example, Monro 1951; Morreall 1983, 1987), others reveal that the element of surprise is not essential, and that there is a different source of pleasure in humorous expectation, as the reader eagerly anticipates what they know will ultimately happen (Eastman 1936; Clark 1987; Latta 1999).

Many instances of such foreshadowing occur in this trilogy, and this narrative technique is often an essential part of the parody inherent in children's comic Gothic. Whether children can actually recognise this aspect of the parody is not the main point, although I believe that many children are very likely to recognize parodies of the comic Gothic in particular, due, in no small part, to the sheer prevalence of the mock Gothic in twentieth-century culture. Many cultural productions have been and still are aimed at children, such as cartoons, comics, films and Television series, from *The Addams Family* (in *The New Yorker*, 1937 onwards, and from 1964 on television and film), and *The Munsters* (1964 onwards), through to *Scooby Doo* (1969 onwards), and *Buffy the Vampire Slayer* (1997–2004), which all repeatedly return to various combinations and amalgamations of figures and features of the Gothic.

What is key here is the amusement of dramatic irony—a vital component in literary examples of "superiority humour"—when the reader is allowed the satisfaction of knowing more than the characters. In the example of the letter already quoted, readers probably know, unlike the prison officer characters who subsequently read the letter, what Valburga's real plans are likely to be as regards Dimanche (kidnapping or some other terrible misfortune). The narrator points out how the prison officer, after reading Valburga's letter before it is sent out, "was deeply moved by such kind intentions." He even "shed a tear," as did his companion as "they agreed that the power of prison to reform even the worst of criminals was truly remarkable" (9). Yet again, the reader has the satisfaction of knowing more than adults in authority. This satisfaction is compounded if the young reader can access all the irony in the letter, as the adult prison officer characters have failed to see through Valburga's letter to the real intent.

Of course, adding to the already paradoxical mix of ambiguities in the comic Gothic, this important element of the parody of melodramatic conventions is also mixed with a typically Gothic level of apprehension and anxiety about what is going to happen to Dimanche. This combines with the pleasures of comic anticipation of a humorous, probably slapstick, resolution, with Valburga receiving her just deserts (the schema/pattern for this has already been set by events in the first book), and thus adds even more to the overall ambiguity of the comic Gothic in children's texts—the incongruous mix of the fearful and the funny.

The irony of narration is also important, being prominent in this trilogy and in contemporary comic Gothic texts for junior readers in general. As Horner and Zlosnik reveal, though in relation to adult Gothic, the comic turn is often located in the telling (narration) of the story itself (2005: 9). In addition to the parody of melodrama in the use of foreshadowing, there is also the strong parody of the overt, intrusive, opinionated and often ironic narrator of melodrama; such parody can be useful in providing comic distance from the horrors of the Gothic. In a review of Branford's texts, Michael Thorn (2002: 1) points out the "lugubrious narrative tone" of the narrator of this trilogy, for children still too young (in terms of reading ability) for Snicket's *A Series of Unfortunate Events*. In addition, the stories, like Snicket's, do lack the usual cheerful tone of most children's tales, certainly those which most obviously contain lots of humour. From the second sentence of the very first book, the narrator addresses readers, after informing readers that Dimanche is an orphan, having lost both her parents at sea.

> And let me tell you right now, this is not one of those stories in which the missing parents turn up in the end. You must just take it from me that every now and then fate deals someone a cruel blow. (Branford 1994a: 7)

Although the stories, true to the spirit of melodrama, do end with the heroine triumphing and villains receiving their comeuppance, there is no happy ending in that Dimanche's parents are indeed lost forever.

This is typical of the comic Gothic, which despite slapstick and farcical episodes, often contains elements of more serious, normally less palatable undertones of life's unfairness, offering a bitter-sweet experience. Indeed, humour, and comedy in particular, have long been recognised as often containing serious themes (Palmer 1994: 120).

Despite this dark element of the comic Gothic, the parody of the conventions of melodrama, which itself parodies romantic literature, and the extensive use of irony mostly serve a playful, humorous function, certainly in books for this age group. Indeed, Nicholas Tucker, in his obituary of Henrietta Branford in *The Independent* (1999), talks of the series as "good humoured melodrama." The trilogy could certainly be seen as a spoof of the bleak Victorian Gothic melodrama, but it is much more than that. Hutcheon (1985: 16–17) points out that parody, in contemporary works, simply does not have to have a polemical edge. Dentith (2000: 16–19), too, agrees that the use of parody does not necessarily mean an attack upon the form parodied. The subtle humour of this parody has more to do with the play with the form—a playful imitation. The humour of this sort of parody for young readers, as Jon Stott points out about other texts, is in the story turning "things upside down" and/or looking at "serious story conventions humorously" (1990: 224). In doing this, such texts are actually self-reflexive and foreground their own textuality, and this can, at least in theory, provide young readers with a subconscious awareness of deliberately constructed literary devices. Irony, in particular, may help produce a certain level of beneficial detachment from any unthinking identification with the ideologies of the text (the use of irony is acknowledged as being useful for creating distance; Muecke 1970: 45) and, above all, there may be an awareness that, as Horner and Zlosnik put it, "nothing is to be taken seriously" (2005: 4).

This playful inversion may be a form of subversiveness (in its play with language and form, rather than satirical attack). So the higher, cognitive forms of humour in these texts can have a less obvious and therefore more effective subversiveness than that of the cruder forms of slapstick and violent, shocking gross-out humour which overtly rejoices in mocking frightening, powerful adults. So parody and irony may serve the function, in these comic Gothic texts for young readers, of creating ludic and liberating effects, the liberation applying to freedom of thought, which lasts far longer than the carnivalesque freedom of temporary time out from societal restrictions.

Examination of the higher forms of cognitive humour in Branford's trilogy for younger junior readers offers a new starting point for the study of the increasingly popular genre of the comic Gothic, and steps away from the earlier critical focus upon the developmental aspects of the low forms of humour contained in the genre, previously centred solely on criticism of Roald Dahl's work. I do not deny the existence, nor the benefits, of lower humorous forms, such as slapstick and ridiculous caricatures, in diffusing any fear engendered by the Gothic aspects of texts. But the humour in these texts can serve other functions than merely ameliorating fear through humour, and also extends beyond the well-documented psychological temporary relief from societal restrictions provided by simpler, cruder forms of humour. In fact, in Branford's trilogy, perhaps unusually for a book aimed at such a young readership, there is surprisingly little recourse to what developmentalists such as Kappas sometimes term early, cruder types of visual humour (Kappas 1967: 69). Branford's inclusion of more complex, higher forms of humour, such as parody and irony, as well as acknowledging young children's cognitive abilities and their perceptions of incongruity, can actually reinforce and even add to the schema for the playful ambiguity of the child Gothic in developing readers. This ludic quality of higher forms of humour in the comic Gothic, then, serves to add even more to the essential hybridity of the Gothic. This clever playfulness is one of the most useful, most unacknowledged and yet possibly one of the most beneficial functions of the humour in comic Gothic texts for junior readers.

ENDNOTES

1. See Kate Kellaway, "Bad Luck, good news," *The Observer*, 18 August 2002.
2. Review in *The New York Times*, 15 October 2000, cited in *The Children's Literature Review*, vol. 79, 2002, pp. 205–206.
3. According to the survey of children's reading, Young People's Reading at the End of the Century, carried out by the National Centre for Research in Children's Literature at Roehampton in London in 1996, Roald Dahl's books were rated as the favourites of all the age groups consulted (see pp. 73–74).
4. Horner and Zlosnik believe that "Gothic writing always concerns itself with boundaries and their instabilities" (2000: 243).
5. Of course, ideas about the fragmentation of the self should be borne in mind here. Obviously, humour preference is, anyway, incredibly individual and subjective, but it is also very dependent upon time, place, and mood.
6. According to Peter Brooks (1995), the rise of the Gothic novel and the birth of melodrama emerged historically at roughly the same time, at the beginning of the nineteenth century.
7. Rimmon-Kenan (2002: 48) states that prolepsis is less frequent than analepsis in literature in the Western tradition.

REFERENCES

Primary Texts

Branford, H. (1994a). *Dimanche Diller*. London: Collins.

_____ . (1994b). *Dimanche Diller in Danger*. London: Collins.

_____ . (1996). *Dimanche Diller at Sea*. London: Collins.

Dahl, R. (1961). *James and the Giant Peach*. London: Puffin.

_____ . (1983). *The Witches*. London: Puffin.

_____ . (1988). *Matilda*. London: Puffin.

Snicket, L. (1999–2006). *A Series of Unfortunate Events* (planned series of 13). London: Egmont.

Secondary Texts

Alderson, P. (2000). *Young Children's Rights: Exploring Beliefs, Principles and Practice*. London; New York: Jessica Kingsley Publishers.

Anderson, C. C. & Apseloff, M. F. (1989). *Nonsense Literature for Children: Aesop to Seuss*. Hamden, CT: Library Professional Publications.

Bakhtin, M. (1984). *Rabelais and His World*. H. Iswolsky (Trans.). Bloomington; Indianapolis: Indiana University Press.

Bassey, M. (1999). *Case Study Research in Educational Settings*. Buckingham; Philadelphia: Open University Press.

Berger, P. (1997). *Redeeming Laughter: The Comic Dimension of Human Experience*. New York; Berlin: Walter de Gruyter.

Boodman, S. (2002). *Children's Literature Review, 79*, 185.

Booth, W. (1974). *A Rhetoric of Irony*. Chicago; London: University of Chicago Press.

Botting, F. (1996). *Gothic*. London; New York: Routledge.

Brodzinsky, D. & Rightmyer, J. (1980). Individual Differences in Children's Humour Development. In P. McGhee & Chapman, A. J. (Eds.), *Children's Humour* (pp. 180–212). Chichester: John Wiley & Sons.

Brooks, P. (1985). *The Melodramatic Imagination: Balzac, Henry James, Melodrama, and the Mode of Excess*. New Haven, CT; London: Yale University Press.

Buckingham, D. (2000). *After the Death of Childhood: Growing Up in the Age of Electronic Media*. Cambridge: Polity Press.

Byars, B. (1993) 'Taking Humor Seriously'. In Hearne, B. (ed.) *The Zena Sutherland Lectures, 1983–1992*, 210–27 Boston: Clarion Books.

Cameron, E. (1981). 'A Question of Taste.' *The School Librarian, 29*(2), 108–114.

Cart, M. (1995). *What's So Funny? Wit and Humor in American Children's Literature*. New York: HarperCollins.

Clark, M. (1987). Humor and incongruity. In Morreall, J. (Ed.), *The Philosophy of Laughter and Humor* (pp. 139–155). Albany: State University of New York Press.

Culley, J. (1991). Roald Dahl— 'It's about children and it's for children'—But is it suitable? *Children's Literature in Education, 22*(1), 59–73.

Cunningham, H. (1995). *Children and Childhood in Western Society since 1500.* London; New York: Longman.

Dentith, S. (2000). *Parody.* London; New York: Routledge.

Dunn, F. (1921). *Interest Factors in Primary Reading Material.* Teachers College Contribution to Education, No. 113. New York: Teachers College, Columbia University.

Eastman, M. (1936). *Enjoyment of Laughter.* New York: Simon and Schuster.

Edmundson, M. (1997). *Nightmare on Main Street: Angels, Sadomasochism, and the Culture of the Gothic.* Cambridge, MA; London: Harvard University Press.

Freud, S. [1905] (2001). *Jokes and Their Relation to the Unconscious* (Volume VIII). *The Standard Edition of the Complete Psychological Works of Sigmund Freud.* London: Vintage.

———. [1927] (2001). Humour, 1927 (Volume XXI). *The Standard Edition of the Complete Psychological Works of Sigmund Freud* (pp. 159–166). London: Vintage.

Hazlitt, W. (1885) *Lectures on the English Comic Writers.* London: George Bell, cited in Morreall, J. *The Philosophy of Laughter,* 65–82.

Hobson, M., Madden, J., & Prytherch, R. (1992). *Children's Fiction Sourcebook.* Aldershot: Ashgate.

Horner, A. & Zlosnik, S. (2000). Comic Gothic. In Punter, D. (Ed.), *A Companion to the Gothic* (pp. 242–254). Oxford: Blackwell.

———. (2005). *Gothic and the Comic Turn.* Basingstoke: Palgrave Macmillan.

Hutcheon, L. [1985] (2000). *A Theory of Parody: The Teachings of Twentieth-Century Art Forms.* Urbana; Chicago: University of Illinois Press.

Jalongo, M. R. (1985). Children's literature: There's some sense to its humor. *Childhood Education, 62*(2), 109–114.

John, M. (2003). *Children's Rights and Power: Charging Up for a New Century.* London; New York: Jessica Kingsley Publishers.

Kappas, K. (1967). A developmental analysis of children's responses to humour. *The Library Quarterly, 1,* 67–78.

Klause, A. Curtis (1987) 'So What's So Funny, Anyway?' *School Library Journal,* 33:6, 34–5.

Kümmerling-Meibauer, B. (1999). Metalinguistic awareness and the child's developing concept of irony. *The Lion and the Unicorn, 23*(2), 157–183.

Latta, R. (1999). *The Basic Humor Process: A Cognitive-Shift Theory and the Case Against Incongruity.* Berlin; New York: Mouton de Gruyter.

Lee, N. (2001). *Childhood and Society: Growing Up in an Age of Uncertainty.* Buckingham; Philadelphia: Open University Press.

Levine, J. (1980). The Clinical Use of Humour in Work with Children. In P. E. McGhee & A. J. Chapman (Eds.), *Children's Humour* (pp. 255–280). Chichester: John Wiley & Sons.

Lurie, A. (1990). *Don't Tell the Grown Ups: The Subversive Power of Children's Literature*. Boston; London: Back Bay Books.

Lypp, M. (1995). The origin and functions of laughter in children's literature. In Nikolajeva, M. (Ed.), *Aspects and Issues in the History of Children's Literature* (pp. 183–189). Westport, CT; London: Greenwood Press.

McGhee, P. (1989). *Humour and Children's Development: A Guide to Practical Applications*. New York; London: Haworth Press.

Meek, M. (1988). *How Texts Teach What Readers Learn*. Stroud: Thimble Press.

Monro, D. H. (1951). *Argument of Laughter*. Notre Dame, IN: University of Notre Dame Press.

Morreall, J. (1983). *Taking Laughter Seriously*. Albany: State University of New York Press.

Morreall, J. (Ed.). (1987). *The Philosophy of Laughter and Humor*. Albany: State University of New York Press.

Muecke, D. (1969). *The Compass of Irony*. London; New York: Methuen and Co.
_____ . (1970). *Irony*. London: Methuen and Co.

Mulkay, M. (1988). *On Humour: Its Nature and Its Place in Modern Society*. Oxford: Polity Press.

National Centre for Research in Children's Literature. (1996). *Young People's Reading at the End of the Century*, London, UK.

Olsen, G. (2003). Reconsidering unreliability: Fallible and untrustworthy narrators. *Narrative, 11*, 93–109.

Palmer, J. (1994) *Taking Humour Seriously*. London; New York: Routledge.

Peck, J. & Coyle, M. (1993). *Literary Terms and Criticism*, 2nd ed. Basingstoke: Macmillan Press.

Petzold, D. (1992). Wish-fulfilment and subversion: Roald Dahl's Dickensian fantasy Matilda. *Children's Literature in Education, 23*(4), 185–193.

Rees, D. (1988). Dahl's chickens: Roald Dahl. *Children's Literature in Education, 19*(3), 143–155.

Reynolds, K., Brennan, G., & McCarron, K. (2001). *Frightening Fiction* (pp. 1–18). London; New York: Continuum.

Rimmon-Kenan, S. (2002). *Narrative Fiction*, 2nd ed. London; New York: Routledge.

Roberts, P. (1997). *Taking Humor Seriously in Children's Literature*. Lanham; London: Scarecrow Press.

Rose, M. (1993). *Parody: Ancient, Modern and Post-Modern*. Cambridge: Cambridge University Press.

Sage, V. (1994). Gothic laughter: farce and horror in five texts. In A. Lloyd-Smith & V. Sage (Eds.), *Gothick Origins and Innovations* (pp. 190–203). Amsterdam: Rodopi.

Spencer, H. (1911) 'On the Physiology of Laughter.' In *Essays on Education, Etc.*, London: Dent, 298–309.

Stephens, J. (1992). *Language and Ideology in Children's Fiction*. London; New York: Longman.

Stott, J. (1990). "Will the real dragon please stand up?" Convention and parody in children's stories. *Children's Literature Association Quarterly, 21*(4), 219–228.

Thompson, J. O. (Ed.). (1982). *Monty Python: Complete and Utter Theory of the Grotesque.* London: BFI.

Thorn, M. (2002). Tied to the action. *Times Educational Supplement,* 5 July, p. 1.

Tucker, N. (1981). *The Child and The Book: A Psychological and Literary Exploration.* Cambridge: Cambridge University Press.

———. (1999). Obituary for Henrietta Branford. *The Independent,* 29 April 1999.

West, M. (1990). The grotesque and the taboo in Roald Dahl's humorous writings for children. *Children's Literature Association Quarterly, 15*(3), 115–116.

4

BETWEEN HORROR, HUMOUR, AND HOPE: NEIL GAIMAN AND THE PSYCHIC WORK OF THE GOTHIC

Karen Coats

As the essays in this volume clearly demonstrate, children's Gothic has become prevalent enough as a phenomenon to represent what can be considered a cultural symptom—an indicator that points to an under-lying trauma, often in such a displaced or condensed way that there is no apparent link between the trauma and its symptom. Interpretations of symptoms always operate as limits, that is, to give an interpretation is to limit what most likely has multiple meanings to the one or two meanings the interpretation generates. This is, in part, one of the reasons why knowing what a symptom means, according to a particular interpretation, doesn't make it go away. What interpretations can do, however, is make a symptom more interesting, or less threatening; they can make us less likely to try to censor or eradicate a symptom that isn't really hurting anyone and is in fact helping certain people to cope with the circumstances of their lives, and allow us to enjoy it. This essay takes such an approach: my goal is to look at children's Gothic as a symptom, to explore some of the possible traumas that produce the Gothic as symptom, and to suggest how the Gothic may help children cope with those traumas in an indirect fashion.

Though my arguments have a wider application, I will focus them by looking specifically at three texts by Neil Gaiman. Certain Gothic motifs in his work, including big old houses with secret spaces, doppel-gangers, dream-visions, and dark tunnels, operate rather obviously as metaphors for unconscious depths, but he also employs Gothic themes through the use of the macabre, the ghostly, and the anti-expected (as opposed to the merely unexpected) event or characterization (such as portraying Death as a cute teenaged Goth girl). Gaiman's work is particularly interesting for this collection as he is bringing Gothic resonances to the whole range of age groups in children's literature, from his picture books (*The Wolves in the Walls*, 2003), to his preadolescent fiction (*Coraline*, 2002), to his work for young adults (the *Sandman* graphic novels series, as well as stand alone novels and graphic novels such as *Neverwhere* and *Creatures of the Night*, various short stories, and his recent film *Mirrormask*, 2005). Gaiman often combines humour and horror, which has been the legacy of the Gothic since its inception, and indicates the close relation between fear and humour as two affective responses to incongruent stimuli. Ethically speaking, Gaiman does Gothic old-school, that is, the demarcations between good and evil are clear, and even when the evil is within, it is soundly defeated and expelled by a problem-solving hero or heroine. Obviously, Gaiman is only one of the many authors using Gothic conventions in his work, and I will be exploring but a small, interconnected sample from among his many works for my readings, but the phenomena he explores are spread across all aspects of children's literature and culture. Though the market undoubtedly has a strong role in creating the desire for the products it has to offer, it is also beyond question that these products are responding to a demand; that is, there is an appetite that they are feeding. So the question is: What needs are being met with these works, and why are they emerging so strongly in the present cultural milieu?

Traditional adult Gothic has tended to give a sinister inflection to fairy tale tropes and motifs, combining elements of horror and the supernatural to produce situations in which the humble subject can become a hero or a heroine, beset on all sides but ultimately (usually) triumphant. This affinity with fairy tales gives us a starting place to consider why the Gothic has become a prevalent form in children's literature in recent years. Bruno Bettelheim and Marie-Louise von Franz have taught us about the unconscious psychic work that the fairy tale is supposed to do for children—to provide concrete images of villains and monsters on which to project undirected anxieties and fears so that they might be contained and dispatched, to facilitate psychic integration, and to assure the child of the possibility of happy endings when present trials are overcome. The dark landscapes, inappropriate lusts, and ravenous villains correspond to the dangerous impulses and aggressions that children actually experience as part of their own mental topographies, and fairy tales offer narratives that put those scary appetites in their proper places, so to speak. Twentieth- and twenty-first-century culture, however, has degraded these once psychically useful tales into little more than "a couple of rodents looking for a theme park" (*Hercules*, 1997), where ogres don't eat children as much as entertain them, an average Joe can have his princess without slaying any dragons, and a schoolgirl will be handed both her kingdom and her prince at the low cost of learning how to walk properly and style her hair. Such sanitizations render fairy tales less able to do their work despite the fact that our unconscious is as murky and the outside world as dangerous as ever they were. In addition, materialist objections, including feminist and Marxist critiques, have cast traditional stories in a bad light; their legitimate concern with the surface values of the tales has led to either dispensing with the tales altogether, or to calling for revisions that fail to pack the unconscious punch needed for the tales to be psychically effective. These circumstances create the conditions for the Gothic in contemporary children's literature to fill the gap that the loss of traditional fairy tale has created.

The initial instantiations of the Gothic as a form are often considered to be a reaction to the Age of Reason, a time when superstitions and folkways were losing ground to scientific investigation and explanation. However, ignoring the irrational, affect-driven aspects of human experience doesn't make them go away, and the force of their re-emergence is often in direct proportion to the force with which they have been repressed. Thus it makes a kind of sense that this is a form that would speak to children, who are themselves involved in a project that will involve them giving up certain cherished beliefs, inventions, and fantasies in light of more reasonable and impersonal explanations. They need to put aside magical thinking, and realize that their evil wishes did not cause their gym teacher to break his ankle, or that the universe didn't decide to rain just because they had an important soccer game. The residue of magical thinking persists, however, well into adulthood, if only for those fleeting seconds when we are caught off-guard by the fulfilment of our wishes for good or ill, before we take ourselves in hand and talk ourselves into the reasonable explanation. By casting these wishes into story form, and taking them to their hyperbolic extreme, we are more readily able to see their absurdity, to turn them into moments for self-deprecating and subsequently empowering laughter.

We find such a dynamic in Gaiman's *The Wolves in the Walls*. While the rest of her family blithely engages in quotidian occupations, Lucy alone hears noises inside the walls of her house. She is convinced that there are wolves in the walls. Why wolves? Remember Max's drawing of a wild thing that he pins to the wall going down the stairs in *Where the*

Wild Things Are (Sendak 1963)? When Max enters his fantasy domain, then, he encounters the creatures of his own imagination. This is why he doesn't fear them, but the point of the story is that they nonetheless must be contained in a private space; mom will not have him acting like a wild thing in her house, so he must learn to control the wild things in his mind. Like Max, Lucy has drawn a picture (many pictures, actually) of her particular bogeyman; she has in fact covered the stair wall with pictures of wolves. In terms of Gothic space as private, haunted space, it is significant that it is the stair wall in both stories, as stairs usually lead from the public spaces of a house to the private spaces, and how many times have we all yelled at the heroine on the horror-movie screen *not to go upstairs?* At any rate, Lucy has conjured her own villain—she has effectively accomplished one of the functions of the Gothic, which, according to Mark Edmundson, is "to turn anxiety, the vague but insistent fear of what will happen in the future, into suspense" (1997: 12). The anxiety that Lucy is experiencing is a common one for children—what if I lose my home, which represents, for most children, the boundaries of their whole world? Most of us can remember this anxiety taking some very particular shape in our own pasts, or we can see shades of it in our children—fear of sounds in the night, fear of monsters under the bed, fear of a certain space (the basement or attic, for instance), fear of the house catching on fire, fear of intruders, etc. are all linked in some way to the anxious residue of the trauma of separation from that first womb-home. What is interesting about this particular anxiety is that it is not at all irrational; rather it will certainly come to pass. Children will lose the presently necessary comforts of their home, their family, and the protection from responsibility that those things afford them; there is a Gothic moment where that vague anxiety must be turned into suspense, and so they had better learn to cope with whatever symptom that trauma has produced.

Gaiman links this vague anxiety to a truly absurd narrative scenario so that he can actually bring it to pass and have Lucy deal with it. But first he exposes (or, more accurately, illustrator Dave McKean exposes) its internal origins, the drawings on the wall, and its position as repressed by the forces of reason. When Lucy tells her mother her fears, her mother offers the much more reasonable explanation that she is hearing mice. Her father suggests rats, and her brother bats. Her brother is, significantly, the most determined to be reasonable, perhaps because he has only just emerged from a belief in the irrational himself: "Firstly," he says, adopting a pedantic tone, "there are no wolves in this part of the world....Secondly, wolves don't live in walls, only mice and rats and bats and things" (2003: n.p.). His hold on the reasonable is childlike and tentative, though, as he says later, "I shall ensure that I sleep with my neck exposed tonight, in case one of them is a vampire bat. Then, if it bites me, I shall be able to fly and sleep in a coffin, and never have to go to school in the daytime again" (n.p.). Impeccable logic, no doubt, even if it is based on faulty premises. Like his parents, however, he adds the ominous warning: "Thirdly, if the wolves come out of the walls, it's all over" (n.p.). The question of what's all over, and who says, are answered "it" and "everyone," respectively. That is, if our unconscious fears do become manifestly present and are allowed to run amok, they will have the last word. When the wolves do come out of the walls, the family panics and moves out, preferring to live in the garden rather than to confront the interlopers. But under this interpretation (limited and limiting, remember?), they really can't do anything about the wolves until Lucy decides to take charge. They are Lucy's wolves, after all.

Realizing that she has left her most important comfort object, a pig puppet, to the unkind ministrations of the wolves, she goes back to retrieve it. After seeing what the wolves are doing to her home, she convinces her family that it would be better to live in the spaces in the walls than to spend another night in the cold garden, but it isn't long before the family, brandishing the legs of a broken chair, breaks out of the walls and reclaims their home. I can't help but be reminded of the retaking of Toad Hall from the weasels here—in both cases, the childlike characters have lost their comfortable homes to menacing representatives of insatiable appetite and unchecked greed. But whereas Badger and company act on Toad's behalf to get him under control, Lucy takes that initiative upon herself. Toad remains a child, but Lucy, like Max, takes the first steps toward growing up by suppressing her wild things. She has temporarily lost her home, but she proves that she has the power to reclaim it, to chase the wolves away. Gaiman slyly suggests that her psychic work in protecting her ego-home from the intrusion of id-dwellers will be an ongoing process when he introduces the spectre of elephants in the walls on the final pages.

The composition of the book encourages readers to take an interpretive stance toward the story. McKean's surrealist mixed-media images engage the viewer on multiple levels but never at the level of a straightforward representation of reality, thus imposing an ironic distance from which the reader can safely and critically view the events. The compositions are technically fascinating, impelling readers to a figure-it-out response: How did he create this effect? What are the objects in this collage and why are they here? Which objects are real and what is computer generated? Faces are made of assemblages rather than seamless wholes, TV images are blurs of colour, and jam jars run off the page to infinity, creating images that are obviously artificial and manufactured and yet as organic and recognizable as dreams; hence we sense that the images are attempts to capture mental states and meanings that require interpretation rather than unthinking absorption. This kind of visual detective work predisposes readers to adopt an analytical attitude to the book as a whole. Thematically, we see how the humans' dusky skin tones mimic the textures of the walls, connecting them with their home and giving them a chunky solidity, whereas the wolves are ink line drawings, making it significant that Lucy is holding a pen on the cover, drawing a wolf whose eyes are eerily real, peeking through holes in her drawing as she looks out at the reader, a mute invitation in her dot eyes. Once readers make the imagistic if not entirely conscious connection that Lucy has somehow literally drawn these wolves out of the walls, it becomes funny rather than scary to think that she and her parents are chased out of their home by them. The metatextuality of the illustrations, if you will, reminds readers that this is a story, as does the repetitive cycle of their conversations, where each family member contributes a similarly formulated answer to whatever question is posed. Their droll acceptance of their predicament and their hyperbolic suggestions for new living arrangements are of the order of children's fantasy games. Gaiman heightens the effect by inserting a random character into the narrative, not for her importance to the story, but to maintain the structure of both illustration and text. When Lucy suggests that they move back into their house, each family member is shown in horrified profile in a quadrant of the page saying "What?" Since Lucy herself can't participate in this incredulity and thus complete the foursquare, Gaiman manufactures a new player: "'What?' said the Queen of Melanesia, who had dropped by to help with the gardening" (n.p.). This kind of unexpected incongruity produces a flash of surprise, which, when discerned to be deliberately disarming and ultimately nonthreatening, heightens the sense of textuality and elicits laughter, as does the scene where the family chases the wolves out of their home.

Gaiman's device of treating what could be a horrible situation with a humorous twist is a move that empowers young readers. The idea that wolves are as afraid of humans as humans are of wolves is of course a fairly standard but decidedly useful cliché, at least when one is menaced by them from the safety of one's armchair. But it is the unexpectedness of the turn-around and its successful outcome that releases psychic tension and results in laughter. Every fairy tale-reading child knows that wolves are a threat to little girls. But the absurdity of wolves playing video games, eating jam, and playing the tuba sets off giggles because it defangs their fears, making them seem child-like. When Lucy and her family send the wolves off in fear for their lives, the inversion is complete—the child reader, like Lucy, is superior to these silly ink drawings, and can send them packing with whatever weapons they find on hand. Therefore, when the elephant footprint appears in the final scene, all that is left, affectively speaking, is humour. Whether or not the readers were a little spooked by the previous home invasion, it has been rendered safe by the ensuing events. Furthermore, elephants don't carry the same fairy tale baggage as wolves, and their size makes the possibility that they are living in Lucy's walls quite silly indeed.

In this book, then, Gaiman uses Gothic conventions to dress up a common childhood fear, and then dresses it down with humour and Lucy's assertive agency in the face of that fear. His story plays in the spaces between the quite reasonable emotional anxiety that children (and adults) feel at the threat of loss, and the irrational forms that fear can sometimes take. We manufacture fearful stories and engage in dark, obsessive daydreams in order to get some mastery over unfocused anxieties; in our narratives we can muster a degree of control over our responses by giving them a specific location in a character or a setting, and producing a narrative arc where anxiety becomes suspense, suspense culminates in the thing we fear actually happening, and we work out possible plans of response where we do not disintegrate into quivering jellies, or maybe we do, but we get back up and move forward. Once we have achieved a sense of superiority over the anxiety through narrative, we may even move into a position where we can laugh about it. This kind of Gothic story helps children because it acknowledges and validates the horror—Lucy was right about the wolves, even though her family pooh-poohed her—even as it domesticates and contains it. And as I mentioned above, the anxiety of loss of home and security that the story responds to is something that will come to pass, repeatedly even, over the course of a child's development. Thus these stories increase children's emotional preparedness for the times when their own wolves come out of the walls.

Besides being a reactionary form of psychic protest against the dominance of reason, the Gothic is indebted to a culture of revolution; thus, the emergence of Gothic is also attributed in part to the ambivalences felt by those who wanted to throw off the oppressive mantle of patriarchal values that suppressed individual freedoms, but were nevertheless frightened by what such freedom would entail. Leslie A. Fiedler opines:

> The guilt which underlies the gothic and motivates its plots is the guilt of the revolutionary haunted by the (paternal) past which he has been striving to destroy; and the fear that possesses the gothic and motivates its tone is the fear that in destroying the old ego-ideals of Church and State, the West has opened a way for the inruption of darkness: for insanity and the disintegration of the self. (1982: 129)

Once again, the forces that haunt the form make it an ideal mode of expression for the emerging adolescent. Like the revolutionary, the child seeks to test and perhaps throw off the stifling ego-ideals that he or she has internalized as a child under the rule of parents, and find ones that will reflect his or her individual desires and sense of self. The problems, of course, are manifold. First, such change isn't accomplished without some resistance on both sides; children don't want to be clones of their parents, so their assertion of their identities will most likely involve some measure of rejection of paternal values. Additionally, though, the ego-ideals that children internalize are reflective of both conscious and unconscious legacies of their parents, so that the things we have repressed about ourselves may in fact be the things that emerge most forcefully in our children, much to our shame and dismay. Even if the parents are utterly supportive of their child's identity choices, the process is painful, because it involves yet another time of separation and sense of some connection lost, with the accompanying grief. Finally, there is no guarantee that the new identity will have uptake or ultimately lead to the life one dreams of having; teens are notorious for trying out multiple provisional identities in order to find one that effectively matches their desire with the requirements of the community they wish to join.

Psychologically speaking, Fiedler was writing both during and about a time when fragmentation of the self was, if not an indicator of insanity and disintegration, then at least an undesirable state of affairs. With today's embrace of postmodernist ideals of self-fashioning, however, such fragmentation can be read as a cultural advantage; chasing cool and adapting to rapidly changing technologies is easier without dragging along the baggage of a fixed and immutable sense of self.

Fiedler's broad and rather dramatic statement is an attempt to make a cultural interpretation of an oedipal trope prevalent in early Gothic fiction—namely, the trope of incest. In a traditional oedipal scenario, mother-son incest is both the ultimate expression of the son's desire and the ultimate violation of the father's law, which sets the limits on who is available to be desired—not mothers and not sisters. As long as the son (and the mother) plays by the father's rules, dark desires remain in the walls, so to speak; they are properly abjected, in Kristeva's terminology, sloughed off as impure and dirty, unthinkable (1980). But Kristeva also reminds us that what has been abjected doesn't simply go away. We are haunted by the persistence of those incestuous desires, and we are haunted by the guilt we feel in having them. Surely not in children's literature! Well, not usually openly, no, but the patterns are there in veiled form, just as the desires themselves emerge in veiled form in our experiential life. Though most critics have focused on the father/daughter, mother/son, or brother/sister incest plots in Gothic fiction, Claire Kahane suggests that these plots often act as mere overlays for "another mode of confrontation even more disquieting" (1985: 336). She continues:

> What I see repeatedly locked into the forbidden center of the Gothic which draws me inward is the spectral presence of a dead-undead mother, archaic and all-encompassing, a ghost signifying the problematics of femininity which the heroine must confront. (336)

She cites Fiedler, who also affirms that "beneath the haunted castle lies the dungeon keep: the womb from whose darkness the ego first emerged, the tomb to which it knows it must return at last" (Fiedler 1982:132; quoted in Kahane 1985: 336).

Because children are in the process of birthing an ego separate from that of their mothers, the mother/child relationship finds various modes of expression in children's literature, including mother/daughter incest anxiety. Both Lacan (1988) and Kristeva (1980) remind us that the mother is the first object of desire for the daughter as well as the son. But female identity is more likely to progress not in the fashion of Electra, as some psychoanalytic models have proposed, but in what may perhaps be the archetypal font of all Gothic fiction—the myth of Persephone. While gathering flowers, the beloved daughter of Demeter is stolen by Hades who erupts from the earth. He rapes Persephone and makes her Queen of the Dead, a position she eventually embraces and comes to like, according to some versions of the legend. But Demeter will not suffer her kidnapping, and she causes the world to go dormant until Zeus demands that Hades release Persephone. He does, but he gives her a pomegranate, three to six (accounts differ) seeds of which she eats, causing her to have to divide her time between her mother and her husband. As a story of female development, this one highlights the deep bond between a mother and a daughter, but it also opens up questions and points to ambivalences. Persephone misses her mother, but she has been made a queen and relishes her power. As for her abduction, she wandered far away from her companions while picking flowers and didn't give up her plucking habit while in the Underworld; according to some versions, she is the one who picked the pomegranate from Hades' garden. Hence, Persephone is caught in the ambivalences that plague all young girls: a desire to remain in a dyadic relationship with their mothers, which is the variant of the incest plot that concerns us here, and a desire to break away and explore things on their own, which is the plot of the revolutionary indicated by Fiedler.

Gaiman's versions of this Gothic drama of female development are found in his preadolescent novel *Coraline*, and his film *Mirrormask*. Both narratives are indebted to Lucy Lane Clifford's eerie short story, "The New Mother" (1882) in which two children are tempted to be naughty by a mysterious stranger who will only show her magical talents to truly naughty children. Their mother warns them that if they are truly naughty, they will prove that they do not love her, and she will have to leave and be replaced by a new mother with shiny glass eyes and a wooden tail. The stranger convinces them that no such creature exists and encourages them to escalate their naughty behaviours, since it is clear that they are not sincerely mischievous, but only want to see what she has in the box attached to her peardrum. She's right, but the little girls are so consumed by their desire to see her secret that they do their best. Though they fail to achieve the level of wilful misbehaviour that the stranger requires, their mother leaves, and the new mother arrives, forcing them to flee their home and live out their lives in the woods behind their house. It's a spooky, cautionary tale that works by playing on very real childhood fears: What if my desires become too much for my mother? What if she withdraws her love? What if she is replaced by an ogress who will devour me? Which is worse—giving up what I want, or giving up her love?

Gaiman plays with these fears as well, but ends in a very different place. Unlike the girls in "The New Mother," Coraline is not naughty, nor does she desire to be. She's just bored. Adam Phillips asserts that "boredom starts as a regular crisis in the child's developing capacity to be alone in the presence of the mother" (1994: 69). Up to a certain point, the developing child is so entangled with the mother that his and her desires are not perceived as separate, at least on the part of the child. When a child develops the capacity to be bored, it is a signal that he or she is in a transitional state, a state where he or she is developing a separate sense of self, a need to assert his or her desires over and against the desires of the mother. Boredom is, in Phillips' words, "that most absurd and paradoxical wish, the wish for a desire" (1994: 68). So long as the boundaries between mother and child are fuzzy and indistinct, the mother fills in the child's desire—he desires her, and he desires as and what she desires. But when he begins the long process of disentangling himself from her, of becoming a subject, he needs to develop his own desires, and sometimes that project momentarily fails.

Hence we see Coraline caught in that liminal moment when she finds herself cut off from her parents' desire, and not yet sure of her own. When she goes school shopping with her mom, we get a fuller picture of the disconnection of their desires. Mum is aligned with the shop assistant and the school's dress code; Coraline wants to assert an individual sense of style by buying some Dayglo green gloves. Coraline's mother ignores her, and Coraline drifts away. When she returns and her mother asks her where she's been, she replies, "I was kidnapped by aliens....They came down from outer space with ray guns, but I fooled them by wearing a wig and laughing in a foreign accent, and I escaped," to which her mother replies in patented distracted momspeak, "Yes, dear" (Gaiman 2002: 24). These small interactions clearly show that Coraline is searching for her own desires, and is in fact alone in the presence of her mother. It is significant, then, that it is immediately after this shopping trip that Coraline first enters the realm of the other mother. It is also significant that it is her mother who has shown her the key and has also shown her that the doorway is blocked. One of the most important things that parents do for children is to educate them in the way of desire, not by fulfilling their desires but by showing how desire may be pursued as a project, not by distracting them out of their boredom but by allowing boredom as an opportunity to explore their own possible desires. When Coraline and her mother view the opened door together, it is blocked by a brick wall; this is not the space of a shared desire, but one that Coraline must pursue on her own.

Coraline's experience in the other mother's world charts the development of a sophisticated sense of desire. At first, she is intrigued by the promise of a world where all of her desires are met with things she likes and finds fascinating. But it soon becomes clear that she will never be allowed to be bored in this world; she will never be allowed to want. Her other parents will never be too busy to stop what they are doing to play with her, but she will never be able to move beyond her other mother's desire. As Coraline explores the grounds around the house, she realizes that everything has actually been constructed, or rather copied, by the other mother, and that the world ends where the other mother stopped making it—the trees first lose their definition, and then everything disappears altogether like a blank piece of paper, and then she finds herself back at the house. She is confined to her other mother's desire. When

Coraline tries to figure out the nature of the other mother's desire, the cat replies, "'She wants something to love, I think', said the cat. 'Something that isn't her. She might want something to eat as well. It's hard to tell with creatures like that'" (65). And this is the true horror of the other mother—for her, love is a regressive desire to consume Coraline. The ghost children that Coraline finds in the closet are mere husks because they didn't learn the paradoxical lesson that Coraline does, that desire doesn't work by getting everything you want. The offer the other mother makes through the rats, "If you stay here, you can have whatever you want" (120) is roundly rejected by Coraline:

> Coraline sighed. "You really don't understand, do you?" she said. "I don't *want* whatever I want. Nobody does. Not really. What kind of fun would it be if I just got everything I ever wanted? Just like that, and it didn't *mean* anything. What then?" (120)

The other mother's desire is devouring, but Coraline is as resistant to it as she is to her father's recipes; unlike the other children, she is discriminating enough to know what she likes, and she also knows, somehow, that being bored is a necessary move in the game.

Gaiman uses multiple womb images to underscore the nature of Coraline's plight. The point of mother/child incest is not the pleasure of sex after all, but the dubious pleasure of regressing into an infantile state of undifferentiation, of plenitude experienced as reuniting with the body you once shared, marking it as a death drive rather than the claiming of one's actual desire. The creatures that Coraline encounters in the other mother's realm are versions of fetuses in various stages of development—the sisters Miss Spink and Miss Forcible regress first to younger versions of themselves, and then to two half-formed bodies in a thing resembling a spider's egg-sac. The other father is also punished with regression of form; when Coraline finds him in the basement, he looks unformed, having lost distinction in his facial features and missing one of his button eyes. When she finally rescues her parents and the souls of the children, they have to pass through a long, dark, undulating tunnel that is at first "warm and yielding...covered in a fine downy fur" and then becomes "hot and wet, as if she had put her hand in somebody's mouth" (135). Mouth, indeed.

Coraline's final test, after successfully escaping from a world where she would have certainly been absorbed into the other mother's consuming desire, is to escape her clutches, literally, once and for all. Here Gaiman uses the ghastly device of a severed, malevolent hand with lethal fingernails that he continually compares to a spider skittering along. Both hands and spiders are traditionally linked to mothers in a child's psycho-symbolic world.

If I may be permitted a personal anecdote and some whimsical interpretation by way of example: My younger daughter, Blair, had a Gothic dream when she was three. She said that her daddy, her sister Emily, and she were being chased by a giant spider, but that I, her mommy, wasn't in the dream. I had learned enough from my elder daughter's drawings of me that I most certainly was in that dream; Emily drew most of her figures with the correct number of arms and fingers, except for me, who always had way too many of these appendages. It makes sense that a mother, who does so much washing and combing and buttoning, etc. for a child, would be represented as having more than the requisite number of arms and fingers, and it is no small leap to think that a breastfed child, especially, might bear a residual image of her mother as nothing but a breast with arms, i.e., a spider. Not very flattering, of course, but there you are.

Whether or not one buys my little story, it is undeniable that, from *Charlotte's Web* to *The Hobbit* to *Harry Potter and the Chamber of Secrets*, spiders figure largely as bloodthirsty maternal symbols. And just as Ron Weasley's fear of them can be linked to Molly Weasley's overprotective streak and her propensity for sending howlers, so Coraline's problem with the spidery hand can be linked to a more sinister mother bent on smothering her child. Coraline has no choice but to dispatch this demon back to hell, which she does by trading on what she has learned about the other mother's inability to resist going after what she wants.

The final text I will explore in my sample is Gaiman's film *Mirrormask* (2005), which I see as a synthesis of the themes he develops in *The Wolves in the Walls* and *Coraline*. McKean partnered with him on all three of these projects, heightening the sinister strangeness of the worlds with his ragged and angular figure and landscape drawings. The breathtaking visual effects of *Mirrormask,* as in *The Wolves in the Walls,* contribute to the thematic density of the works, creating an aesthetic mood that intensifies the story's effect. Like *Coraline, Mirrormask* is centrally focused on a mother/daughter plot. Unlike Coraline, though, Helena means to be nasty to her mother. Helena is in an adolescent moult. She is resisting her place in her father's circus, and, lashing out at her mother in typical teen girl fashion, screams that she wants to run away from the circus and join "real life." When her mother claims that Helena will be the death of her, Helena replies, "I wish I was." Of course her mother collapses that very night and has to go to the hospital for an unspecified but apparently serious problem. Helena is undone with guilt, which occasions her journey into a dream-world of her own making. Instead of her drawings coming out of the walls like Lucy's, Helena enters the world composed of the drawings on her walls and finds there a world of doubles. Her mother has both a white and a dark queen double, the white queen, significantly, being asleep. Helena sees an opportunity for reparation—if she can find the charm that will waken the white queen, she can atone for being so nasty to her mother and her mother will be well. But Helena does not take the blame for her fractured relationship with her mother entirely on herself. Both mother and daughter are out of balance; the good, kind side of them is sleeping, while the evil, sinister side is taking control. Whenever Helena peers through a window from her dream-world into her real life, she sees the runaway princess of the Land of Shadows, her dark double, yelling at her dad, making out with a guy and burning all of Helena's drawings in an attempt to prevent Helena's return to her real world. When Helena meets the Queen of Shadows, she finds her to be like Coraline's other mother, bent on possessing her and turning her into an automaton. Interestingly, the cost for both Helena and Coraline is the loss of their eyes; Coraline's other mother wants to replace Coraline's eyes with buttons, whereas Helena's eyes fill in with an inky black blankness. Helena makes an eloquent plea for her beleaguered double, requesting that her mother let her make some of her own choices, but the evil queen flatly refuses, and Helena realizes that they must both be destroyed in order for her world to survive.

Helena is clearly more entangled with her real mother than Coraline is. At a pivotal moment in Helena's quest, her mother comes to her and they muse over whose dream this actually is. Her mother thinks it is her dream, brought on by the anaesthesia they are using for her surgery. She even asks Helena if she has dreamed her a boyfriend, indicating the companion that Helena has picked up on the way. Helena is clearly embarrassed by this, but it is a telling moment in the psychic drama of separation; her mother clearly has some of the controlling traits of the Queen of Shadows, thinking it is she who has procured a boyfriend for her daughter. Helena insists that this is her dream, and she uses that belief as an impetus to change the landscape. In other words, she can only make progress when she has asserted that she is the dreamer of her own dreams. Nonetheless, she uses the same words her mother used on her when she finally expels her evil twin: "You couldn't handle real life." Helena's recovery of her mother would be less decisive than Coraline's in developmental terms, then, were it not for the appearance, in real life, of her dream boyfriend. Whereas Coraline's mother/daughter incest plot ends with her rebirth and a firm expulsion of her other mother from her world, Helena's ends with the finding of an appropriate male substitute.

What is perhaps most interesting from a psychoanalytic point of view here is that even though both Coraline and Helena have good, wise, loving parents who recognize and support their need to grow away from them, they still need to go through harrowing psychic dramas of separation from them in order to achieve their own desire. Part of that drama is their recovery; not only must each girl find a way to assert her identity apart from her parents, but she must also find a way for them to be part of her without being all of her. Gaiman maintains a clearer ethical stance in his fiction than many Gothic writers for children; his villains are truly nasty, and his heroines are steadfast in their work to defeat them. This may be yet another function of the Gothic for outwardly stable, well-loved children. Their worlds do not provide them with circumstances that adequately represent for them the violent, bleeding cut that is psychically necessary for them to learn to be alone in the presence of their parents. Their outer lives give them no actual contexts for the fear that accompanies the inner dramas and psychic losses that are an inevitable legacy of growing up. Well-made Gothic can fill in those gaps, giving concrete expression to abstract psychic processes, keeping dark fascinations and haunting fears where children can see them, and mingling the horror with healthy doses of humour and hope.

REFERENCES

Clifford, L. L. [1882] (2005). The new mother. Reprinted in J. Zipes, et al. (Eds.). *The Norton Anthology of Children's Literature* (pp. 568–582). New York: Norton.

Edmundson, M. (1997). *Nightmare on Main Street*. Cambridge, MA: Harvard University Press.

Fiedler, L. (1982). *Love and Death in the American Novel*. New York: Stein and Day.

Gaiman, N. (2002). *Coraline*. Dave McKean (Illus.). New York: HarperCollins.

———. (2003). *The Wolves in the Walls*. Dave McKean (Illus.). New York: HarperCollins.

———. (2005). *Mirrormask*. Dave McKean (Director), Destination Films and Jim Henson Company: Sony Pictures.

Hercules. [1997] (2000). Ron Clements & John Musker (Directors), Walt Disney Studios: Walt Disney Video.

Kahane, C. (1985). The Gothic Mirror. In S. N. Garner, C. Kahane, & M. Sprengnether (Eds.), *The (M)other Tongue: Essays in Feminist Psychoanalytic Interpretation*. Ithaca, NY: Cornell University Press.

Kristeva, J. [1980] (1982). *Powers of Horror: An Essay on Abjection*. Leon Roudiez (Trans.). New York: Columbia University Press.

Lacan, J. (1988). The family complexes. Carolyn Asp (Trans.). *Critical Texts,* *5,* 12–29.

Phillips, A. (1994). *On Kissing, Tickling, and Being Bored: Psychoanalytic Essays on the Unexamined Life.* Cambridge, MA: Harvard University Press.

Sendak, M. (1963). *Where the Wild Things Are.* New York: Harper & Row.

5

ON THE GOTHIC BEACH: A NEW ZEALAND READING OF HOUSE AND LANDSCAPE IN MARGARET MAHY'S *THE TRICKSTERS*

Rose Lovell-Smith

I open my essay with a swift but, I hope, convincing argument that the beach is a Gothic[1] site in Aotearoa/New Zealand. The beach has another existence, of course: we know it as that bright and sunshiny place complemented by hot cars, hot asphalt, ice creams, children, lilos, surfers, sand, sandals, sandwiches, sunburn. But the New Zealand family also likes to get together at the beach for Christmas—and, famously, one of Mahy's ghosts in *The Tricksters* is quite incredulous about celebrating "the family" at Christmas. "You might just as well celebrate battle, murder and sudden death," he remarks (Mahy 1986: 92). Such violent events, of course, do regularly and notoriously occur in families at Christmas time; as do, at New Year, riots and fights, most often at beach resorts, and, at both Christmas and New Year, drownings and road accidents, a common part of our midsummer festivities, and two of our favourite ways of dying.

The beach is thus, in Aotearoa/New Zealand, a place of recent memories of violent incidents and significant encounters. And in the remoter past, the beach was very often the place where you met the other (Figure 1). When water travel was much the easiest and cheapest option, living places and settlements clustered on coasts and waterways. So beaches are where Maori met Pakeha; where they talked and translated and traded and fought; where animals and goods were imported and exported; where waka (canoes) and ships were sometimes attacked or

Figure 1 Meeting the other: Maori bargaining with a Pakeha on a New Zealand beach. John Williams, c. 1845. Courtesy of Alexander Turnbull Library, Wellington.

wrecked, and crew or passengers rescued or drowned. Coastal places today often exhibit histories of loss and violence in their small cemeteries, memorials, and plaques, and in their quota of abandoned homes and farm or business buildings, isolated and ruined, overtaken by the development of land transport. Beaches may not look like probable Gothic sites at first, then, but on second thoughts reveal themselves as the bits of New Zealand with the longest and most violent histories. These are definitely among our haunted landscapes.

That this is so has been recognised by storytellers from the beginning. Māui, the Polynesian trickster, was born incomplete, an aborted foetus, a mere clot of blood (many tricksters have unpromising beginnings).[2] Perhaps he was always, in the mind's eye of the Maori teller and listener, born at the beach; certainly in our modern iconography, in children's books like *The Birth of Maui* by Glenda Kauta (1984), he is often depicted as having been born at the beach (Figure 2). Believed dead, wrapped in his mother's topknot and thrown into the sea, he drifted there, cared for by its gods or spirits or creatures, finally recovered for humanity among the seaweed and wreckage of the tideline—in some tales by a god, in some by a relative, for instance, by his own grandfather. With regard to Maori tales of Māui, Margaret Orbell remarks that "in Māori belief an aborted foetus or stillborn child might turn

I te whānaunga mai o Māui,
i pōhehe tana whāea a Tāronga, kua mate kē.

When Māui was born,
his mother, Tāronga, thought he was dead.

Ka tapahia tana tikitiki ka takaia te pēpi ki roto,

She cut off her topknot and wrapped the baby in it,

I a ia e karakia ana, ka peia atu te tikitiki ki te moana.

then saying a prayer, she pushed the topknot on to the sea.

Figure 2 Maui born and abandoned at the beach. Pp. 3–5 of *The Birth of Māui: Te Whānaunga Mai o Māui.* Glenda Kauta, illus. Janet Piddock, 1984. Trans. into Māori by Mārara Te Tai. Auckland: Reed Methuen, 1984. 3–5.

Figure 3 Birth of Maui as Gothic event in *Maui: Legends of the Outcast*. Chris Slane's artwork, Robert Sullivan's text, 1996. np. Courtesy of Chris Slane and Robert Sullivan, and Random House, New Zealand.

into a spirit of an especially dangerous kind (atua kahukahu)." Because Māui has not died, as Orbell points out, he "is not himself such a spirit." But, she continues, "the resemblance is there, and makes for ambiguity" (1995: 114). The potential Gothic dimensions of the Māui stories, especially the possibility that Māui's entire history may be seen as a kind of haunting,[3] are exploited powerfully by Chris Slane and Robert Sullivan in their 1996 comic-book version of the Māui stories (Figure 3). The birth-myth of Māui also marks many other New Zealand fictions, including Keri Hulme's *The Bone People* (1983) and my focus text in this paper, Margaret Mahy's *The Tricksters* (1986), in both of

Figure 3 (*Continued*)

which a lost son emerges from (is reborn from) the sea. When Mahy's trickster character, the ghost of dead Teddy Carnival, re-emerges in tri-partite form as the three Carnival brothers, the three are brought back to life by various factors which include, I think, the presence of a rela-tive, a descendant of Teddy's sister Minerva, on the beach—a clear echo of Māui's story. Māui leaves his traces, too, in Patricia Grace's *Potiki* (1986) and *Dogside Story* (2001), books where beach setting and family context seem just as important as they are in *The Tricksters*.

The beach is an old story site, then, and the simplest explanation for a New Zealand Gothic beach would be that local histories of vio-lence are here married with transatlantic traditions, for the beach is to New Zealanders a place for family time, whether harvesting kai moana (food from the sea), boating, playing and exercising, holidaying, or socialising. It thus functions as "home," an extension or replication of domestic space.[4] The Gothic beach is not a concept canvassed so far in histories of the meanings of the seaside as marginal place, "engineered paradise" or "site of transformations"[5]—the opposite is rather the case—but among the multiple meanings assigned to this important cultural icon, acknowledgement of its ambiguous, sinister, haunted, and conflicted sides is well overdue. New Zealand theorist Steve Matthewman has argued that the beach as "site of escape, leisure, and new identity formation" is not empty space but (citing Fiske 1983) "literally awash with meaning" (Matthewman 2004: 36), but his emphasis on it as a littoral, *and* as a liminal, zone which is "neither here nor there" (36; citing Jones 1999), is that it "fosters new freedoms" (36), and this capacity of the beach "is strongly signalled in all Cultural Studies beach reading" (36).[6] Indeed, Matthewman's position is that the "freedom" the beach offers New Zealanders is in part a benefit conferred by its *absence* of history, by the way it "cannot be built on like land" and thus escapes "thorny questions of rightful ownership" of the land which tend to arise in ex-colonies[7] (47)—a stance which appears to be the very opposite of my own position. Yet some of these comments, written *before* controversy erupted when Maori moved in 2004–2005 to claim ownership of the foreshore and seabed, now simply look outdated. And in fact, Matthewman's construction of the beach is not always so far from mine; for example, he records Maori opposition to the practice of removing sand from one iwi's (tribe's) beach to grace another beach— opposition so far disregarded by the local government bodies involved. This acknowledgment of Pakeha disregard for Maori consciousness of inherited responsibility for, and guardianship of, the tribal resource which is their coastline in fact anchors Matthewman's beach in a history of conflict more solidly than he himself allows for.

Likewise, Matthewman notes that people regularly drown at beaches (42). Piha, he says, is not merely the iconic Aucklanders' beach but "New Zealand's most dangerous beach" (46) as well—although this, apparently, is something that we love it for. Myself, I suspect there is more than one point of view on that danger, and I wonder if women writers and/or writers for children, likely to see themselves as responsible for children and their safety, might be more sensitive to other nuances in our idea of the beach; certainly Matthewman's iconic beach offers an unlikely context for the feelings of *danger*, of psychic imperilment, and of the uncanny, which flood across Margaret Mahy's beach in *The Tricksters*. It appears that Mahy, like some other New Zealand women writers,[8] like Jane Campion in her film *The*

Piano (1993), and like another Christchurch children's writer, picture book creator Gavin Bishop,[9] goes to a somewhat different beach from Matthewman.

Might children's literature—from the beginning, in New Zealand, closely allied with retelling Maori traditional tales—provide more significant intertexts for Mahy's novel than the kind of sources generally accessed by cultural studies like Matthewman's? Diane Hebley's chapters on "Ocean and Island" and "Harbour and Beach" in her survey *The Power of Place: Landscape in New Zealand Children's Fiction, 1970–1989* describe seascapes as pervasive in New Zealand children's fiction.[10] In earlier children's fiction, she notes, beaches and harbours feature in historical narratives as points of arrival and departure for emigrant protagonists setting out to build a new life (Hebley 1998: 25). In the 1980s, however, the focus shifts to "being here" (29), and the sea, often dangerous to cross in stories of emigration, has already acquired its particular local ambiguity as both *producing* and *reducing* ("by the coming and going of ships for travel and trade," 29) our commonly recorded settler society's feeling of isolation in a faraway place. In the 1980s, too, island settings begin to demonstrate a "sense of the mysterious" (40); supernatural elements appear, often drawn from Maori or Polynesian sources. Harbours, says Hebley, as "encircling" places ostensibly offering shelter and protection, may also become places of danger: beaches, which she regards as "essentially linear, a line of demarcation between land and sea, setting boundaries and limits" offer "the simple pleasures of swimming and picknicking" but also "change and revelation, arrival and departure" (Hebley 46).[11] Hebley's survey therefore brings us closer to many elements of the beach in Mahy's *Tricksters* than Matthewman's does.

Yet *The Tricksters* begins where any Arthur Ransome book begins, at the start of the summer holidays. Teddy Carnival, the ghost in this story, is something of a companion to the Hamilton children who come to Carnival's Hide every summer; they believe he dived off the very rock they themselves always dive off and drowned right there, where they always swim. On arrival at Carnival's Hide, they go down to the sea to greet him and tell him he is no longer alone. "What are they looking at?" asks Anthony Hesketh, the visitor from England who will turn out to be a surprise Carnival family member, when he sees this annual ritual. "Oh, it's a private ceremony!" replies Jack, the Hamiltons' father. "Rather like a game in a graveyard. That's the very rock where Teddy Carnival dived and disappeared." Anthony responds: "There's a definite charm about frisking around the edges of doom. I've played in a few graveyards myself." "We've always been very happy here, ghost or not," says Jack, defensively (Mahy 1986: 20).

The conversation neatly suggests transatlantic, Gothic (or graveyard) literary roots, as well as local ambiguity of feeling about the seaside. A literal graveyard, the seaside in *The Tricksters* is also Matthewman's traditional resort of social freedom, site of the annual "beach carnival"—an occasion replicated on a small scale in *Tricksters* by the Hamiltons' fancy-dress party on the beach before Christmas—and of the minor riots and pub fights also acknowledged in *The Tricksters*. Mahy thus positions her novel as inheriting mixed traditions, a point I will expand on briefly before moving to my main argument, that Mahy's exploitation and modification of those traditions locates her book as a necessarily—and unmistakably—New Zealand product. In particular, Mahy's seaside house and beach setting adapt and modify the transatlantic trope of the Gothic house into a more distinctively New Zealand site.

That the cultural inheritance evoked by Mahy is a mixed or multi-stranded one is most evident in Teddy Carnival's return. Believed dead, Teddy was abandoned by his father, like Māui by his mother, to the ocean. With a Gothic touch, Mahy positions a small undersea cave below the Hamiltons' diving rock, arranging that from this cave, this pathway into the world of the dead, Teddy Carnival will begin his return.[12] Harry's, our heroine's, first encounter with the ghost is the sensation that her hand has entered a different world at the back of this cave and been grasped there by another hand. Her sensation recalls *Wuthering Heights*, where Lockwood's hand passes through the window from domestic space to wild space and is grasped by a child/other: "my fingers closed on the fingers of a little, ice-cold hand!" (Brontë 1847: 23). A second field of reference opened up by this underwater cave, however, is Maori belief that after death the spirit travels to the far north of the North Island of New Zealand, where, at Te Reinga, the wairua or spirits of the dead clamber down a cliff face with the help of a pohutukawa tree branch or root and watch for the waves of the sea to wash aside the seaweed and reveal an underwater cave entrance, their route to the underworld of the dead. Indeed, when Māui tries—as his last and greatest trick—to defeat death itself by entering the body of goddess of this realm, Hine-Nui-te-Po, intending to reach her heart and kill her, although he is really entering her vagina, his death is generally represented in children's books in pictures showing him crawling into a cave or cleft.[13]

The mixed field of reference evoked by Mahy's setting, then, is a way of laying claim to and revising a transatlantic cultural complex in ways that make it specifically local, at the same time constructing

New Zealand as a nation of Polynesian heritage. But in this scenario, what becomes of that literary topos so indubitably European in origin, the haunted or Gothic house? This is the focus of my discussion henceforth, and my argument is that while many characteristics mark Carnival's Hide as a "Gothic" house in *The Tricksters*, these characteristics are nevertheless significantly modified by Mahy's text. Here it is useful to draw on one of the earliest descriptions of the phenomenon of the Gothic house, Chapter 1 of *The Haunted Castle* (1927) by Eino Railo, where it is noted that "The Haunted Castle" or "old 'Gothic' castle" (7) contains the essential "collection of family portraits," subterranean vaults and passages, and a hidden key which proves to open "a secret trap-door" (7)[14]; while Clara Reeve in *The Old English Baron* (1778)[15] is credited by Railo with adding the first suite of sealed-off, reputedly haunted rooms to the edifice (8); and to Ann Radcliffe, in various novels, is attributed the development of the full picture of the Gothic home in all its romantic, ruinous and melancholy state (9–13).

Such features undergo change in the antipodes, as will be seen: the abandoned house functions intermittently as family beach, portraits become photographs, the trap-door leads *upwards* to Harry's attic bedroom. Nevertheless Gothic tropes haunt the house called Carnival's Hide—after all, photographs, just as effectively as old family portraits, can suggest that family history is at stake.[16] I will concentrate my attention on Mahy's modification of just three remarkably persistent features of the Gothic house: the difficulty of getting into it; its mysterious or labyrinthine extensiveness (this house is somehow bigger on the inside than the outside); and its remoteness and isolation in a lonely, rural, perhaps wild and uncivilized, even desolate, setting. Examples of "the Gothic" will be drawn from nineteenth-century texts likely to be known to many Mahy readers. Finally, I will note the significance of other modifications of the Gothic expressed through the figure of Harry/Ariadne. All these changes contribute to Mahy's particular vision of a New Zealand Gothic beach.

The classic Gothic house, of course—the one that is difficult to get into by definition, as it were—is the castle or fortress. It is also often difficult to get out of, containing within itself, or forming for its inhabitants, a prison. Kate Ferguson Ellis, in fact, begins her book *The Contested Castle* thus: "The strand of popular culture we call the Gothic novel can be distinguished by the presence of houses in which people are locked in and locked out" (1989: 3).[17] The claim is partly convincing. For numerous examples of domestic confinement, one need seek no further than *Wuthering Heights*; again, in Bram Stoker's *Dracula* narrator Jonathan Harker records in his diary:

> I explored further; doors, doors, doors everywhere, and all locked and bolted. In no place save from the windows in the castle walls is there an available exit.
>
> The castle is a veritable prison, and I am a prisoner! (2003: 172)

In *Jane Eyre*, Thornfield, a house with battlements, is a kind of vestigial Gothic castle; Wuthering Heights may be no castle, but it is strongly built of thick stone. Walls, doors, gates, and windows often present barriers to ingress and egress in *Wuthering Heights*, as in other Gothic houses: chains, locks, massive keys, uncooperative servants or grumbling chatelaines who cover vast distances to unwillingly open groaning or creaking doors are classic Gothic phenomena. Thus in *Dracula*, Harker, abandoned by the driver who has brought him to the castle, finds himself waiting before a massive door with no bell or knocker; he hears:

> a heavy step approaching behind the great door, and [sees] through the chinks the gleam of a coming light. Then there was the sound of rattling chains and the clanking of massive bolts drawn back. A key was turned with the loud grating noise of long disuse, and the great door swung back. (163)

Similarly, on his first visit to Wuthering Heights Lockwood cannot persuade Heathcliff to open the gate until his "horse's breast is fairly pushing the barrier" (2)—and Joseph, the servant, is extremely rude when asked to look after an unexpected visitor.

Carnival's Hide in *The Tricksters* is another house protected by a gate—a five-bar gate which has to be opened and shut every time anybody arrives at or leaves the house—but is remarkably permeable and undefended otherwise. Doors and windows are generally open, allowing the wind to move in and out of the house freely, the veranda offers an intermediary or half-way zone (people quite commonly exit or enter the house via a veranda window) and this wooden house is also a sounding board faithfully transmitting non-human temperature changes and winds and rains, as well as human movements and actions and voices and words, to anyone who cares to listen. Interestingly, the winds that blow inside Mahy's house are not without Gothic precedent—Eino Railo devotes considerable attention to these invisible forces (1927: 12)—and one is again reminded of *Wuthering Heights*, where stormy weather outside is apt to be matched by stormy emotions within. But the interior winds described by Railo seem to threaten an intrusion of uncontrollable violence, often functioning to extinguish "the heroine's lamp as though trying to crush in her the last beam of hope" as he remarks (13).

In Mahy's vision, however, these winds suggest in a more general way the "naturalness" of changeable emotions: Christobel, heard waking up, for instance, comes "closer and closer like a southerly storm" (1986: 58), while the nor-wester that keeps the Carnival's Hide sitting room "alive and murmuring" (31) is often a benign-seeming force. Carnival's Hide is, indeed, well-lit, open, and hospitable (as well as haunted) and by its physical form represents, in my view, tolerance of emotional expression within the family, as well as the relatively loose and permeable boundaries of the family itself. In contrast, the classic Gothic house, as in *Wuthering Heights*, contains an isolated and inward-looking family kept under patriarchal control, and considerable hostility and a high degree of opacity or unreadability are shown to outsiders. Merely to open a window is an occasion at *Wuthering Heights*—indeed, can be virtually a story in itself. Mahy's windows, conversely, frequently open up the inside to the outside, and vice versa.

A second familiar characteristic of the Gothic home modified by Mahy is its mysterious inwards extensiveness, as Railo remarks of Radcliffe's works, "the castle doors and passages [...] are extremely numerous, winding and narrow, so that they form a veritable labyrinth" (1927: 11). Mahy refers us to this motif by her heroine's name—Harry short for Ariadne—and a maze motif is also evoked, though by no means especially well developed, by the physical house at Carnival's Hide. Such internal swellings-out of the Gothic domestic space as cellars and attics, long complicated passages and locked, unexpected or secret rooms, hidden stairs, priest's holes, abandoned west wings, grottoes and caves in the garden or environs connected by secret underground passages to the house, and so forth, are represented at Carnival's Hide only by Harry's attic bedroom. For Carnival's Hide *is* extended in space, but extended *outside*, where the washhouse and loo are, as well as the whare down by the beach, a special place up on the hillside where Harry and Felix meet, the sailing boat and boat ramp where Charlie passes his days, and, of course, the beach itself, a near-private space where the family spends whole days and often entertains visitors. The family at Carnival's Hide is larger, fuller of secrets, differences, distances, tensions, and untold histories than may appear on first view: this is the main meaning of those extensive but mysterious spaces found *within* the Gothic house. But in Mahy's version these emotional factors also prove to build the family out into the world. An outward-turning family first laid the Hamiltons *open* to their current internal tensions, and similarly *open* to hauntings by the undead past; but they are also *open* to various outsiders and visitors who will in time prove to be sources of resolution and healing.

Thirdly and finally, what of the remote, rural, uncivilised, feature-less, the *unmarked* surroundings of the Gothic house? Whether in the form of high mountains, as in *Dracula*, where Jonathan Harker discovers that his host's castle stands "on the very edge of a terrible precipice" (Stoker 2003: 172)[18]; or of the wild moorland, rocky crags, and bogs that surround Wuthering Heights; or of the sea, as in Scott's *The Bride of Lammermoor* and Daphne Du Maurier's *Rebecca*, this encircling desolation is another factor making the house both difficult to get into, and difficult to get out of. Predictably, then, the reader of *The Tricksters* finds that Carnival's Hide is a lonely place a long way from towns or main roads. It is surrounded by wildish hills and stands by the sea, on "a ragged coastline of tiny bays and indentations" (Mahy 1986: 19). In my view this traditional isolation of the Gothic house, apart from plot, functions in removing persecuted heroines from human assistance, mainly offers an interpretation to the reader of wider society as wilder-ness. An isolated house implies the primacy of family origins, but also, that only *within* the family can the subject hope to find or make mean-ing of their (her) life. The implication of social alienation is a familiar, if depressing, feature of the literature of urbanised and industrialised societies in the last two centuries. Within the family, says the Gothic house, problems must be resolved, terrors faced, tyrants overcome, one's inheritance claimed, and one's true identity established[19]; the outer world offers only a wilderness of non-meaning.

Here Mahy's modifications to Gothic tradition are, once again, both local and significant. The sea at Carnival's Hide signifies not an uncross-able waste but rather what it has always been to Maori and settler, a highway for waka, ships, ferries, and small boats, and a playground for bodily and spiritual recreation. Here Harry delights in her skill and strength as a swimmer, here Charlie the sailor finds companionship and, eventually, his life's partner.[20] As Matthewman also recognised (2004: 49), the Polynesian idea of the Pacific is not of tiny islands con-fined by a vast, empty and meaningless ocean, but rather, in the words of Epeli Hau'ofa, "a large sea full of places to explore" sustained by an "underlying assumption that the sea is home" (1993: 8); I have heard Maori, making much the same point, remark that Cook Strait was not a barrier but a motorway.

Although Mahy's dead do re-emerge from the sea, then, her boundary-crossers fit into a South Pacific setting as remarkably social (if mysterious) ghosts: they make themselves at "home," are welcomed, indoctrinated into the family history, and, as is the case in many traditional trickster stories, produce both disruptive and beneficial effects. Thus, though Mahy's ocean setting is mysterious and changeable and her shoreline remains a significant transition zone, Mahy's family, as signified by its location beside not-exactly-desolate waters, proves a markedly benevolent and ill-defined family—one might say "ragged" at its edges, as the local coastline is. The Hamiltons on holiday deal with many outsiders, including Anthony Hesketh, a visitor from England who came to check out his colonial connections and ancestry. Indeed, he is welcomed so efficiently and warmly that he begins to look, by the closing pages of the book, as if he might become an even realer family member by marrying Christobel. Emma and Tibby, two extremely awkward arrivals, are made equally welcome. Even the mysterious Carnival brothers are permitted to "bunk down in the whare" (Mahy 1986: 71)—a nice phrase encapsulating treasured local ideas of rough and ready but warm-hearted Kiwi hospitality and ample room in the family circle. All are fed and fed generously and in detail; the Christmas catering is not neglected by the narrator. Mahy's idea of home thus allows many intrusions by, and assigns considerable importance to, "outsiders" (the Hamiltons, after all, are no relations of the Carnivals; two unconnected families assist each other in this novel).[21] The surrounding world, natural and human, also often offers additional resources for enlightenment and renewal: Mahy repeatedly records changeable beauties of light and weather modifying seascape and landscape, and repeatedly notes the setting forth of many characters on land and sea journeys, which thus become associated, especially Harry's swimming, with the family's internal journey to enlightenment and change.

The reader derives from Mahy's modified Gothic setting, then, a relatively optimistic and integrated idea of family and of the family's connectedness to wider geographical and social worlds: a local modification of transatlantic traditions which also, I think, represents Polynesian modification of Pakeha worldviews. The Hamilton family benefits from Jack and Naomi's relaxed parenting style, which contrasts with Edwardian settler-patriarch Edward Carnival's crazed exercise of absolute authority over his children Teddy and Minerva. And yet, Mahy's family retains secret spaces as well; this book is sharply aware of the dangers of the exercise of male privilege Jack allowed himself by beginning a relationship with his daughter's best friend Emma. This family secret above all others gives the Tricksters power over the family at Carnival's Hide.

My discussion of Gothic house and beach must finally deal, of course, with the main source of their fundamental differentness—their *hauntedness*. Here my analysis turns away from Railo's description towards theories of the Gothic informed by feminist thought. For, as Jane Austen well understood, the realm of the Gothic house is the realm of the patriarch, and women and children are frequently its victims. Here Mahy's sense of the possibility of change is carried mainly by one character, Harry, the family member who opened the way for the ghosts to get through. Harry/Ariadne holds the clue to the family maze: it is she who, with fantasies both compensatory and aspirational, inscribed in her own Gothic romance an overheated, imagined world whence Ovid, Felix, and Hadfield embodied themselves and returned from the dangerous past. But Harry as a constant and imaginative occupier of the many-sided spaces of the beach where she sun-bathes, runs, and swims also occupies fully the local, Kiwi holidaymaker side of *The Tricksters'* narrative space. She thus becomes rather like a beach herself, having made of herself a meeting place, an extended hand, a pathway through, a site of reconciliation, a space both littoral and liminal, a junction where along a ragged edge a long-established genre finds congenial mental lodging places and forces itself through into new being in quite other forms and settings.

Harry and the Gothic house must therefore be importantly associated. In discussing *The Tricksters* I have so far worked from the assumption that details of a Gothic house and setting are mainly a symbolic representation of the family that lives within: a family traditionally the father's family, just as the house traditionally belonged to him as well.[22] This kind of symbolism, found in an especially pure form in Edgar Allen Poe's knowing description of the house of Usher at the beginning of *The Fall of the House of Usher*, was extended by Sandra Gilbert and Susan Gubar (1979) with their claims about the importance of the upstairs imprisonment of *The Madwoman in the Attic* to the symbolic presentation of the heroine of *Jane Eyre*.[23] Mahy's use of the house, however, while accommodating that classic trope where described details of the house suggest the bodies and being of its main inhabitants, makes a further radical change. I believe it is primarily Harry's body and Harry's sense of being which control, and ultimately wield power over, the symbolic field of Mahy's "uneasy" (1986: 150) Gothic home.

To rehearse the relevant imagery briefly, Carnival's Hide is first seen "enclosed in a great, green summer bouquet of poplars and silver birches" so that only its roof is visible on first sight. Harry is seen similarly obscured, on the next page, "half hidden by her glasses and her curtains of reddish-brown hair" (3, 4). The word "curtains" used here of Harry's hair, the house that spreads "around itself a gentle skirt of shade" (4) mean house language is being used for Harry's body, and the house is being dressed like a girl. The "fringe" of purple and green ringing the veranda is another word which suits Harry's body but is here applied to her home: "a single central dormer window, a little extra eye," high up in the front of the house is of course not just any window but Harry's special window, suggesting Harry's insights and her watchful role in her family, just as the underwater cave which is described as "like a black submarine eye watching her" (25) at the opening of the book, and the third or pineal eye which Harry later refers to in conversation with Felix (149), are signs of the return of Harry's inventiveness onto herself, as her own creations bring her under their now-separate gaze.

The position of Harry's room in the attic is therefore suggestive of much more than the rage of Charlotte Brontë's hidden "madwoman." Its height matches Harry's status as older teenager, already growing up and out of her family but still linked to them under a common roof; it enables, too, her position as eavesdropper and listener-in, for from her attic outpost Harry hears much that goes on in the house. It suits her self-assigned superior role of observer and writer, looking down on a family she would very much like more power in and over. Yet the attic also represents Harry's solitude, ironically enough an effect of being the reliable daughter, one who can safely be a bit neglected by a disturbed, over-busy mum and dad with something to hide. Carnival's Hide will eventually be released from its ghost in a struggle during which the house (which increasingly, in Mahy's narrative, resembles a living being) convulses itself to the point of redecorating itself. But it will come to represent in the process many aspects of Harry's (rather than any patriarch's) personal power, including her creative power, which is what gave the Carnival brothers their chance to return so disturbingly to their old home, and the power of her confused yearning to assert herself on the family stage as an enchantress more to be wondered at than her dominant, attention-hogging older sister Christobel. The house and Harry therefore transform themselves and release themselves, together; her loneliness is symbolically ended, for instance, when Christobel makes a significant visit to Harry in her attic fortress towards the end of the book.

Other critics have already commented on the astonishing degree of power Mahy assigns her young heroines—but nothing shows this, in my view, so clearly as the way Harry's body becomes *the* body symbolically represented by the house at Carnival's Hide. Indeed, it is *her* house—an idea Mahy recently took hold of again in *Alchemy*, when she made high school student Jess Ferret the literal, legal owner of her parents' house. By the virtues of superior powers of observation, knowledge and imaginative creation, rather than by transfer of title deeds, Harry likewise becomes the true owner of Carnival's Hide.

The Tricksters takes place at Midsummer, Christmas, and New Year, for reasons I have already canvassed, but it also takes place, to return to my starting point, at the beach; in this case, at a small beach with an old and abandoned house nearby which is used by a well-off city family for a holiday home, a familiar enough scenario to New Zealand readers. There really seems no reason why, in terms of plot or family dynamics, the uneasy trinity of ghostly Ovid, Felix, and Hadfield should not have re-emerged in the house or garden at Carnival's Hide to haunt the Hamiltons; the drama of Harry's transition to self-assurance, to adulthood, to sexual experience, to family acknowledgement, could well have been staged mainly within the house as well. Teddy Carnival *was* actually killed in the garden by the gooseberry bushes, after all. But what happens, of course, is that the Tricksters take Harry the swimmer's hand and cross the beach to return to life, and their reappearance and presence there is known first and most fully to, and is most threatening to, Harry. They bring with them various kinds of summer holiday peril: Harry fights off rape by Hadfield on the dark beach; Christobel when painted for the beach party is close to absorption into Ovid's fantasy as he remakes her into a doll to fit his own disturbed needs; Felix and Hadfield, playing out the inner drama of Ovid's divided self, come to blows at the edge of the sea itself. The Carnival brothers are indeed, as Felix puts it, "tied to that strip of beach" (224), and when reassembled in the single person of Teddy Carnival are last seen there, too, by Harry: her final glimpse of the assuaged and reunited spirit of Teddy is of a kneeling man on the other side of a beach bonfire from her, who "streamed with water as if he were the source of many springs" (243)—a watery dislimming of Teddy into the oceans of anonymity and death.

As I have tried to show, Mahy, an author often accused of writing like a foreigner,[24] shows an accurate sense of her local New Zealand heritage in thus alternating the setting of her tale of haunting between the Gothic home and that other domestic space and elemental meeting place, the beach. If her ghosts are *tied to* that site, it is because Mahy's wide knowledge of mixed cultural heritages in Aotearoa and her skills as a reader of culture enabled her recognition of the beach as a local and significant Gothic site and tied her characters there.

ENDNOTES

1. The range of meanings I am attributing to the word Gothic will become clear in the course of my discussion. In brief, I take the Gothic to be a literary strategy produced in the European consciousness after the era when mental disturbance could plausibly be assigned religious or

supernatural interpretations and origins, and before the emergence of modern theories of psychology, particularly the idea of an unconscious mind. It is a way of encompassing or imaging in fictional narratives extremes of emotional experience and mental aberration brought about by extraordinary connections and/or disconnections between characters often of the same household or family. Associated with these, as ways of speaking the unspeakable, elements appear in narrative like excessive interest in death, living death, and hauntings, various forms of doubling, and the intrusion of other horrific, irrational, or inexplicable elements into an apparently ordinary world, that is, a world initially presented to the reader with the literary trappings of domestic realism. I am also in agreement with Eugenia C. DeLamotte's "perception that the Gothic vision has from the beginning been focused steadily on social relations and social institutions and that its simultaneous focus on the most private demons of the psyche can never be separated from this persistent preoccupation with the social realities from which those demons always, in some measure, take their shape" (1990: vii).

2. See Laura Makarius, "The Myth of the Trickster: The Necessary Breaker of Taboos" pp. 66–86 in Hynes & Doty (1993), here, p. 77.

3. Margaret Orbell, in her discussion of the figure of Maui, also notes the significance of his name, for the word maui means left and left hand, and that associates him with the "noa [profane, ordinary] side of the body, as opposed to the tapu [sacred] right side" (1995: 115). This association of the Maori trickster hero with left-handedness is interesting to contemplate in relation to the strange personification of dead Teddy Carnival in three forms, one of whom, Hadfield, representing the instincts, has his heart on the "wrong" (or right) side, in this the mirror image of his twin Felix, representing the feelings, whose heart is in its normal position on the left side of the body. About all three Tricksters in Mahy's novel hangs a strong sense of wrongness—Hadfield is left-handed, or "sinister" as he himself says (1986: 70)—and on first sight of the trio, Harry "knew at once that they had crawled out of a wrong gap in the world" (53).

4. The possible "domestic" equivalence of beach and home is suggested by the proximity of a significant house close to the beach in many of the stories I mention in this chapter. Keri Hulme's abused boy, the mute Simon, for example, "The vandal, the vagabond, the wayward urchin, the scarecrow child" (1983: 37) is first discovered by Kerewin in The Bone People not actually on the beach but hiding in her seaside house. With its aspects of a fortress, tower, or castle, this house suggests the Gothic house in eighteenth- and nineteenth-century novels and tales and also many later descendants in popular culture.

5. Lena Lencek and Gideon Bosker's study The Beach (where I found these two phrases, pp. xx and 223) is subtitled The History of Paradise on Earth and introduces itself as product of a "love affair" (1998: xiii); its

account of the beach is generally upbeat, the only exception being a vivid evocation of an American Marine's landing on the blood-soaked strand of Tarawa in the Gilbert Islands in November 1943. But in Lencek and Bosker's account, barbed-wired coastlines and grisly war landings only increased the longing of post-war populations to escape to beaches to have fun—a contradictory state of mind neatly exemplified in the two meanings evoked by the word "bikini" (see pp. 217–222). On the other hand, the Romantic poet Mary Robinson included in her 1800 *Lyrical Tales* a poem called "The Haunted Beach" which may be the first narrative set on a Gothic beach; it is discussed by Jacqueline M. Labbe (2004, pp. 151–152). The motif of the Gothic beach may well also have an Australian dimension; in the last scene of Rowan Woods' film *Little Fish*, Lionel's recently dead body is posed on the beach in holiday-maker mode while other characters swim.

6. Other studies Matthewman refers to are Ann Game (1991), "Sense of Place: Bondi" in *Undoing the Social: Towards a Deconstructive Sociology*, Milton Keynes: Open University Press, pp. 166–185; Craig McGregor (1994) "The Beach, the Coast, the Signifier, the Feral Transcendence and Pumpin' at Byron Bay" in D. Headon, J. Hooton, & D. Horne (Eds.), *The Abundant Culture: Meaning and Significance in Everyday Australia*, St Leonards, NMSW: Allen & Unwin, pp. 51–60; John Pilger (1989), "On the Beach" in *A Secret Country*, London: Jonathan Cape, pp. 6–17; Rob Shields (1991), *Places on the Margin: Alternative Geographies of Modernity*, London; New York: Routledge; John Urry (1990), *The Tourist Gaze: Leisure and Travel in Contemporary Societies*, London: Sage.

7. In making this claim Matthewman acknowledges Stephen Turner (1999) "Settlement as Forgetting."

8. See, for example, Janet Frame's *State of Siege* and Kirsty Gunn's *Rain*. Janet Frame's frightening story of social isolation and mental disintegration is set in a seaside bach; in *Rain* we find the contradictory safeness/unsafeness of the family summer holiday at the seaside fully exploited again, but in terms of a coming-of-age or getting-of-wisdom story shape rather than a persecuted-heroine story.

9. In Gavin Bishop's picture book *The Horror of Hickory Bay*, which also has a Christmas Day setting, the beach, that is, the seaside landscape itself, comes to monstrous life and begins to devour its human visitors (and other things). Bishop's artwork associates the bloated and indifferent parents of its child heroine, India Brown, with the greedy, heartless landscape. Here, as in *The Tricksters*, as in *The Piano*, there is a connection between art, self-expression, the beach, and violent and frightening narrated events. An unexpected image in *The Horror of Hickory Bay* is that of India Brown's violin, prominent in many illustrations. Perhaps it represents the kind of "food" for the spirit that India Brown is "still hungry" for even after a Christmas dinner. She takes it down to the beach

with her and stands it up in the sand at the water's edge with bow upright alongside, where it is threatened by the rising waves caused by the awakening of the "Horror," but stands bravely up against them. The image uncannily resembles scenes in *The Piano* where Jane Campion's heroine plays her piano on the beach, against the waves of the sea, as it were. (Art is the way the silenced one finds a voice, it seems. DeLamotte remarks that "women's Gothic was from the beginning obsessed with the interrelated social and psychological constraints on women's freedom to make themselves known through the act of "speaking 'I,'" 1990: viii).

New Zealanders tend to find *The Piano* silly and over-romantic (see Mary Paul's report of the reaction of a graduate film class, "Her Side of the Story," 1999: 94). Bishop's earlier version of Campion's seaside vision is perhaps a more Kiwi one, humorous, self-deprecating, and ironic. In it the Horror is refashioned by India Brown's terrible music and undergoes a form of rebirth (like Maui, like the heroine of *The Piano*, who undergoes a resurrection from the depths of the sea, and like Teddy Carnival, who is also remade) though the Horror's resurrection is comic, and comically reductive, as he suffers dismemberment and diminishment into a romantic landscape feature of the beach. Odd as this book is, Bishop reports that he receives more correspondence about it from children than about his other books (Bishop, personal communication). Like Patricia Grace and Keri Hulme, novelists I have already mentioned, Bishop has Maori ancestry.

10. Her figures establishing the dominance of seascapes in children's novels are 57% seascape settings in the 1970s, 54% in the 1980s (Hebley 1998: 23).

11. She also notes James K. Baxter's claim that "the beach symbolises a no-man's-land between the conscious and the unconscious" and that for teenagers the beach offers "sexual adventure" (Baxter, "Symbolism in New Zealand Poetry" 61, quoted in Hebley 1998: 46).

12. In Mahy's mythology, a volcano-world, for the book is set (to New Zealand readers) near Christchurch on Banks Peninsula, on the shores of a sea-drowned ancient volcanic crater.

13. See, for example, Peter Gossage, *How Maui Defied the Goddess of Death* (1985: n.p.); Christ Slane and Robert Sullivan, *Maui: Legends of the Outcast* (1996 n.p.); Robert Sullivan and Gavin Bishop (illustrator), *Weaving Earth and Sky* (2003: 78–79).

14. Railo's main source at this point is Horace Walpole's *The Castle of Otranto*.

15. It earlier appeared in 1877 under the title, *The Champion of Virtue: A Gothic Story*.

16. Anne Williams remarks that the Gothic house "embodies the family history" (1995: 45).

17. Ellis's next sentence reads, "They are concerned with violence done to familial bonds that is frequently directed against women" and her paragraph

concludes with a statement of her thesis: "It is when the home becomes a "separate sphere," a refuge from violence, that a popular genre comes into being that assumes some violation of this cultural ideal." While I agree that the Gothic is a literary "complex" (in Anne Williams's term, see *Art of Darkness*: 23) that deals with gender issues and the nature of home and family, I think Ellis exaggerates the importance of female perceptions of violence and danger to women within and outside the home in producing this genre; Williams's argument that there are both male and female forms of Gothic narrative points to the need for a more complicated theory of the Gothic. If "the mythos or structure informing this Gothic category of "otherness" is the patriarchal family," a thesis, as she notes, "widely intimated," then "the power of the patriarchal family structure is far greater and more extensive—more central—than has been recognized," and "organizes human experience at many levels" (Williams 1995: 22).

18. "A stone falling from the window would fall a thousand feet without touching anything!" he records, and all that can be seen is "a sea of green tree tops, with occasionally a deep rift where there is a chasm" (Stoker 2003: 172).

19. With regard to the question of identity, it is notable that Harry/Ariadne is one of a very long line of Gothic heroes and heroines unsure of their own real name.

20. I enjoy the way what had seemed a boys-only zone, Charlie's and Robert's sailing, is reassigned to a male-female partnership by the end of the book. There seems a determination in Mahy's construction of local culture that spaces which might easily and inadvertently have been demarcated as masculine or feminine space should be quite casually shared in her novel. Mahy's sea, too, known, meaningful, signifying, reminds me of the comment Perry Nodelman (1988) makes on a famous footnote from Roland Barthes' *Mythologies*. He quotes Barthes' "In a single day, how many non-signifying fields do we cross? Very few, sometimes none. Here I am, before the sea; it is true that it bears no message. But on the beach, what material for semiology! Flags, slogans, signals, sign-boards, clothes, suntan even, which are so many messages to me" (Barthes 112, quoted in Nodelman 1988: 9). Nodelman remarks: "What Barthes forgets here is the extent to which even the sea itself bears messages, for those equipped with appropriate contexts" (9). Indeed.

21. Christine Wilkie-Stibbs claims that the Hamiltons are descendants of Edward Carnival, who built the house, but I can find no evidence for this relationship in the text. The mistake may be taken as instructive. Strangely, Wilkie-Stibbs also seems not to have noticed that Charlie is a family member, for she introduces him only as Robert's friend (2002: 44).

22. It is on the basis of this understanding that Anne Williams argues persuasively that the Gothic house so often embodies not just patriarchal power but also its inbuilt downfall.

23. See especially their comment on p. 347: "not only is Thornfield more realistically drawn than, say, Otranto or Udolpho, it is more metaphorically radiant than most gothic mansions: it is the house of Jane's life, its floors and walls the architecture of her experience." Also on 348: "These upper regions, in other words, symbolically miniaturize one crucial aspect of the world in which [Jane] finds herself. Heavily enigmatic, ancestral relics wall her in; inexplicable locked rooms guard a secret which may have something to do with her; distant vistas promise an inaccessible but enviable life."

24. I base this statement on memories of conversations with students, teachers, and librarians disappointed by the lack of local setting and reference in Mahy's stories. For a long time I was disappointed myself. Disappointment has also been expressed overseas, for instance by David Rees, whose *What Do Draculas Do* (1990) is quoted by Tessa Duder: "Rees was...critical of what he regarded as a lost opportunity 'to reveal a unique place and culture' to the outside world: 'if readers expect New Zealand to be a central issue, as Australia is in the work of Patricia Wrightson and Ivan Southall, they will be disappointed'" (Duder 2005: 187). Duder notes that interviewers prior to Mahy's successes in the 1980s often asked Mahy "why her stories were not 'New Zealand'" (190). Her own comments on the reception of *The Changeover*, with its recognisably Christchurch setting, are illuminating about the conditions Mahy works under. "Few reviewers anywhere remarked on the consciously New Zealand setting of *The Changeover*, a first in Margaret's writing" she says, for, as she points out, a "New Zealand commentator, even unaware of Margaret's story but familiar with the bleak local publishing environment and the attitudes of overseas editors, would not have made such observations. ('I think it was *The Changeover*,' Margaret has said, 'where the editor said it's wonderful to have a New Zealand story and then proceeded to cut out a lot of New Zealand references')" (Duder, quoting interview with Mahy, 188).

REFERENCES

Bishop, G. (1984). *The Horror of Hickory Bay*. Auckland: Oxford University Press.

Brontë, C. [1847] (1980). *Jane Eyre*. Oxford: Oxford World's Classics.

Brontë, E. [1847] (1998). *Wuthering Heights*. Oxford: Oxford World's Classics.

Campion, J. (Writer & Director). (1993). *The Piano*. New York: Miramax Films.

DeLamotte, E. C. (1990). *Perils of the Night: A Feminist Study of Nineteenth-Century Gothic*. New York: Oxford University Press.

Duder, T. (2005). *Margaret Mahy: A Writer's Life*. Auckland: HarperCollins.

Ellis, K. F. (1989). *The Contested Castle: Gothic Novels and the Subversion of Domestic Ideology*. Urbana; Chicago: University of Illinois Press.

Frame, J. (1967). *A State of Siege*. Christchurch: Pegasus.

Gilbert, S. & Gubar, S. (1979). *The Madwoman in the Attic: The Woman Writer and the Nineteenth-Century Literary Imagination*. New Haven, CT: Yale University Press.

Gossage, P. (1985). *How Maui Defied the Goddess of Death: Te Taki a Maaui i a hine-Nui-Te-Poo*. (Translated into Maori by Merimeri Penfold). Auckland: Lansdowne.

Grace, P. (1986). *Potiki*. Auckland: Viking Penguin.

———. (2001). *Dogside Story*. Auckland: Penguin.

Gunn, K. (1994). *Rain*. London: Faber & Faber.

Hau'ofa, E. (1993). Our sea of islands. In E. Waddell, V. Naidu, & E. Hau'ofa (Eds.), *A New Oceania: Rediscovering Our Sea of Islands* (pp. 2–19). Suva, Fiji: University of the South Pacific.

Hebley D. (1998). *The Power of Place: Landscape in New Zealand Children's Fiction, 1970–1989*. Dunedin: University of Otago Press.

Hulme, K. (1983). *The Bone People*. Wellington: Spiral.

Hynes, W. J. & Doty, W. G. (1993). *Mythical Trickster Figures*. Tuscaloosa: University of Alabama Press..

Kauta, G. (1984). *The Birth of Maui: Te Whānaunga Mai o Māui*. (Translated into Maori by Mārara Te Tai). Janet Piddock (Illus.). Auckland: Reid Methuen.

Labbe, J. (2004). Romance and violence in Mary Robinson's *Lyrical Tales* and other Gothic poetry. In C. C. Barfoor (Ed.), *"A Natural Delineation of Human Passions": The Historic Moment of* Lyrical Ballads (pp. 137–156). Amsterdam: Rodopi.

Lencek, L. & Bosker, G. (1998). *The Beach: The History of Paradise on Earth*. New York: Viking Penguin.

Mahy, M. (1986). *The Tricksters*. London; Melbourne: Dent.

Matthewman, S. (2004). More than sand: Theorising the beach. In C. Bell & S. Matthewman (Eds.), *Cultural Studies in Aotearoa: Identity, Space and Place* (pp. 36–53). South Melbourne; Auckland: Oxford University Press.

Nodelman, P. (1988). *Words about Pictures: The Narrative Art of Children's Picture Books*. Athens: University of Georgia Press.

Orbell, M. (1995). *The Illustrated Encyclopedia of Māori Myth and Legend*. Christchurch: Canterbury University Press.

Paul, M. (1999). *Her Side of the Story: Readings of Mander, Mansfield and Hyde*. Dunedin: University of Otago Press.

Poe, E. A. (1986). *The Fall of the House of Usher and Other Writings: Poems, Tales, Essays and Reviews*. D. Galloway (Ed.). Harmondsworth: Penguin Classics.

Railo, E. (1927). *The Haunted Castle: A Study of the Elements of English Romanticism*. London: George Routledge.

Reeve, C. [1778] (1967). *The Old English Baron: A Gothic Story*. J. Trainer (Ed. & Intro.). New York: Oxford UP.

Slane, C. & Sullivan, R. (1996). *Maui: Legends of the Outcast: A Graphic Novel*. Auckland: Godwit.

Stoker, B. (2003). Dracula. In A. Williams (Ed.), *Three Vampire Tales: Dracula, Carmilla, and The Vampyre* (pp. 149–460). Boston: Houghton Mifflin.

Sullivan, R. (2003). *Weaving Earth and Sky: Myths and Legends of Aotearoa.* Gavin Bishop (Illus.). Auckland: Random House.

Turner, S. (1999). Settlement as forgetting. In K. Neumann, N. Thomas, & H. Ericksen (Eds.). *Quicksands: Foundational Histories in Australia and Aotearoa New Zealand* (pp. 20–38). Sydney: New South Wales University Press.

Wilkie-Stibbs, C. (2002). *The Feminine Subject in Children's Literature.* New York: Routledge.

Williams, A. (1995). *Art of Darkness: A Poetics of Gothic.* Chicago: University of Chicago Press.

Woods, Rowan (Director). (2005). *Little Fish.* Australia: Icon Films.

6

HIGH WINDS AND BROKEN BRIDGES: THE GOTHIC AND THE WEST INDIES IN TWENTIETH-CENTURY BRITISH CHILDREN'S LITERATURE

Karen Sands-O'Connor

They must have had a vacation in a trailer, she and Dad, but it can't have been much of a vacation, because all she remembered was rain, an incessant drumming on the roof, moisture everywhere, damp sheets...and some delicious shiver of fear, she had no idea why: secrets, and murder, and horror. But it wasn't real. It was safe, it was a story, she could enjoy it. (Pullman 1990: 76)

By the time Philip Pullman wrote *The Broken Bridge* in 1990, the lines between safety and fear, fiction and reality, and enjoyment and terror had been blending for well over a hundred years. The notion of the West Indies as a place haunted by the ghosts of the British colonial past goes back at least as far as Charlotte Brontë's 1847 novel *Jane Eyre*. In creating the now-famous "madwoman in the attic," Bertha Mason Rochester, Brontë made clear the links between destructive British capitalism and the demise of the West Indian. As Tiffin and Lawson point out, "Imperial relations may have been established initially by guns, guile and disease, but they were maintained in their interpellative phase largely by textuality" (3). Twentieth-century British children's fiction, however, softens or even erases the negative historical connections between Britain and the West Indies without eliminating their common ghosts.

Valdine Clemens notes that "Although writers have been producing Gothic fiction fairly continuously for the last two centuries, the readership for Gothic horror has expanded significantly in such crisis periods, when the public mood becomes uneasy and pessimistic, and when re-evaluation of the national identity seems to take on a particular urgency" (1999: 5). The urgency in twentieth century children's fiction is to contain the West Indian subject at a time when British control over the island nations was becoming increasingly tenuous. The 1930s, as Jed Esty notes, was one of these moments:

> "colonial unrest" did not become especially important for Britain until the 1930s, when the military challenges in Europe began seriously to divert resources away from the empire. It was also in the 1930s that Britain's strategic vulnerability was exacerbated by severe economic depression. In 1931, Britain was forced to go off the gold standard and the pound's value was drastically and suddenly reduced. (2004: 37–38)

White British subjects in twentieth-century children's novels are depicted, using Albert Memmi's terminology, as "benevolent colonizers" (1965: 43); but these colonizers, no matter how benevolent, can yet never feel entirely comfortable because "the benevolent colonizer can never attain the good, for his only choice is not between good and evil, but between evil and uneasiness" (43). Post-World War II fiction is equally uncertain. Just as earlier British authors were responding through the Gothic to the breakdown of empire, later British authors are struggling with the redefinition of British character. Paul Gilroy argues that in post-war dialogue, "What must be sacrificed is the language of British nationalism which is stained with the memory of imperial greatness" (1996: 270), but the use of the Gothic in literature of the end-of-Thatcher era points to the difficulty of this task. The colonized (or formerly colonized) West Indian subject is the cause of the British characters' disease, and is variously depicted as absent, terrifying, or responsible for their own miserable fate. The British writers in this chapter try to wash their hands of the West Indies, but it keeps coming back to haunt them.

"THIS CRUMBLING HALF-VEGETABLE GLOOM": THE DEATH OF THE WEST INDIES

In the nineteenth century, novels about the West Indies dealt primarily with the issue of slavery and its often bloody aftermath; the novels of authors such as G. A. Henty did not, perhaps, portray a tolerant, happy, multicultural West Indies, but they depicted it as *alive*, teeming, in fact, with people and issues and problems. Rebellion on one island, such as French-owned Haiti, led to fears of the same for other islands, no matter what imperial government was in charge. The sea provided a crucial setting, but not the only one; the islands of the West Indies were real places with names and ports and mountain ranges. Pirates burying treasure on desert islands were doing so in the vaster reaches of the Pacific; West Indian pirates were capturing cargoes of rum and goods from their clashes with British merchant ships. Interaction, not abandonment, was the key to Victorian fiction about the West Indies. This mirrors the contemporary political interaction with the West Indies, which was quite active for the British at least until the Jamaican Morant Bay Rebellion of 1865.

After 1865, however, the British government became increasingly involved in its eastern empire, and more or less abandoned its West Indian colonies to their fates. By the early part of the twentieth century, this political abandonment began to be reflected in literature as well, but with a Gothic sense of unease. The unease is invariably connected with race, often in quite discordant ways. Patrick Brantlinger suggests that this was a period of Imperial Gothic, and that "The three principal themes of imperial Gothic are individual regression or going native; an invasion of civilization by the forces of barbarism or demonism, and the diminution of opportunities for adventure and heroism in the modern world" (1988: 230). All these are present in *A High Wind in Jamaica* (1929) and *Peter Duck* (1932). The West Indies is described, nonetheless, as "a kind of paradise for English children" (Hughes 1929: 8); the Gothic elements in these novels serve to accentuate the differences between English and West Indian versions of reality, but also to indicate the impossibility of exorcising the ghosts of Britain's history.

Novels in the early part of the century, such as Richard Hughes's *A High Wind in Jamaica* and Arthur Ransome's *Peter Duck* show English children in Caribbean settings described with a Gothic combination of lushness and terror. This was a Gothic trope going back at least as far as the nineteenth century, as H. L. Malchow notes: "The *concealing* nature of the dense tropical world allowed the imagination of the white interloper and the distant novelist alike to color what they could not themselves observe with an apprehension-driven gothic sensationalism" (1996: 50). In Hughes's book, the terrible lushness is intimately connected with race.

And the scene is this: coming to Derby Hill on some business or other, and wading waist-deep up to the front door, now lashed permanently open by a rank plant. The jalousies of the house had been all torn down, and then supplanted as darkeners, by powerful vines: and out of this crumbling half-vegetable gloom an old negress peered, wrapped in filthy brocade. (1929: 4)

The two white owners of this decaying mansion are being starved to death by their former slaves. It is into this world that Hughes brings his main characters, the Bas-Thornton and the Fernandez children.

The children, however, are not sufficiently impressed by the terror of the West Indies. They play upon the fears of the former slaves and are ignorant of the fears of their parents, making the terror seem merely the imaginings of superstitious grownups. In fact the children are creators, rather than victims, of the Gothic. They create fear in the minds of others, but are never fearful themselves. In two separate incidents, this fear relates to the black population of Jamaica. Hughes writes, "once a negro really was drowned in the pool....The great advantage of this was that no negro would bathe there again, for fear the dead man's 'duppy,' or ghost, should catch him. So if any black even came near while they were bathing, John and Emily would pretend the duppy had grabbed at them, and off he would go, terribly upset" (1929: 11). Later, Emily discovers a community of runaway former slaves, and finds herself an object of fear: "Encouraged by the comfortable feeling of inspiring fright she advanced" (15). John, and more particularly Emily, are gods in their world (Emily in fact later decides she *is* God), and Jamaica's tangling vegetation and murky pools serve as settings in which the children can wreak their vengeance. Indeed the West Indies is a "paradise"—for English children.

Nonetheless, there is a force more powerful than the godlike English children, and that is the West Indian weather. In the case of Hughes's book, it is the eponymous "High Wind in Jamaica" that blows the children, almost literally, out of the island and back to England. While Emily and the other children become more self-confident after living through both an earthquake and a hurricane, their parents worry that they have been psychologically damaged by this blindly destructive weather. Mrs. Thornton says to her husband, "You know, I am terribly afraid what permanent *inward* effect a shock like that may have on them. Have you noticed they never so much as mention it? In England they would at least be safe from dangers of that sort" (46). Terror, for the white adults, lives in Jamaica; England is safe from its dangers.

The children are sent to boarding school; however, along the way they are kidnapped by pirates and remain in the West Indian sea for months. For the first time, the children experience fear, but it is the confused fear of sex and sexuality, and much of it is sublimated into dreams by Emily. However, even here, the horror of sex is mixed up with race, even though the pirates are largely European. The pirates come down into the hatch with unnamed evil intentions toward the girls and Emily turns them away by biting the captain's thumb until it bleeds; later she has a related dream:

> One night (and that was the worst of all) she had rushed out to rescue [her cat] and her darling faithful Tabby had come up to her with the same horrible look on his face the captain had worn the time she bit his thumb, and had chased her down avenues and avenues and avenues and avenues of cabbage-palms, with Exeter House at the end of them never getting any nearer however much she ran. She knew, of course, it was not the real Tabby, but a sort of diabolic double; and Margaret had sat up in an orange tree jeering at her, gone as black as a negro. (151–152)

Emily begins the novel with a sense of superiority over the black population of Jamaica, but behind it, underneath it, is the fear that she is being laughed at by them, is not really in control at all. Hughes's children's paradise has become a nightmarish memory for the maturing Emily, just as it is for end-of-empire Britain. Although the children do reach England, Emily is left with a haunting reminder of the ordeal she has endured when she serves as a witness in the trial of the pirates. In the final pages, as the pirates are sentenced to the gallows, Hughes suddenly introduces a "negro cook"; the cook makes a speech to the pirates that furthers Hughes's underlying message about racial relations between Europe and the West Indies.

> "We have all come here to die," he said. *"That"* (pointing to the gallows) "was not built for nothing.... *You* know that I die innocent: anything I have done, I was forced to do by the rest of you. But I am not sorry. I would rather die now, innocent, than in a few years, perhaps guilty of some great sin." (278)

Bill Ashcroft, Gareth Griffiths, and Helen Tiffin link the European conquest of the West Indies with piracy in *The Empire Writes Back* when they write:

> In the Caribbean, the European imperial enterprise ensured that the worst features of colonialism throughout the globe would all be combined in the region: the virtual annihilation of the native population of Caribs and Arawaks; the plundering and internecine piracy amongst the European powers; the deracination and atrocities of the slave trade and plantation slavery, and the subsequent

systems of indenture which "stranded" Chinese and Indians in the Caribbean when the return clauses of indenture contracts were dishonoured. (2002: 144)

Hughes lays sin, the death of innocents, and other terrors at the feet of the European "pirates" who have stolen the West Indies, and death is the only escape.

Because of the violence and underlying sexuality of *A High Wind in Jamaica*, many argue that Hughes's novel is not a children's book at all (see Victoria de Rijke's "Reading the Child Invention" for a history of the book's publication and marketing); and although I do not necessarily ascribe to this notion, I introduce Hughes's book in part to show its parallels to another book written just a few years later, one that is clearly within the children's canon: Arthur Ransome's *Peter Duck*, the third book in the *Swallows and Amazons* series. *Peter Duck* is subtitled *A Treasure Hunt in the Caribees* and concerns the adventures of the four Walker and two Blackett children treasure hunting in a schooner with their adult companion Captain Flint and a seasoned sailor who saw the treasure hidden many years before, Peter Duck. Unlike Hughes's novel, *Peter Duck* is not a Gothic novel; it is an adventure story with an aura of safety—readers of the series know that the Walker and Blackett children may come into dangers, but they are competent and clever enough to work out solutions on their own. However, although the sense of fear and terror is kept to a minimum in Ransome's book, when it is present it shows up in ways strikingly similar to the horror in *A High Wind in Jamaica*. David Adams calls this type of book a "colonial odyssey" and argues that "the uncanny content of these novels offers access to some of the deepest anxieties motivating imperial conquest" (2003: 6).

One of the major differences between the two novels is that Ransome's story presents an *empty* West Indies. There are no ruined plantations on Crab Island; no people at all, in fact, and the children feel free, comparing themselves to Columbus, to name the mountains and other landmarks they see after each other and even after their pet monkey. Todorov, discussing Columbus, indicates that naming and empire are intricately linked: "The first gesture Columbus makes upon contact with the newly discovered lands (hence the first contact between Europe and what will be America) is an act of extended nomination" (1982: 28); and Daphne Kutzer argues that the Walkers and Blacketts are deliberately aping the traditions of empire when she writes, "The nature of the play his children (and their friends, the Blacketts and the D's) indulge in further suggests that the children are comfortable with both the values and the language of empire" (2000: 108).

However, despite the control that the children seem to have over the land, the threat of danger is present, making itself visible in the island's vegetation and natural setting. "They met nothing really dangerous," Ransome writes (1932: 235), but still the grownups feel uneasy because of the wildness of the islands.

> [T]he parrots were startled and a flock of them rose together into the air above the trees, so that the explorers could not see them, but only heard the wild screaming of them high above the green feathery screen that shut out all but small patches of the sky.
>
> It was hard going in places, with the thick undergrowth and the tangles of climbing plants.
>
> "I don't believe we ought to have brought you children," said Captain Flint. (235)

Titty, the main girl character in the series, also displays unease, although hers is more sublimated than that of the adults. When she sees a blazed tree, she "found herself wondering who it was who asked the executioner to sharpen his axe and cut boldly...it was queer the way things came shooting into your mind just when you were really thinking of something quite different" (238). The West Indies is "queerly" connected with death for Titty. Just as in *A High Wind in Jamaica*, the flora and fauna of the island itself remind the characters that the Caribbean is no place of safety.

In Ransome's novel, too, it is a hurricane that changes the fortunes of the children. Hughes's hurricane kills a servant and a cat, among other creatures, and precipitates the departure of the children to England. Ransome's hurricane is less destructive (no one dies), but it does unearth the treasure the children had been hunting. The treasure consists of four bags labeled, "Mallies, Bonies, Niggers and Roses" (331). When the bags are opened, they contain pearls, bad, good, black, and pink. The treasure itself is small, and may seem to the reader unworthy of the journey that the children attempt. However, it is significant that, as Raymond Betts points out, "the Caribbean consisted of a string of islands poetically described as pearls—hence, plunder worth the struggle" (1975: 42). Betts was writing about the West Indies during the nineteenth century; the fact that the Swallows and Amazons see little worth in the treasure, and more in the journey itself, is not insignificant.

Finally, *Peter Duck*, despite ignoring the people of the West Indies, does not fail to comment on race. The Swallows and Amazons are followed down to the West Indies by a gang of pirates led by Black Jake. One of these pirates is black, introduced to the children by Peter Duck as "Mogandy, the nigger, blacker'n Black Jake" (Ransome 1932: 162). Mogandy is presented as black both inside and out. When the pirates board the children's ship after the treasure is found, Mogandy (now called "Fighting Mogandy," 346) is in the thick of the action. And although the text suggests that he is "crouching" (346) until he attacks Peter Duck, the illustration (done by Ransome himself) that accompanies the fight tells a different story. Mogandy, standing and with one fist raised, is in the center of the picture, completely alone and defiant (347). He is more monstrous than the monsters; he is the only one who mentions killing and he does so several times (twice on 348, once on 351). The person he wants to kill is not an adult but one of the children, Bill, who had once been cabin boy on the pirate ship. Thus, the greatest fear of those once in league with the pirates is racial violence. Even in a West Indies now conveniently emptied of its non-European population, racial fears haunt the English characters.

The fight with the pirates and the fear it produces ultimately sends the Swallows and Amazons back to England. Ransome comments that "It was no longer their island and theirs alone. Earthquake and landslide had not been enough to make this kind of difference. It was the coming of the *Viper* that had changed the island for them" (365–366). As long as the children could play at being Columbus, claiming empty islands for themselves, the West Indies is a paradise; but interaction with other people (and races) kills their interest, and the children head home to the safe harbors of England. The island, as Sarah Spooner argues, has remained "unknowable": "Despite all their best efforts in marking, mapping and pathfinding, it has remained silent, secret and unknowable. The unknowability that was enticing on their first arrival has become something much more threatening as the island resists European attempts to grasp and control it" (2004: 225). In the very act of turning back, they can erase the uncomfortable fears they have felt.

> Long before they were halfway home across the Atlantic they were beginning almost to forget the wild turmoil of those last two days on the island, earthquake, and hurricane, and landslide, and the coming of the *Viper*, and the horrible hours when they knew that Captain Flint and the pirates were on the island together. Even the horror of that last day of all, when the *Viper* had crept up on them, and the pirates had brought down their mainsail, and they had thought that all was up, until the waterspout that they had feared themselves had suddenly made an end of their enemies, seemed now like a dream or something that had happened not to them but to somebody else. (Ransome 1932: 409)

Edward Said argues, "One must remember, too, that when one belongs to the more powerful side in the imperial and colonial encounter, it is quite possible to overlook, forget, or ignore the unpleasant aspects of what went on 'out there'" (1994: 157). Ransome's language in this excerpt indicates the underlying potential for Gothic terror in *Peter Duck*, a terror that is intimately tied up with race, violence, and the history of colonialism even while it attempts to erase the past into a nightmare that dissipates with the sun.

"ALL THE GOLDEN YEARS HAD COME TO THIS": MISCEGENATION AND THE GOTHIC

Novels written by white British authors after World War II and the breakdown of the British Empire have a very different focus, as the nightmare of colonialism can no longer be placed "out there." Rather than setting novels in the West Indies, these authors begin to recognize the growing West Indian communities within Britain itself. However, despite the change in setting, the Gothic fears and terrors present in earlier twentieth-century novels do not dissipate. Philip Pullman's *The Broken Bridge* (1990) is an excellent example. *The Broken Bridge* is the story of a young girl, Ginny, who is the product of an English-Haitian marriage. She believes her Haitian mother to be dead, and is living happily in Wales with her father at the time the novel takes place, in a relationship that Ginny describes as being "close, almost like brother and sister, like equals" (Pullman 1990: 8). This equality, between race, gender, and age, would not last long. From the beginning, Pullman uses Gothic elements in his novel to indicate the ruin that a mixed-race liaison can bring to everyone involved or connected with it. The eponymous bridge of the title is a recurring and mysterious element that serves to remind the main character of her inability to ever fully connect with either her English or her Haitian heritage. The bridge has been repaired, but its old name still sticks. Ginny finds out the truth about her past, but can never be whole or innocent again; as she herself thinks, "All the golden years had come to this, and there was no going back now" (174).

Race, sexuality, and the absent mother are the key elements of the novel; they are also the most heavily Gothicized. The book's largest mystery concerns Ginny's parentage; there are no traces of her mother except in her own face, and Ginny feels that makes her empty inside. While she is "proud of her mother and the color she'd inherited and the exoticness in her blood" (7) she also feels (along with a black friend whose adoptive parents are white) that "looking black, they'd each grown up feeling white" (12). In order to make a deeper connection with her mother, Ginny pursues art (her mother was an artist), but even here wonders if "there might be a difference between the way white people paint and the way black people do" (41), and is not sure what this means for her own work. Ginny puzzles over which side of her ancestry to align herself with when she says, "It was my English ancestors who sold my African ancestors into slavery. Where does that leave me? Am I innocent or guilty or what?" (81). Pullman never provides a direct answer to this question, but amidst helpless adults it is Ginny who must ultimately bear the responsibility for the damage done in the past.

Ginny also discovers that she was born out of wedlock and that her father had left his first wife to be with Ginny's mother, who eventually abandoned them both. Ginny has a white half-brother who suddenly comes to live with them after the death of his mother. Ginny feels anger at "being shoved aside by this invisible cuckoo, this white son and heir of a proper marriage" (86). Pullman's linking of the West Indian with illegitimacy is, according to Paul Gilroy, not coincidental: "West Indians, for example, are seen as a bastard people occupying an indeterminate space between the Britishness which is their colonial legacy and an amorphous ahistorical relationship with the dark continent and those parts of the new world where they have been able to reconstitute it" (1996: 250). Ginny cannot forgive either her new brother, Robert, or her father until she goes up to Liverpool to meet her father's parents, who turn out to be horrible racists. Her grandmother tells her, "God knows it's not your fault, dear, but to think of my boy, my son, my only child, wallowing in colored filth when he had a decent home, a pretty wife, the best background a man could have....Well, he'd never have done it if she hadn't tempted him" (Pullman 1990: 171). Malchow indicates that attitudes such as these tend to showcase British anxiety: "Anxieties about self-identity and the preservation of individuality provoked a more intense awareness of the 'unnatural' in human relationships—that is, of sexual perversion and racial 'miscegenation,' which often implied the subversion or even reversal of the assumed-to-be-natural power-relationships of class, gender, and race" (1996: 127). The grandparents' attitudes toward Ginny's mother led indirectly to Ginny's father's imprisonment (for kidnapping his daughter after his parents make accusations of abuse about him). Her parents' mixed-race liaison, an illegitimate but passionate relationship, leads to more than a decade of secrets.

Her attempts at connecting to her absent mother lead her into terror that is foreshadowed early on in the novel. One of her memories is of swearing on her mother's deathbed to keep a secret:

> She was very frightened. She thought about it that night and couldn't get it out of her mind. She imagined a deathbed as a special sort of bed which was delivered to the house when it was time for you to die, and you'd know everybody would know, and slowly it would get closer to bedtime, and you wouldn't want to go to bed, but you must, you had to, it was time. What happened on the deathbed was too horrible to think of. (Pullman 1990: 43)

Secrets and death are further mixed up in her quest for her mother when she hears the story of the broken bridge and the baby abandoned there to freeze to death after a car accident. Ginny is told this story by a friend while she is riding on a "ghost train" (69) at a fair. The setting plays into Ginny's feeling of being haunted by the past; as Jerrold Hogle points out,

> hauntings can take many forms, but they frequently assume the features of ghosts, specters, or monsters (mixing features from different realms of being, often life and death) that rise from within the antiquated space, or sometimes invade it from alien realms, to manifest unresolved crimes or conflicts that can no longer be successfully buried from view. (2002: 2)

Hogle goes on to note that, "the frequent goal of that journey in the Gothic…[is] the recovery of a lost or hidden maternal origin" (10). The ghost train substitutes here for the antiquated space, but ghosts, specters, and monsters will all play a part in the unraveling of the secrets of Ginny's past.

She learns about voodoo, which she connects with her mother, at the same time as she thinks she is uncovering the secrets of the bridge. When she determines for herself that Joe Chicago, a local gangster with a head that "seemed almost inhumanly large, the features coarse and blunt like a giant's" (Pullman 1990: 14), a veritable monster, is the man who stole the jacket that covered the baby, she confronts him. As she does so, she feels her identity "fading and vanishing, and there was the god in her place, the loa, Baron Samedi, mighty and terrible" (143). Joe Chicago gives Ginny, in her voodoo god incarnation, the jacket. Lizabeth Paravisini-Gebert suggests that the use of voodoo in British texts concerning the West Indies is "symbolic of the islands' threatening realities, of the brutality, bizarre sacrifices, cannibalism, and sexual aberrations that filled the imagination of authors and their audiences with lurid, terror-laden imagery" (2002: 234). Ginny uses a religion she does not understand to inflict terror on Joe Chicago, and in so doing she allies herself with the negative West Indies.

But Ginny does not know what to do with the jacket once she has it, and wonders why she suffered the transformation into the god of death.

> What did Baron Samedi want it for? The idea came to her of burning it, taking it up to Gwynant on a winter's night and setting fire to it, as a sacrifice to propitiate the spirit of the lost dead child.

> It was all confused in her mind with the slip she'd made when she was talking to Helen: *He wrapped me up in it.* If she was the baby, what did that make the jacket? Her mother? (Pullman 1990: 146)

The only logical conclusion Ginny can find for this confusion of religion, violence, and death is to connect it to her mother.

In the end, however, Ginny's knowledge and understanding prove incorrect, both in terms of the secret of the broken bridge and her mother. Ginny's mother, Anielle Baptiste, is alive and did, in fact, abandon her many years before. She refuses to acknowledge Ginny when she sees her. After this, Ginny realizes that Joe Chicago is not the thief of the baby's jacket, and returns it to him; when he answers the door, Ginny sees standing behind him "something out of a nightmare: a corpse, a ghoul, swathed in graveclothes with a vacant mouth and hollow staring eyes" (187). The ghoul is Joe's own mother, who is afraid of Ginny. Like the grandmother who could not accept her, Joe's mother is frightened of Ginny, whom Joe describes as a "little girl" (188). But fear leads to negative consequences; as her father tells her, "The reason for all this is quite simple, Ginny: it's fear. Fear is why it happened, fear is why I haven't talked about it. That's the reason for everything" (196). Ginny is the only one who can erase this fear.

But it is only by abandoning her connection with her mother that Ginny can come to any sort of peace with herself. After reconciling with her father, Ginny considers her mother's rejection of her and says, "So what? It doesn't matter. I've never had her, so I can't miss her, really" (207). She trades voodoo for a safer god: "Maybe art itself was a kind of voodoo, possessing you, giving you supernatural powers, letting you see in the dark" (211). After she has made these choices to move away from her connection with her mother, Ginny reasserts herself as part of her English family.

> Think about her grandparents. Maybe it would be possible to meet them with Dad somewhere neutral, somewhere safe and public, where Grandma would feel constrained to be rational. They were

so desperate and unhappy; maybe she and Robert and Dad were strong enough to take charge of bringing the family together. Perhaps it was time to start healing. (217)

"The family" can include Ginny, but not her mother; and it is Ginny, because of her mixed-race status, who must heal the wounds of the past. The West Indies is fully cut off from this process, and the West Indian in Britain must "become English" in order for the past to be rendered harmless.

Like more traditional Gothic novels, these twentieth-century British novels for young people closely link sexuality and death amid scenes of ghostlike ruin. Unlike traditional Gothic novels, however, there is little escape for these children from the hauntings of history. Whether written before or after most West Indian nations became independent, children's novels about the West Indies or West Indians by white, English writers are filled with a Gothic sense of foreboding. The child characters in the novels face real dangers when they try to make contact with the Other, and most often their best option is to retreat, leaving destruction in their wake. But like the broken bridge that haunts the main character in Pullman's novel, the child characters cannot completely leave the horror behind; instead, they carry fear with them as they run from the history their predecessors left dangerously incomplete.

REFERENCES

Adams, D. (2003). *Colonial Odysseys: Empire and Epic in the Modernist Novel.* Ithaca, NY: Cornell University Press.

Ashcroft, B., Griffiths, G., & Tiffin H. (2002). *The Empire Writes Back: Theory and Practice in Post-colonial Literatures*, 2nd ed. London: Routledge.

Betts, R. F. (1975). *The False Dawn: European Imperialism in the Nineteenth Century* (Volume VI). Europe and the World in the Age of Expansion. Minneapolis: University of Minnesota Press.

Brantlinger, P. (1988). *Rule of Darkness: British Literature and Imperialism, 1830–1914.* Ithaca, NY: Cornell University Press.

Clemens, V. (1999). *The Return of the Repressed: Gothic Horror from The Castle of Otranto to Alien.* Albany: SUNY Press.

de Rijke, V. (1995). Reading the child invention (in conversation with A. Zacharkiw). *Children's Literature in Education, 26*(3), 153–169.

Esty, J. (2004). *A Shrinking Island: Modernism and National Culture in England.* Princeton, NJ: Princeton University Press.

Gilroy, P. (1996). "The whisper wakes, the shudder plays": "Race", nation and ethnic absolutism. In P. Mongia (Ed.), *Contemporary Postcolonial Theory: A Reader* (pp. 248–274). London: St. Martin's.

Hogle, J. E. (2002). Introduction. In J. E. Hogle (Ed.), *The Cambridge Companion to Gothic Fiction* (pp. 1–20). Cambridge: Cambridge University Press.

Hughes, R. [1929] (1999). *A High Wind in Jamaica*. New York: New York Review Books Classics.

Kutzer, M. D. (2000). *Empire's Children: Empire and Imperialism in Classic British Children's Books*. New York: Garland.

Malchow, H. L. (1996). *Gothic Images of Race in Nineteenth Century Britain*. Stanford, CA: Stanford University Press.

Memmi, A. (1965). *The Colonizer and the Colonized*. Boston: Beacon Press.

Paravisini-Gebert, L. (2002). Colonial and postcolonial gothic: the Caribbean. In J. E. Hogle (Ed.), *The Cambridge Companion to Gothic Fiction* (pp. 229–257). Cambridge: Cambridge University Press.

Pullman, P. (1990). *The Broken Bridge*. New York: Knopf.

Ransome, A. [1932] (1987). *Peter Duck*. New York: Godine.

Said, E. (1994). *Culture and Imperialism*. New York: Vintage.

Spooner, S. (2004). Landscapes: "Going foreign" in Arthur Ransome's *Peter Duck*." In K. Lesnik-Oberstein (Ed.), *Children's Literature: New Approaches* (pp. 206–227). New York: Palgrave.

Tiffin, C. & Lawson, A. (1994). Introduction: The textuality of empire. In *De-Scribing Empire: Post-colonialism and Textuality* (pp. 1–11). London: Routledge.

Todorov, Tzvetan. [1982] (1999). *The Conquest of America: The Question of the Other*. Norman: University of Oklahoma Press.

7

THE SCARY TALE LOOKS FOR A FAMILY: GARY CREW'S *GOTHIC HOSPITAL* AND SONYA HARTNETT'S *THE DEVIL LATCH*

Anna Smith

If childhood is a time for learning to properly inhabit a culture, universally an experience where the means employed to cultivate the proper has been embellished through stories playing on infantile fears. Yet American horror writer H. P. Lovecraft once argued that the most primal of all human emotions was fear, and that even sophisticated readers retained a primitive "fear of the unknown" (cited in Sandner 2004: 102). The weird tale survives, he wrote, because neither rationalism nor Freudian psychoanalysis is sufficiently powerful to dispel the fascination for being terrified out of one's wits. So while adulthood ostensibly signifies the time where these childish tales ought to be put away, wherever there is a "fire" today, you can still expect to find children and adults listening to scary stories to drive away the greater dark.

Fear thrives on distorting the familiar: nothing is more terrifying for a child than to find that ghosts, aliens and bad fairies can haunt a *real* bedroom, a school, a neighborhood. Making connections between stories and places is thus an integral part of childhood, one could almost say an integral right of growing into one's culture. That these pathways between imaginative tropes, texts, and places are highly varied, though, is what makes children's literature so arresting. In this paper, I take two contemporary Australian writers who also draw from the infinite reservoir of the unknown which had attracted Lovecraft in the 1920s. Gary Crew and Sonya Hartnett address the family through the literary genre known as the Gothic, attending to the darker side of human experience through opening their characters to that frightening void between finite knowledge and infinite mystery.[1] I will examine the ways in which Crew and Hartnett locate their families, and I shall conclude by taking a precognitive leap into the future to imagine what one possible scenario might be for the Gothic as a mode of writing children's literature.

Recently, John Stephens and Robyn McCallum (2001) drew attention to the difficulty in establishing a local discourse of horror/mystery in Australian writing for children. Taking the collection of Gothic tales edited by Gary Crew and published under the rubric of *Dark House* in 1995, the authors concluded that most of the horror tales in Crew's collection assume the lack of Australian-specific chronotopes. Even a more substantial narrative like Carmody's *The Gathering* (1994), they argue, leans toward the fantastic and a generalized sense of place; and while Judith Clarke's novel *The Lost Day* (1997) attempts to make a stronger play for social realism in the story of a boy who vanishes under frightening circumstances, its author nevertheless found herself bereft of a tradition of local models of horror and mystery to draw on. Similar observations could be made about two New Zealand texts published in 2005: Gary Cross's *Borderland*, and Ken Catran's *Something Wicked This Way Comes*. *Borderland* boasts a haunted house north of Dargaville, a grotto in the bush, a mural that sucks real people into its frame, a demon sprite, and a threatening old man. Like many tales in the genre, it features a crumbling family, so ten years on from Crew's *Dark House* collection, post-*Buffy*, post-*Angel*, unhappy misfits and uneasily reconstructed families still constitute the social matrix that births the modern Gothic horror. While the family in *Borderland* appears to be on the edge of breaking up, Rosie and Lucas fill in their holidays by defeating a power-crazed Uncle Silo and a rapacious spirit born when Silo quarrelled with his son many years ago. Over the course of the narrative, evil is vanquished, and justice done. Briefly, the family comes together to fight against Silo; yet their success fails to stave off the inevitable separation and divorce.

As for *Something Wicked*, it again draws on Gothic, horror and fantasy for its effects. The sense of place here is rather muted; there are wallabies in the local hills, and abandoned gold mines suggest an Australian setting, although the author doesn't belabor this. "The Apron," an opening to an old mine, features as the portal between this world and the darkness beneath. This time, however, the ailing family is less dominant. Catran's intimate community is made up of those who align themselves with the forces of good—the Light of the Pure Force. A reader may find suggestive parallels between *Something Wicked* and

The Gathering, in that both texts lose their grip on realism at the very point of contact with the universal forces of good and evil. It needs to be said, however, that this focus doesn't necessarily condemn modern fantasy, as Stephens and McCallum do, to conservatism; in fact, Catran's need to have his protagonist Brad Foster learn the nature and limits of good and evil from scratch suggests that children today are not necessarily equipped to recognize the difference, and that allowing the complex nature of making ethical decisions to be explored is an increasingly important aspect of fiction for children, especially for teenagers. In any case, while the Gothic can be seen in these texts as a shifter, each age and culture adapting the genre for its own purposes, and despite the power of context to alter narrative content, most often Gothic writing continues to be allied with sick or scary families and communities.[2]

Gary Crew's treatment of a boy's search for his missing father has all the classic ingredients of a Gothic mystery: *Gothic Hospital* is one of the most self-consciously textual Gothic stories to appear for the younger reader.[3] There is nothing in this book to ground it in the southern hemisphere or more precisely in Australia. Whereas Sonya Hartnett is careful to set her two families in a recognizably Australian city suburb complete with pet cockatoo, failed native gardens, middle-class pensioners, and tram stops; Crew's Johnny Doolan and his family could live anywhere vaguely urban. Crew gets to work at once with his sleight-of-hand that readers know so well from *Strange Objects* and *Inventing Anthony West*. Johnny Doolan has lost his formerly happy nuclear family: his sister dies, apparently of TB, his parents argue incessantly and then split up; Johnny takes refuge in an attic room and a pile of old Gothic novels. Somewhere around the second page, he explains how an illustration in Stoker's *Dracula* came to life, infilling as if it were an illustration in a magic paint-book.

Brooding mountains, a dark pine forest, and a ruined nineteenth-century castle complete with spooky graveyard: all classic Gothic furniture happily imported from the fictions of old Europe. Johnny's arrival in the castle is framed by a sign that reads: "GOTHIC HOSPITAL: AN INFIRMARY FOR ORPHANS." The device of entry into this familiar textual landscape is hardly the point; Crew's narrative markers indicate what we already knew: this is a story with a well-rehearsed trajectory, where if the orphan-protagonist keeps his wits, he will find what he is looking for, or else will perish trying. The graveyard, then, marks both the point of origin for Johnny's search for his father, and its return. And if the Gothic has any determining feature, it is in its claims to deal with unfinished business: with hauntings, returns, doublings, and with secrets that won't go away—things undead, in other words.

Indebtedness to the Gothic in *The Devil Latch* (1996b) is considerably less textual. No one seems to read anything except for Curtis who studies computer manuals. Kitten Latch might be the devil of the title, but he is no Dracula; he has blonde hair for one thing, and seems to eat real food like the rest of his family. The Latch family are, however, very odd. Kitten's grandfather, former patriarch and bully, is dying of a creeping stiffening that will eventually strangle him if his grandson does not get there first. Hartnett gives us plenty of reasons why Kitten might want to kill Paul Latch; trapped in mutual cruelties, the two men can no more leave each other alone than Agatha, Paul's sister, can prevent herself from spoiling Kitten because of his angelic looks. Hartnett's Gothic pays its dues to a different rendition of "scary," one where the physical and emotional dangers are more real than textual, and where the kiss Aimee receives from Kitten could equally be a slash of fangs.

> He draws her close, envelops her as if with wings....She does not resist him or the kisses over her face and when he tilts her chin up, she lets him, exposing the flesh of her throat. He kisses her there and then bites her, so she feels a handsome pain. It is a pressure that starts softly and then grows until she almost cries out, and suddenly it is gone. When she goes home that day she will wear the marks of the devil, the clinging smell of oil, the bruising of her neck. (Hartnett 1996b: 72–73)

The implicit violence that borders actual physical injury here is one of Hartnett's most powerful trademarks. Most of her narratives range over the territory of psychological cruelty, prodding at her characters as if to test their behaviour in the face of "handsome pain." Exemplary of this studied observance is the opening of the novel where we first meet Kitten watching a wasp destroy a praying mantis:

> Kitten props his chin on his hands. The wasp is a swarming insect, and it swarms over the mantis. Its assault remains urgent even after the mantis has weakened and ceased to defend itself, and Kitten feels the beat of teardrop wings against his face, hears the furious buzz....The wasp begins to disassemble the mantis before the defeated is dead...clumsy with its angular load, [it] is not difficult for Kitten to catch and crush under his hand. Predator and prey are left as one, against the peeling paint. (3–4)

As obvious as this scenario may seem in a tale of devilry and enchantments, its invitation to read the struggle between predator and prey in larger terms certainly intends to leave the reader trapped in a suffocating family narrative, but it hardly inserts itself into a *literary* tradition in order to allow the particular nature of that scariness to emerge.

Thus *The Devil Latch* can be termed "textual" in only the most attenuated of senses, whereas Crew's *Gothic Hospital* is continually calling up literary ghosts: Dr. Doolan's new girlfriend resembles an actress from *Flowers in the Attic*; the train passes through a murky town that reminds Johnny of Jekyll and Hyde; the station of fake sweets seems like the witch's cottage in Hansel and Gretel. *Great Expectations, Oliver Twist, The Secret Garden, The Wizard of Oz,* and Oscar Wilde's *The Importance of Being Earnest* are among the throwaway references in Johnny's account of his adventures that, naturally, are performed in front of the psychiatrist an anxious father has hired for his son—yet another overworked piece of textual machinery. That Johnny finally dismisses these confessions as nothing more than an exercise in bibliotherapy hardly justifies Crew's Gothic confection, but it is at least consistent with his using inherited and moribund parameters to tell a story:

> something's wrong [says Johnny Doolan]. There's a terrible commotion. Gorms are running everywhere, out of the front door, across the courtyard. There's yelling and screaming....
>
> "It's Gorman. He's escaped. He's escaped from the library. He climbed up on the fiction shelves and crawled through a fan light. Run. Run for your lives... "
>
> "Quick," Jasmine calls. "Zac, get your crutch!" Zac does as she says right away. He grabs his abandoned crutch from among the graves and runs up the stairs and together they ram the thing through the door handles, trapping Gorman inside.
>
> Then Zac skips down from the portico and gives me a look, and one of his grins, and he says, "Well, Johnny, while the villain's still locked in, maybe it's time to close this book. OK? Let's slam it shut right now. You see? We can do that now. We're all free and he's locked in. If you do it now, you give our story a happy ending.... You ready?" (Crew 2001: 223)

This is not to say that *Gothic Hospital* fails because it is excessively derivative. In fact, there is no value in suggesting that this is a novel that fails at all; rather, that its mechanics, its Gothic indebtedness, simply predisposes its resolutions to be less emotionally powerful for most readers than Hartnett's.

What generates Crew's Gothic narrative is the missing father and the son's dream-quest to find him. The further Johnny ventures into the landscape of the book, the more he sees its grotesque inhabitants to be clumsy disguises of his real experience. The head of the hospital appears in a suit that resembles his own father's; the witless gorms, bearing the name of their abusive progenitor Gorman, recall the helpless poor of Dr. Doolan's dangerous philanthropy in the real world; Jasmine wears a blue ribbon exactly like Johnny's sister's. One-eyed Uno and one-legged Zac add resonance to the suggestion that if Gothic Hospital is empty of sick children, it's simply humming with the baroque fall-out from an oedipal scene. Castration anxiety and fears of a devouring doctor/father figure, and uncanny resemblances between things that are familiar and those weirdly out of place cannot help but affirm the Gothic's enduring indebtedness to Freudian dysfunctionality. The ambiguity of this latter expression is deliberate. In his early work, Freud never disguised the fact that his interpretation was sired by taking the anomaly and turning it into the narrative of a general, universal condition: a dysfunctional narrative of dysfunctionality, if you will.[4] Clearly, Crew has made use of Freud's scary oedipal tale, and what better place to house it than in a ruined children's hospital left over from the nineteenth century? And isn't Zac's wooden crutch a telling memento of what Lacan would have referred to as the "orthopedic support," a support that in Johnny's case is represented by the Gothic structure of the quest narrative itself?[5]

Among Crew's diverse writing talents is the obsession for constructing purely artificial imaginary worlds that seem to float on the page like bright, curling transfers. Youthful adolescent fantasy is treated in this way in the novella, *Inventing Anthony West* (1994). Two thirteen-year olds literally fashion a drop-dead gorgeous boy out of magazine cutouts. It is an accepted convention of the genre that Gothic writers cut figures from the dark imagination of popular, as well as literary culture, which is why the trademark of a Gothic text is the curious, resurrected feel that animates the characters: a trace of that return from the dead (a limp, a stutter, or a coterie of peculiar eccentricities) remains to mark their behaviour with the sign of the *made-up*.[6] When Crew pursues the fantasies of two young women as they share their imaginary worlds with the delicious Anthony, his strength as a writer lies in the flatness and artificiality he is able to call up: the scary place of the zombie, the undead, the vampire are humorously reduced here to two friends quarrelling over a piece of paper. Ultimately, the live Anthony who appears at the close of the narrative represents nothing more than the inherited shadows of a fantasy master narrative that refuses to die yet is doomed to repeat itself on a foreign continent. Kate and Libby's dreams are constructed by Hollywood movies and worn-out clichés salvaged from popular culture. If the Gothic bears the mark of the inauthentic with

Crew, it does so in part because of the difficulties in divesting the genre of its European past.

It has frequently been said of Gothic tropes that they not only "transfer an idea of otherness from the past into the present," but because of this action, they inevitably import an anti-historicising context into the contemporary (Sage & Smith 1996: 1). While this is undoubtedly the case in *Gothic Hospital*, the point at issue is rather one of emotional fitness. So what if Johnny's family has fallen to pieces and he is forced to read for company and comfort? And that Dr. Gorman has plans to cut out his heart and exchange it with Kurt's? As readers, we like stories to be made up, but we like them to be real too, and Johnny Doolan's limping conversations with his therapist, while certainly fabricated, are just as certainly not "real." *Gothic Hospital* lacks an affective charge because it lacks a genuine emotional ground, and so cannot arouse the reader to identify with either the pre-text for the story, or the characters themselves. Consequently, while Johnny, Zac, Jasmine, and the rest float hypnotically on the surface of the reader's mind, pictures of near-whimsy, their shallow representation evades all attempts at identification and thus cannot begin to offer either enlightenment or consolation. Moreover, the fact that Dr. Doolan never appears during the narrative, serving only as an off-stage device, suggests that the Gothic has been used by the writer not so much in order to illuminate—or add to—the genre, but simply as a device to lead the reader to unpack the mystery of the missing father.

With Crew's *The Diviner's Son*, published a year later in 2002, once again the crumbling of the family is what is at stake, except that the conventional inherited landscape of Europe has this time been exchanged for nineteenth-century Tasmania, the Gothic now reproduced as an unsolved murder and the troubling figure of the diviner's son who channels voices from the spirit world. It reads as less shallow, less self-consciously textual than *Hospital*, for in this outlying fragment of Australia where women's voices are almost as muted as those of the indigenous population, such local details re-animate and ground the Gothic through an interweaving of horror with colonial history. Granted, its readership is more teenaged than *Hospital*'s, nevertheless, alongside *The Lace Maker's Daughter* (2005), *The Diviner's Son* goes some way to consolidating a local Australian version of a Gothic landscape and more importantly, to encouraging a new generation of writers to tell the truth of their own scary stories.

This is exactly what Sonya Hartnett, a generation younger than Crew, has been doing ever since she began her writing career. Just as drawn to illuminating fractured families, but a fiercer writer than Crew, Hartnett also remains fascinated by the Gothic's unrivalled capacity to uncover dysfunctional relationships. Despite achieving the masterful rural Gothic of *Sleeping Dogs* (1997), her translation of the uncanny generally rejects formal, as well as supernatural, lineaments of Gothic tradition. In *The Devil Latch*, random native objects acquire that menacing resonance traditionally associated with Gothic landscapes. Instead of a pine forest and snow-covered crags, Hartnett offers the glimpse of a nervy bird without tail feathers, oleander leaves that can poison, and Kitten Latch's antique farm tools perfectly restored. Unlike Crew's Gothic, too, Hartnett's compels the reader to undergo scarification. Her style is confrontational; atmospherics that are psychically violent threaten not only her characters, but the reader's equanimity. Deprived of the shelter of a narrative that takes one into a labyrinthine textual landscape and then simply locks the bogeyman within the book, *The Devil Latch* works by stripping away normalcy and leaving us—not with resolution, but with real horror merely temporarily suspended. I was interested to see that while rejecting the whole convention of a resolution based on understanding—a breaking through to some kind of subjective truth no matter how superficial—Hartnett nevertheless does effect a temporary reconciliation where Kitten decides his encounter with the two white-coated, angel-seeming psychiatrists is actually a meeting with the "natural parents" he feels he has never had. It's hardly bibliotherapy, but at least Kitten is offered an opportunity to construct a shelter against lovelessness with the help of a paternalistic couple acting in his apparent best interests:

> This is what they do to him: they open his head and drag out the twins, who writhe and scream and crash their teeth, clutching with their claws at the curve of Kitten's skull. When they are freed they are wrenched apart and their long arms lunge for each other, desperate for their old embrace....The natural parents step upon the small soft bodies until the whimpering twins are silent and dead.
>
> When Kitten wakes up they tell him he's not a devil any more, he's just an ordinary boy. He is no longer called Kitten: now he is Christopher....
>
> An ordinary boy: Christopher. Kitten sighs.
>
> Well, it will not last forever. (Hartnett 1996b: 170–171)

Violent though his rehabilitation may be, in medication and surveillance Kitten has found a measure of relief. The reader who completes this book, then, recognizes the veracity of Kitten's devil, the truth of his subjective horror, and admits to its pervasive social existence. Wherever children are abandoned and mistreated, there devils be also. And if there is a struggle between good and evil being explicated here, it is seen not as a set of inherited literary tropes, but in the infinite permeability between the vulnerable human skin of the child, and the potent adult will to power that can emerge unbridled, destructive, and inventively cruel.

CONCLUSION

Unquestionably, the Gothic genre lends itself particularly well to dramatizing narratives of lost and broken families. Contemporary writers for children and teenagers have adopted Gothic chronotopes with the same finesse with which they have appropriated other adult modes of writing. The covert question that drives this paper, however, has little to do with whether we are beginning to see a local tradition of children's writing which could broadly be called Gothic. Rather, it seeks to investigate whether the "Gothic" can stand for anything other than a failed or psychotic family. Do scary narratives, in other words, always have to address—and spring from—scary families?

In part, this question was prompted by reading Jackie French's *In the Blood*, the first of a trilogy published in 2001.[7] Here in a futuristic society with a recognizably Australian setting, the villain is a vampire happily married to a non-vampire and living in an innocuous rural community. In fact, the cover illustration with its ruined Gothic castle and sunset flight of bats is a fake: a contrived, virtual world that sucks the viewer in through its power of illusion. The truly scary monsters in French's series belong to a highly centralized urban ruling system that wilfully experiments with the human gene pool in order to breed the perfect civil servant. In this reconstituted fantasy that hybridizes chronotopes from science fiction, fantasy and horror, the Gothic component seems to have been liberated from its suffocating dysfunctional family, and shifted instead to play, through the figure of the vampire, the exemplary mutant, symbol of neither decadence nor conformity but instead representing a surreptitious resistance to an ideology of control and standardization.[8]

By no stretch of the imagination could either Kitten Latch or Johnny Doolan be read in the same way: Kitten is too psychologically damaged; Johnny too naïve to serve as figures of resistance to an ideology of normality. What French offers is a departure from both horror and standard Gothic conventions, and the first novel's success may simply be due to her choice of locating the series in the future, echoing John

Marsden's time setting for the *Tomorrow* series.[9] On the other hand, because she has chosen to inject one conventional genre (sci-fi/futurist) with another (the Gothic), the way forward for writers of supernatural fantasy for children and young adults—however the supernatural is conceived—may well now lie in blending a number of antipathetic chronotopes into a new arrangement that owes loyalty only to itself. As Walter Kendrick says of Nina Auerbach's *Our Vampires, Ourselves*, "each age fashions vampires in its own image…[and that] truly, we always get the vampires we deserve" (1995: back cover). The figure of the hybrid, the mutant and the cyborg are of course, closer to realization today than when H. G. Wells wrote *The Island of Dr Moreau*, when Philip K. Dick's speculative story about "precognitives" first appeared in 1956, and nearly forty years later, when Donna Haraway conceived of the liminal identity of the cyborg.[10] And if the scientific imagination was slower to gain entry into material time, these strange figures from biology and science fiction nevertheless entered literary history immediately through interbreeding with older textual conventions from Gothic Europe and America. Today, along with classical Gothic tropes of dysfunctional families and supernatural horrors, children and teenagers can read about vampires who are social exemplars, and families whose life-blood is being drained by corporation-sponsored geneticists. If teenagers nevertheless continue to identify with the outsider status of liminal creatures straight from the Gothic imagination,[11] they can equally be edified through reading about risky behaviours without having to put their family lives on the analyst's couch. Contra Johnny Doolan, Kitten Latch—and Angel and Willow, for that matter—unorthodox protagonists don't have to spring fully-armed from dysfunctional families.[12] A vampire isn't always a predator; nor a revenant the sure sign of an unresolved past. Some of the most recent juvenile Gothic fantasy and sci-fi horror allow readers to enjoy the ride without assuming a prefabricated set of issues implicit in the representation of vampire, werewolf or blood witch that must be worked through by needy individuals, families and social groups.[13] Granted, that magnetic pull of reading horror—so immediate sometimes that the skin literally crawls—will hardly disappear, nor should it; but as accompaniments to the enigmatic, painful family spaces of writers like Hartnett, Gothic tales for teenagers and younger readers ought to be free to experiment with less predictable, less classically dysfunctional outcomes.

Offering vicarious identification in association with a narrative trajectory that persistently surprises suggests that the best writers of Gothic literature for children and adolescents allow room for scary language to find its own haunting container. Fiction, then, is the ultimate sign of mutation; sooner or later, it will throw up a sport that will neither be recognized by its predecessors or the society it is expected to reflect. This is not to say that realism is an inferior form of writing, but simply that the Gothic imagination remains far more unpredictable and arresting than we postmodern critics have assumed.

ENDNOTES

1. As many formal definitions of the Gothic as there are critics, the best cumulative exposition of the genre currently available is probably David Punter and G. Byron's edited text, *The Gothic* (2003).

2. The notion that the figure of the vampire was associated with syphilis being a classic case in point. Consult Rebecca Stephens on "Blood Culture: the Heretic, Vampire and the Jew" (2002). And note the powerful fear linking vampirism with contagion in Bram Stoker's *Dracula* and Sheridan le Fanu's portrait of the Countess Carmilla. See http://www.nthposition.com/bloodculture.php.

3. Cornelia Funke's *Inkheart* (2003) is an exception; however, its readership is considerably more sophisticated than that of *Gothic Hospital*.

4. Note the transition between Freud's *Studies in Hysteria*, written with Breuer in 1895 and his later text, *The Interpretation of Dreams*. In the former, he treated the hysteric's neurotic symptoms as the result of painful repressed memories of their own literal seduction by a paternal figure, or of their idiosyncratic seduction fantasies. In both cases, these symptoms were believed to be anomalous, and thus in need of a "cure." By 1900 with the publication of *The Interpretation of Dreams*, this hypothesis gave way to the theory of the Oedipus complex that made the threat of parental seduction a universal—and normative—psychic structure.

5. See Jacques Lacan, "The Mirror Stage as Formative of the Function of the I," (1977).

6. Witness Mary Shelley's *Frankenstein, or the Modern Prometheus* ([1818] 1993; London: Pickering); Robert Louis Stevenson's *The Strange Case of Dr Jekyll and Mr Hyde* (1886); Freud's interpretation of Hoffman's "The Sandman," and the Coppelia myth (in Helene Cixous, "Fiction and its Phantoms: A Reading of Freud's *Das Unheimliche* [1976]).

7. By Angus & Robertson, 2001 (Pymble, New South Wales). Followed by *Blood Moon* (HarperCollins, 2002) and *Flesh and Blood* (Angus & Robertson, 2004).

8. A similar statement is made in Octavia Butler's *Fledgling* (2005). Shori is a young black female vampire genetically modified to withstand the sunlight. She is the novel's protagonist and heroine, not its dysfunctional predator.

9. The first of Marsden's series being titled *Tomorrow, When the War Began* (2002).

10. H. G. Wells, *The Island of Dr Moreau* (1896). Philip K. Dick, "Minority Report" (2002). Donna Haraway, "A Cyborg Manifesto: Science, Technology and Socialist-Feminism in the Late Twentieth Century" (1991).

11. Elaine O'Quinn is particularly good on the way teenagers intuitively associate their own emotional and physical changes at puberty with the transforming figures they read about in supernatural and Gothic fiction. See her "Vampires, Changelings, and Radical Mutant Teens" (2004).

12. Jes Battis argues that the new extended "families" present in both *Angel* and *Buffy* are symptomatic of the failure of the nuclear family and the concomitant growth of intimate social groups based on mutual interest and shared identities. See his *Blood Relations* (2005), particularly the final chapter.

13. Annette Curtis Klause's *The Silver Kiss* (1992) is of this order. Its resolution, where the young vampire Simon willingly destroys himself, reflects a conventionally "Gothic" ending.

REFERENCES

Auerbach, N. (1995). *Our Vampires, Ourselves*, Chicago: University of Chicago Press.

Battis, J. (2005). *Blood Relations*, New York: McFarland and Co.

Breuer, J. & Freud, S. (1974). *Studies on Hysteria*. J. Strachey & A. Strachey (Trans. & Eds.). Harmondsworth: Penguin.

Butler, O. (2005). *Fledgling*. New York: Seven Stories Press.

Carmody, G. (1994). *The Gathering*. New York: Dial.

Catran, K. (2005). *Something Wicked This Way Comes*. Auckland: Scholastic.

Cixous, H. (1976). Fiction and its phantoms: A reading of Freud's *Das Unheimliche*. *New Literary History, 7* (3), 525–548.

Clarke, J. (1997). *The Lost Day*. Sydney: Puffin.

Cross, G. (2005). *Borderland*. Auckland: Reed.

Crew, G. (1991). *Strange Objects*. Port Melbourne: Mammoth.

———. (1994). *Inventing Anthony West*. St. Lucia: University of Queensland Press.

———. (2001). *Gothic Hospital*. Melbourne: Lothian.

———. (2002). *The Diviner's Son*. Sydney: Pan Macmillan.

———. (2005). *The Lace Maker's Daughter*. Sydney: Pan Macmillan.

Dick, P. K. (2002). Minority report. In *Minority Report*. London: Gollancz.

French, J. (2001). *In the Blood*. Sydney: Angus & Robertson.

Freud, S. (1954). *The Interpretation of Dreams*. J. Strachey (Trans.). London: Allen & Unwin.

Funke, C. (2003). *Inkheart*. Anthea Bell (Trans.). London: The Chicken House.

Haraway, D. (1991). A cyborg manifesto: Science, technology and socialist-feminism in the late twentieth century. In *Simians, Cyborgs and Women: the Reinvention of Nature* (pp. 149–181). New York: Routledge.

Hartnett, S. (1996b). *The Devil Latch*. Melbourne: Penguin.

———. (1997). *Sleeping Dogs*. Ringwood, Victoria: Penguin.

Klause, A. C. (1992). *The Silver Kiss*. New York: Dell.

Lacan, J. (1977). The mirror stage as formative of the function of the I. In *Ecrits: A Selection* (pp. 1–7), Alan Sheridan (Trans.). New York: Norton.

Lovecraft, H. P., 'Introduction to Supernatural Horror in Literature,' 1927. In *Fantastic Literature: A Critical Reader*, ed. David Sandner. Praeger, 2004, pp. 102–105.

Marsden, J. (2002). *Tomorrow, When the War Began*. Sydney: Pan Australia.

O'Quinn, E. (2004). Vampires, changelings, and radical mutant teens. *Alan Review, 31* (3), 50–56.

Punter, D. & Byron, G. (Eds.). (2003). *The Gothic*. London: Blackwell.

Sage, V. & Smith, A. L. (Eds.). (1996). *Modern Gothic: A Reader*. Manchester: Manchester University Press.

Sandner, D. (Ed.). (2004). *Fantastic Literature: A Critical Reader*. New York: Praeger.

Shelley, M. [1818] (1993). *Frankenstein, or the Modern Prometheus*. London: Pickering.

Stephens, J. & McCallum, R. (2001). "There are worse things than ghosts": Reworking horror chronotopes in Australian children's fiction. In A. Gavin & C. Routledge (Eds.), *Mystery in Children's Literature* (pp. 165–83). Houndmills; Basingstoke: Palgrave Macmillan.

Stephens, R. Blood culture: The heretic, vampire and the Jew. Retrieved January 2007, from http://www.nthposition.com/bloodculture.php.

Stevenson, R. L. [1886] (1999). *The Strange Case of Dr Jekyll and Mr Hyde*. M. Danahay (Ed.). Peterborough, Ontario: Broadview.

Stoker, B. [1896] (1983). *Dracula*. Oxford: Oxford University Press.

Wells, H. G. [1896] (1993). *The Island of Dr Moreau*. B. Aldiss (Ed.). London: Dent.

8

HAUNTING THE BORDERS OF SWORD AND SORCERY: GARTH NIX'S *THE SEVENTH TOWER*

Alice Mills

Over the past 16 years, Garth Nix has established himself as a leading Australian writer of Gothic fantasy for children and adults. Nix's fantasy quest novels mingle elements from sword and sorcery and Gothic horror, with the horror element at its most potent in *Sabriel* and its sequels. He has been a prolific author, at his best when working on the larger scale of trilogies and series novels; it is in these longer books that his talents as an accomplished storyteller and builder of richly varied imaginary worlds are best demonstrated.

Sabriel brought Nix into prominence as a fantasy writer when it won the 1995 Australian Aurealis award as the most outstanding adult and (jointly) young adult fantasy of the year; in 1997 it was chosen as an ALA Honor Book. In both Australia and the United States, it became a bestseller. Nix's next book, *Shade's Children*, a much darker work of dystopian speculative fiction, was an ALA Best Book for young adults and a CBCA notable book. The success of *Shade's Children* and *Sabriel* in the U.S. marketplace attracted the attention of Lucasfilms, who approached Nix to write a "fantasy franchise" that could be translated from book form into film or television series or perhaps a computer game. Nix developed Lucasfilms' initial idea into a six-volume series, *The Seventh Tower*, which proved to be another commercial success in the United States; to date, however, no film, television, or game spin-offs have eventuated. These books have not attracted critical acclaim. Stylistically they are not Nix's best work, their prose workmanlike and sometimes clichéd, their pace rapid, their focus on exciting adventures and cliff-hanger endings to chapters rather than on depth, reflectiveness, or subtlety. Nevertheless, cumulatively, these six volumes present a Gothic narrative of some complexity, especially with regard to the ending.

The Seventh Tower, each volume published in large print, primarily targets a child audience of 8 to 12 year olds. The plot, involving two 13-year-old protagonists, carries only the slightest hint of sexuality, but supplies plenty of ordeals, chase sequences, and fights. The sword and sorcery element of the plot is most obvious in its weapons (blades and magical beams of light), its Gothic element most obvious in the many trips through the Castle's secret passages and the host of sinister, shadowy creatures that infest it. The novel's hero, Tal, is almost 14, an age critical for the Chosen inhabitants of the Castle: at this age, all Chosen have to travel to the spirit-world, Aenir, to give back the shadowguard that has protected them since infancy and capture another Aenirian creature to serve as their Spiritshadow for the rest of their lives. Such is the Chosen's traditional, unquestioned way of life, until Tal learns that the Castle is full of lurking unbound Spiritshadows who are conspiring to destroy the magical Veil of darkness whose function is to keep Tal's world safe from any Aenirian creatures who, manifesting as Shadows here, need light to survive. Another strand of plot concerns Milla, a thirteen-year-old warrior maiden of the Icecarls, who live outside the Castle on the planet's inhospitable, icy surface. Their lives are based on the endless peregrinations of the great seal-like creatures, the Selski, which provide them with food, clothing, and oil. Milla and her people hate and fear the Spiritshadows that have been brought to the Castle by the Chosen and, after a series of adventures with Tal, she leads her Icecarl forces in an invasion of the Castle to force the unbound Spiritshadows back to Aenir.

As in many other Gothic tales and almost all sword and sorcery novels, the multiple quests of Milla and Tal (to gain a Sunstone each; to heal Tal's mother and rescue his father and siblings; to find out the cause of the mysterious disappearances of so many Chosen; to gain a Spiritshadow; to tell the Empress the truth about her realm; and so on) all end in success. Tal and Milla are apparently too young to feel sexual attraction towards one another or to wed, but Tal becomes Emperor, thanks to his discovery of the assassinated Emperor's Sunstone ring and his overthrow of his opponents, and Milla becomes leader of the Icecarl warriors. Tal heals his mother, rescues the rest of his family and restores the Veil of darkness to full potency, so that black night can keep protecting his world. The hidden Spiritshadows have been exposed and most of them cast out; at the end of the book, the Castle is still in process of being purged. The dual slave system on which the Chosen's pampered lifestyle depended, alien Spiritshadows as personal companions and human Underfolk as menial servants, has been abolished. All now seems well, or is in process of being put right, even though some of the Chosen are finding it difficult to accept Tal as their new Emperor and to renounce slavery. Spiritshadows no longer assail and prey upon the Chosen in their own Castle, and the Icecarls need no longer be wary of any contact with the Castle's inhabitants, since these Aenirian creatures cannot cross between the worlds of their own volition.

A little reflection upon the state of the Castle that Tal now rules and the world whose safety Milla and he have assured, should indicate that all is not as well as the book claims. As Nix repeatedly explains, the world under the Veil is perpetually dark, lit only by Sunstones and Selski oil, and by the feebler lights of ice creatures such as luminescent moths. Milla and Tal have dispelled the treacherous Shadows from their world but have not restored daylight to release the world from the coating of ice that has covered it since the Veil was first established. Instead, the cost of safety is perpetual night. Symbolically, night carries overtones of horror, fear and secrecy, and complete darkness is greatly feared by the Chosen; it is, then, a peculiar outcome of Tal's quest that safety and success derive from the restoration of the Veil.

Equally ominous is the Castle's continued dependence on Sunstones to provide light, power, and magical tools and weapons. These stones can only be found on the spirit-planet, Aenir, where they are harvested and then hung to grow to full size on the Castle Towers which protrude into the sunlight through the Veil. Thus Tal's success in freeing his world from Aenirian Spiritshadows in no way means that traffic between the worlds is halted. His restoration of the Veil actually guarantees the continual need for Castle dwellers to revisit Aenir and harvest the stones in order to maintain light and power supplies on their own planet. If the Castle dwellers continue to believe in their unquestioned right to harvest these stones without payment or permission, there remains the possibility of resentment on the part of the Aenirians against these invaders. With the need for visits to Aenir to collect stones will come the temptation for human visitors to enslave Aenirian creatures anew, as they strive for political advantage in the Castle. That was how the troubles that Tal faces began, after the first war against Aenir, when the human victors had set up the magical Veil over their planet and banned the importation of Spiritshadows: an ambitious young woman sought help from Sharrakor, Lord of Aenir, to assassinate the Emperor, and her act of transporting Sharrakor to the Castle led to his secretly taking control. Tal has restored the Veil and renewed the ancient ban on taking Aenirians as Spiritshadows, but his success seems all too likely to set up conditions for a repetition of the betrayals, conspiracies and other abuses of power that he has just overcome. Even now, at the sixth volume's ending, some of the Chosen are finding Tal's reforms very difficult to accept: how long before it all repeats?

The implications of the novel's resolution thus render it deeply uncanny, as Freud defines the term. Throughout the six volumes, Tal and his allies understand themselves as champions of good against a force of evil which is increasingly revealed as monstrous, criminal, alien, bestial, and shape-shifting, battening on the corruption of those in authority and lurking in good Gothic fashion in the Castle's secret places. The volumes gradually disclose that it is the Chosen who have brought this evil into their world, some knowingly and many in ignorance, and that the history of the first war against Aenir has been deliberately suppressed to encourage the bringing of more Aenirians across. Thus it is the Chosen themselves who have brought about the return of the repressed in the form of the second Aenirian invasion and the second Aenirian war that Milla and Tal fight. In restoring the Veil to full strength and banning Spiritshadows from the Castle, Tal is repeating just what was done unavailingly at the end of the first Aenirian war. The novel's happy ending can thus be read as a delusory moment of optimism—in the dark—before the whole cycle threatens to repeat.

In restoring the Veil, Tal can also be understood as failing to heal the planet. No human in the novel, Chosen, Icecarl or Underfolk, expresses any qualms about the restoration of the Veil. As the volumes gradually reveal the history of the two worlds, it becomes apparent that Tal's planet was not always icebound. Rather, the climate of a fertile world was transformed as a result of the Veil's creation. The Icecarls (though not their matriarchal leaders, the Crones) think of their harsh living conditions, their endless crossings of the ice in pursuit of the Selski, as natural; but in fact, the ice is only a thousand years old, as is their culture. When Tal succeeds in restoring the Veil to full power, he perpetuates the Icecarls' struggle to survive. He may pride himself on freeing the Castle's slaves but he has knowingly confirmed the Icecarls' life of bondage to the ice. Paradoxically, these Icecarls pride themselves on their lives of freedom, circling the planet, far from the confines of the Castle and all its corruption, far from alien Shadows. Even Milla, who has learned the whole truth of her people's condition in her journeys with Tal, is represented as very content with her new position as leader of the Icecarl warriors, returning to her life of danger and hardship, now that the Veil has been restored. There is a chance, with Milla and Tal's victory, for sunlight to shine again, which would remove any critical need for humans to visit Aenir for Sunstones and at the same time would put an end to the empire of ice, but the novel does not even broach the possibility.

All of these features of the text are suggestive of Freudian repetition compulsion, which is evident on a smaller scale in the fate of one of the Veil's Guardians. There are six Chosen Guardians of the six Keystones that maintain the Veil, named after the colours of the rainbow. The seventh, Violet Keystone, takes the form of the Emperor's Sunstone picked up from his ancient skeleton by Tal on his travels. Each of the other Keystones is located in a room at the top of a Tower and there, remote from everyday life in the Castle, the Guardians are being successively trapped and imprisoned within their stones. Tal's father is one such Guardian, but is absent from the novel as a character in his own right. The book introduces as a character only the Guardian of the Red Keystone, trapped within the watery globe of her Keystone. She is described as repetitiously circling the interior of her prison, half-crazed, unable to free herself. Her frantic circlings can be seen, in the Freudian reading that I am proposing, as a microcosmic version of the macrocosmic, unending, planet-encircling migration of the Icecarls, but she is under no illusions as to her plight. The fact that the majority of Icecarls do not know their own history and are given no choice whether to continue circling the planet is disregarded in the general jubilations at the end of the novel.

Margery Hourihan points out the ideological effects of closure in quest narratives such as *The Seventh Tower*:

> It is the point in a text where loose ends, doubts and uncertainties are removed, and the significance of the story appears clear and coherent, the point where the myth establishes its meanings upon the reader. The closure is ideological as well as narrative and aesthetic; it makes the values inherent in the structures and narrative point of view seem to "go without saying," to be simply natural. (1977: 52)

It is all too easy to yield to the power of closure in Nix's story, not to question the values presented there as self-evident truth, but the volumes provide enough information to cast doubt on the necessity and virtue of the Icecarls' lifestyle of grinding hardship. Is it, perhaps, better understood as a symptom of self-imposed madness as pitiable as the Guardian's frantic revolutions in her sphere?

Freud's "On the Uncanny" suggests some psychological answers to the puzzle of why Icecarl Crones and Chosen alike are so set upon the retention of the protective Veil, even though no Aenirian can cross over to Tal's world unaided and the danger might be equally well protected against by allowing sunlight to permeate the world once more (since none of the humans is prepared to live in the absolute safety of complete darkness). Freud builds part of his psychoanalytic theory of the uncanny on the odd relationship between the two words, *heimlich* and *unheimlich*, such that the word unheimlich means both the uncanny and the homely and familiar. The novel's ending lays stress on the familiar homeliness of the human world after Tal's victory. The Icecarls can happily maintain their traditional lifestyle and Tal himself can once again enjoy the company of his beloved family, now that all that is unheimlich is in process of being expelled. Throughout the novel, Tal has felt intensely nostalgic for the lost paradise of his family life; now, it seems, as he walks through the Castle in the closing pages towards his family quarters, he may have achieved the humanly impossible task of finally dissociating the unheimlich from the heimlich for himself, his family and all the humans of his world.

Like the remainder of the novel's happy endings, this domestic conclusion repays closer scrutiny. The last pages suggest that Tal can keep his childhood place at home with his loving father and mother and at the same time function in the adult world as Emperor. The story breaks off before he actually reaches home, so that Nix does not have to show how functioning as an Emperor can be reconciled with family life. It also avoids any ongoing relationship between Milla and Tal. For the latter part of the novel, each has worn half of the imperial Sunstone ring that is the Violet Keystone, and it might seem fitting for them to end up as Emperor and Empress, but Milla suddenly gives Tal her half of the ring at the end, contenting herself with a lesser Sunstone to take back to her clan. There is no prospect, then, of joint rule, nor is there any direct mention of a possible sexual relationship between them. In contrast, the beings that they have acquired as companions in Aenir have kept one another company for centuries in the form of storm clouds, and as Spiritshadows find it hard to be separated from one another. The delight with which the male and female clouds embrace at the end emphasizes the lack of ardour between Tal and Milla, or perhaps their repression of ardour, apparent in their shadowy doubles but inadmissible to their conscious minds. The human characters' turning away from relationship with one another seems odder still when the models on which Nix based Icecarl society are taken into account. For Arctic dwellers, early marriage and childbearing were essential for the survival of the community, and a large group of single women of child-bearing age choosing to become dedicated warriors, like Milla and the Icecarls' Shield Maidens, would not have been tolerated. On several levels, then, the novel avoids the development of its human characters towards post-oedipal sexuality.

Apart from the absence of ongoing relationship between hero and heroine, *The Seventh Tower* appears to present a typical sword and sorcery oedipal quest with Gothic trappings: the son is called to initiation into manhood, leaves home, and finally gains ultimate power. There is plenty of evidence in the six volumes to support this reading, until that last movement of retreat beneath the sheltering Veil. The Sunstones, used by Chosen as weapons, can be understood as phallic in their punitive, powerful beams of light. The seven Towers protruding from the Veil into the sunlight, can be read as phallic erections; in search of a Sunstone to enable him to enter the adult world, Tal climbs one of these Towers and is cast down, losing his place in Chosen society and (it seems) his last chance to act the hero, take his father's place and rescue his sick mother. For a Freudian reading, the puffy, shape-changing creatures that the thirteen-year-old Tal and Milla gain as Spiritshadows are suggestive of newly expanding body parts, newly grown breast tissue and a newly vigorous penis. Tal's Spiritshadow, in particular, expands and contracts a lot in the course of his adventures. Particularly apt for a Freudian interpretation is the novel's emphasis on blinding, whether caused by exposure to total darkness or to brilliant sunshine, or attack by a Sunstone beam of light.

The Chosen fear permanent blinding, as it would demote them instantly to slave status. It is notable that all the actual blindings in the novel are inflicted by older men in positions of authority. This tallies well with Freud's comments in "On the Uncanny" as to the close symbolic connection between blinding and castration, the father's threat to the son eager to supplant him during the oedipal period of psychosexual development. *The Seventh Tower*, in a Freudian reading, abounds in images of castration, starting with the unpleasantly intense rays of punishment directed at Tal by his corrupt seniors as punishment for his supposed act of disrespect. If Tal's climb up the tower in quest for a Sunstone has phallic overtones, the moment when a monstrous Spiritshadow casts him down from the heights to probable death has overtones of castration. The book's final, decisive combat takes place on an equally phallic erection, the pillar within a whirlwind in Aenir from which Lord Sharrakor is cast down to his death. Such episodes all suggest an oedipal narrative, with Tal as hero ultimately gaining the position of Emperor, father-figure ruling over all the Chosen.

Yet this reading is ultimately unconvincing. Why, if Tal succeeds in his oedipal quest, does he reinstate the Veil? Why do Tal and Milla renounce those large, puffy cloud-creatures, leaving them behind in

Aenir? If we examine the novel closely, it becomes doubtful if Tal is indeed an oedipal hero or whether there are any post-oedipal subjects operating within the story. I would argue that beneath the sword and sorcery heroic adventures, subverting them, lies the uncanny, and that Tal's final victory is in effect a surrender to Gothic darkness. Considered critically, the hierarchy of the Chosen in the Castle does not present a model of post-oedipality. While the Castle's population understands itself as a hierarchy, Underfolk at the bottom, then layers of power and status from lowly Red to imperial Violet, these Chosen are in fact all secretly controlled by an alien monster, Sharrakor. Some of the Chosen have families of their own and a few carry the responsibilities of guarding the Keystones (a once-a-year tune-up job), teaching, judging, and torturing other Chosen, but none of them works for a living. Their activities are those of dilettantes, infantilised by the slave systems that take away any responsibility for their own personal safety and any need for exertion. Food and other supplies are provided by the Underfolk. The Chosen lead pampered parasitic lives of ignorance; none of them seems aware of any other human beings living outside the Castle's walls. Even those seemingly in authority prove to be other than responsible adults. The Empress and her brother, nominal rulers of the Chosen, turn out to be querulously senile when Tal finally meets them. The torturer, a monster of a man, is alive only because half of his body is made up of Spiritshadow matter, and he claims towards the end of the novel that he is as much nightmare-victim as torturer, forced to take on the Spiritshadow body to save his own life. This seems a somewhat spurious rationalisation, but there is no doubt about the innocence of the man whom Tal long believes to be the source of all the Castle's evil, Sushin. This Chosen's human consciousness, we learn late in the story, has been set aside for decades while a Spiritshadow possesses him, body and mind, and issues commands in his name. When the Spiritshadow is expelled, Sushin remembers nothing of what he has done as Castle despot. Thus the seemingly evil Chosen are not fully responsible for what is done in their names, though the senile Empress and her brother acted in full awareness of their evil when, nearly a thousand years ago, they sought Sharrakor's help to overthrow the then-Emperor. The novel's good adults, such as Tal's mother and father, are easily overcome and rendered powerless. Even Tal's Great-Uncle Ebbit, who has great stores of knowledge and saves him at many a point of crisis, has been cast down from his eminence among the Chosen and has survived only because he is regarded as a harmless eccentric.

Tal and Milla might seem the obvious candidates for post-oedipal subjects, at the end of the book, were it not for the restoration of the

Veil and their separation from their cloud companions and each other. In restoring the Veil of darkness, Tal arguably castrates not only his subjects and the Icecarls but also himself. This leaves Sharrakor as the only candidate for post-oedipal subject, but while he is the most powerful older male character in the novel, his role as secret ruler collapses into that of fomenter of panic and dread, destroyer of the Castle's traditions in the guise of maintaining them. He is a shape-shifter, alternating among the three shapes of dragon, human, and "mind-drill," operating within and outside the human bodies that he possesses. Like all of the Spiritshadows that the Chosen bind to themselves, he appears to function as a double for his Chosen, the Empress, communicating her commands, enforcing her will. Doubts as to the trustworthiness and controllability of these Shadows multiply in the course of the novel until Milla and Tal learn that many of them are not under human control but free, malicious, and murderous. They can thus be understood as living out Freud's theorisation of the double as an attempt by humans to preserve themselves against the powers of death that then becomes the "harbinger of death" (Freud 1961: 235). Here oedipal hierarchy collapses into Gothic mystery; what was understood as an external, adult authority turns out to be a threat assailing that humanity from within, attempting to destroy human society rather than rule it.

Nix's novel contains few metaphors beyond its system of rainbow colours for the seven levels of Chosen and their Keystones and Towers, and the gradients of light in their hierarchy within their colour, from dim to brilliant. An exception to the general sparseness of Nix's prose is the extended metaphor of the Castle as body. Far below the Chosen levels, below the Underfolk levels, lies magma whose heat is channelled through the Castle in the form of steam. The central heating channels, some wide enough to contain several human beings, others much narrower, are described as a blood circulatory system. Symbolically, then, the Castle is a gigantic living organism with steam and water for blood. The Chosen live inside this body, almost all of them unaware of the wealth of Gothic-style secret passages behind their walls, under their feet and over their heads. If the Castle is a body within which the Chosen live, its symbolic brain appears to be the punishment globe in the Hall of Nightmares, where Chosen are punished via the manipulation of their dreams. This is a sick body, then, troubled by nightmare and attacked from within by alien Spiritshadows like multiplying bacteria (though Nix does not develop his metaphor this far).

If the Castle can be construed as a body full of human beings, it must be a maternal body, full of offspring who refuse to be born. The Chosen's annual visit to Aenir is enacted in spirit form only, while their bodies remain in suspended animation at home. Such procedures are more like uncanny, temporary premature burials than births into new life, especially when Tal and Milla hide their bodies in ancient coffins to keep them safe while visiting Aenir. I have previously commented on Tal's climbing of the Tower as an oedipal quest, but it can also be understood, if we read the Castle as maternal body, as a symbolic birth through a difficult dark passage into dazzling sunlight, away from the comfortable, familiar, warm world of the Castle interior as womb. As he climbs through the Veil, the struggling Tal cannot draw breath. All this is suggestive of birth, but rather than establishing a place for himself beyond the symbolic mother, Tal keeps returning to the Castle. Even when he has cured his own sick mother and the sick Castle-as-mother, he shows no wish to move on physically. A few of the other Chosen climb the Towers, once a year, to tend the Keystones briefly and then return. At the start of the novel, the outside world is not a place to which any Chosen wishes to go, unless forced to do so; by the last page, Tal is comfortable visiting Milla's Icecarls but still identifies himself as his mother's son, as a Castle dweller. He appears to have no doubt that his final goal is to return beneath the Veil. Similarly Milla, who alone among the Icecarls has seen the sun, felt the rain and walked on grass in Aenir, wishes for nothing more than to return to her familiar world of darkness and chill.

The Crones, the telepathic matriarchs of the Icecarl clans, have the power to intervene in bad dreams and wake sleepers, tossing them higher and higher until they wake, aroused by the pleasure and excitement of the game. This act of waking sleepers by heaving and tossing them upwards, can be considered a form of psychological midwifery, bringing the suffering sleeper out of unconsciousness into the waking world. But these Crones, who can wake individuals from nightmare, refrain from intervening in the Chosen's lives once the Spiritshadows have been dispelled. Even though they could be midwives of the planet's rebirth to light and fertility, even though they have helped wake the Chosen from a nightmare-ridden sleep of ignorance, they themselves, along with all the other human inhabitants of the planet, lapse into renewed sleep under the Veil as birth canal and shroud.

In his essay "On the Uncanny," Freud speaks of the terrible, uncanny allure of the mother's womb. Nix's singular achievement, in *The Seventh Tower*, is to write what appears to be a somewhat clichéd, formulaic sword and sorcery tale with Gothic trappings, each of whose seemingly oedipal quest elements collapses into the uncanny, and ultimately into the paradise—or is it a Gothic nightmare—of return to the mother's protective and enshrouding darkness.

REFERENCES

Freud, S. (1961). On the uncanny (Vol. xvii). *The Standard Edition of the Complete Psychological Works.* J. Strachey (Ed. & Trans.) London: The Hogarth Press.

Hourihan, M. (1977). *Deconstructing the Hero: Literary Theory and Children's Literature.* New York: Routledge.

Nix, G. (2000a). *The Seventh Tower: Aenir.* Sydney: Scholastic.

_____. (2000b). *The Seventh Tower: Castle.* Sydney; New York: Scholastic.

_____. (2000c). *The Seventh Tower: Into Battle.* Sydney: Scholastic.

_____. (2000d). *The Seventh Tower: The Fall.* Sydney: Scholastic.

_____. (2000e). *The Seventh Tower: The Violet Keystone.* Sydney: Scholastic.

_____. (2001). *The Seventh Tower: Above the Veil.* Sydney: Scholastic.

9

UNCANNY HAUNTINGS, CANNY CHILDREN

Anna Jackson

The first Harry Potter film ends, as a proper school story should, with everyone on the platform, bags packed, saying their farewells, ready to go home; except that, as Harry says, "I'm not going home. Not really."[1] For Harry, the boarding school of Hogwarts, despite being haunted not only by the mostly benign school ghosts but also by Voldemort, the embodiment of evil, is home in a way that suburban life for him can never be home.

For most of the last century, the uncanny has been understood in terms of Freud's definition of *unheimlich* as not quite the opposite of *heimlich*, and so perhaps it might not seem surprising that the Harry Potter books, the twentieth century's most successful Gothic publishing phenomenon, should be set in a school, that home-away-from-home. Nor perhaps is it surprising that Buffy should slay her vampires on the grounds, or just a little out of bounds, of Sunnydale High.[2] Much has been made not only of the homelike qualities of the fictional schools of pop-Gothic texts like these, but of the familiarity, the homelike-ness, of the school genre itself.[3]

In this chapter, I discuss three children's novels that are all about hauntings, that all draw on Gothic conventions to evoke a real sense of the uncanny. Two of the novels, *The Time of the Ghost* (1981) by Diana Wynne Jones and *Charlotte Sometimes* (1967) by Penelope Farmer, have boarding school settings, while the third, *The Haunting* (1982) by Margaret Mahy, moves between the comfortably domestic home of the Palmer family and the more unsettling household of the children's eerie Scholar relatives (and there is much play on the word scholar, and use of scholarly as a family adjective), in a way that also invites a reading in terms of an interplay of heimlich and unheimlich, the home-like and the un-homelike.

However, the school setting can also be understood in relation to the English word "uncanny." Just as the German word unheimlich seemed to have little to do with the word heimlich until Freud teased out the significance of the etymological link, "uncanny" doesn't usually operate as the opposite of the word "canny." Like the German unheimlich, the English uncanny means both unusual and unnatural—spooky, eerie, unsettling. Canny, as a recently republished children's book *Cannily, Cannily* (French 1981) helpfully informs the reader on its back cover, means "knowing, sagacious, shrewd, astute; skilled or expert, frugal or thrifty." The words are not quite opposites, since the quality of uncan-niness seems to belong to a situation or event, as an *effect* the situation or event produces, whereas canniness is a quality that properly belongs to a person. It might make sense, however, to understand the uncanny as that which cannot be understood cannily; as those events, situations or phenomena that do not allow for a knowing, sagacious, shrewd, and astute reading of them.

So far, this recognition of uncanny as the opposite of canny only takes us back to Freud's starting point, the definition of the uncanny, or the unheimlich, by the German psychologist Jentsch in his paper examining the sensation of the uncanny published in 1906. As Freud notes,

> Jentsch did not get beyond [the] relation of the uncanny to the novel and the unfamiliar. He ascribes the essential factor in the production of the feeling of uncanniness to intellectual uncer-tainty; so that the uncanny would always, as it were, be something one does not know one's way about in. The better orientated in his environment a person is, the less readily will he get the impres-sion of something uncanny in regard to the objects and events in it. (1985: 341)[4]

Freud's own return to the etymological roots of the word in German and the idea of the homelike within the un-homelike allowed him to "get beyond" Jentsch's conception of the uncanny and connect it to his theories of repressed childhood fantasies underpinning adult identity, reading various uncanny motifs such as damaged eyesight, severed hands and the "double," all as symbols of the infantile fear of castration by one's father. Going back to Jentsch's starting point, however, returns us to a definition that, although based on the German use of the word, relates particularly well to the etymology of the English word for what was clearly a shared concept, recovering the idea that canniness is what we lose in the face of the uncanny.

Furthermore, by following Freud's example with the word unheim-lich, and looking at the various shades of meanings contained in the word "uncanny" as well as its English etymological opposite "canny," it is possible to "get beyond [Jentsch's] relation of the uncanny to the novel and the unfamiliar" in a new way, which I think throws some light on the frequency with which hauntings appear in the plots of children's and young adult fictions. In particular, considering the uncanny in relation to the concept of canniness helps to explain why hauntings are parti-cularly prevalent in novels exploring the theme of personal identity.

The *Oxford English Dictionary* dates the use of the word "canny" to 1637, and it was used in the seventeenth century primarily to suggest prudence, particularly in matters of government or worldly affairs. "Uncanny" seems to have been a true opposite, up to the eighteenth century meaning careless, or incautious. In the eighteenth century, however, at the time when the Gothic genre was established in England, "uncanny" takes on its association with the supernatural and is associated also, for the first time, with the unfamiliar. "Canny" at the same time is increasingly used in association with women, and comes to mean more broadly cunning or wily, occasionally even with the suggestion of supernatural abilities. More commonly in the eighteenth century it is used as a synonym for shrewd, picking up on the earlier sense of worldliness, and implying an ability to look out for one's self, with "an eye to the main chance." Canny is a word which has increasingly come to mean a cleverness that is not just about knowing things, but is about a particular sort of capability, the capability to manipulate people and events in your own self-interest. It is to do with self-possession—a self-possession that makes you capable of acting powerfully in and on the world. And if we understand canny as a type of self-possession, suddenly it makes perfect sense that issues of identity should be explored through narratives of hauntings, narratives about being *possessed*.

Margaret Mahy's novel *The Haunting* opens with the surprising idea that Barney, recognising he is about to be haunted, should feel this a *babyish* thing to be happening to him, something he had thought himself to have grown out of (1982: 1). Although in fact it is quite true that hauntings are a much more common theme of children's fiction than of adult literature, this representation of a haunting as a baby-ish phenomenon is a novel move on Mahy's part, a twist that comes right at the start of the plot. Usually, it is the ghost plot which disrupts what would otherwise be a cosy, domestic story, or a familiarly generic school story. The ghost plot turns a story about family life or school politics into something that is both more introspective and more open to extraordinary pressures rather than the ordinary social pressures of family and school. The ghost plot is what compels the central character to reconsider issues of identity—to grow up.

And in fact Barney's haunting this time round does turn out to be quite different from his haunting by imaginary friends when he was younger. This haunting is decidedly uncanny, in several key aspects at once, right from the start. It begins not as a ghost but as a failure to appear as a ghost, leaving Barney himself "half expecting to be crushed into a sort of rolled-out gingerbread boy" (2)—marvellously uncanny in the combination of familiar fairytale motif and utterly strange appropriation of the motif to describe not even quite a sensation but the imminence of a sensation. Then the ghost itself appears as "a flat paper doll" (2)—dolls being one of the uncanny motifs that Freud associates with the death-wish. Finally the ghost materialises as an actual figure resembling a human figure, but "old-fashioned and strange" (2)—Gothic in its embodiment of the past. Particularly pertinent for a Freudian reading of its uncanniness is the way in which it then proceeds to repeat the same, eerie message over and over again: "Barnaby's dead! I'm going to be very lonely" (2). The narrative insists here that "It wasn't just that it said the same words that it had said earlier. Its very tone—the lifts and falls and flutterings of its voice—was exactly the same. If it had added, 'This is a recorded message,' it would not have seemed very out of place" (3).

For the rest of the novel, the haunting works rather differently, coming to be understood more as a sort of telepathy. It is never explained why it should first operate like a recorded message rather than a direct communication. In terms of plot, this detail is misleading. The main narrative purpose of this recorded message effect seems to be simply to evoke a sense of the uncanny. In all three of the novels I am looking at, a sense of the uncanny precedes the introduction of other Gothic motifs, and in each novel it is very clearly related from the start to the central theme of the protagonist's uncertain sense of identity.

The appearance of the ghost in *The Haunting* reminds Barney of his own feeling, when he was haunted as a younger child, of having lost his sense of self.

> It seemed to be having some difficulty seeing Barney so that he felt that *he* might be the one who was not quite real. Well, he was used to feeling that. In the days before Claire he had often felt that he himself couldn't be properly heard or seen. (2)

A sense of identity, or the possession of a sense of self, is shown to depend quite a lot on being noticed by other people. Family, and especially the role of the mother, is treated as tremendously important, but it is significant that Claire is Barney's step-mother, not his birth mother. Possession, in the sense of belonging, is shown very much as a result of the kinds of domestic, daily attentions family members pay to each other, whether or not they are biologically related. This, at any rate, is the argument Claire makes when, bursting in on the scene, she arrives just in time to save Barney from being completely possessed by his Great-Uncle Cole, the uncle whose "haunting" of Barney is here described more as a hunting.

> She was just in time, thought Barney, still aware of the spirally winding power building up in Cole. Another moment and he might have become a black hurricane and blown the house to pieces and carried off Barney like a hunter carrying off his prey. (103)

When Cole challenges her use of the possessive, when she calls Barney "my Barney," she calls on these daily attentions:

> "He's mine all right!" Claire replied. "Everyone in this family belongs to everyone else—belongs *with* everyone else, rather. I've looked after him for a year now—ironed his shirts, made his school lunches, told him stories. I made that dressing-gown he's wearing, whereas no one knew you were alive this time last year. But what matters most is that he *wants* to be ours and he doesn't want to be yours. That's what counts." (106)

But while it was the lack of these daily attentions that Barney felt caused his earlier hauntings, this kind of belonging is challenged by another kind of belonging, the belonging of family history and genetic inheritance.

> "But look at us!" said Cole. "Barney and I—we're almost like the same person seen at different times during the same life. Don't we look as if we belong together?" (106–107)

This second kind of belonging can be felt as a possession, and is indeed imposed on Barney as a possession. It is this claim that makes Barney's own reflection in the mirror appear to him as a "horror," the physical resemblance dissolving into a substitution, when Cole's expression takes over and he gazes out from Barney's reflection. Cole claims Barney as his own with the argument: "I have been closer to you than anyone else in your life. I am your reflection—remember?—and you are mine" (102). The "you are mine" here nicely reads two ways, as "you are my reflection," and as a more general statement of ownership, or possession, "you are my own."

If canniness is the kind of clever knowingness that makes a person able to act powerfully in his or her own self-interest, then it fits that this uncanny possession of Barney by his Great-Uncle Cole should make him powerless to act. This is something that the self-possessed Tabitha remarks on throughout the novel. "Don't just lie there suffering," she instructs Barney, and when he does seem to do little more than that, she "became impatient with him...because he was doing nothing about it" (52). Barney's lack of action—"not reading or drawing or anything" (72)—causes Claire to become concerned about him, even when she knows nothing about anything as uncanny as a haunting. When Cole finally arrives to carry Barney off with him, Barney seems powerless to resist him, and Claire, who is not related to Cole or to Barney, is able to act, sweeping in with her shopping bags to confront Cole as Barney cannot. Part of her confidence of course comes from her assumption that Cole is just another ordinary person, with nothing uncanny about him. For a moment it seems as if, coming in from the world of supermarket shopping in this way, she will overcome Cole, but when he presents her with the uncanny proof of his powers, she "shuddered all over" and, although a moment later she "was herself again," she no longer has the confidence to resist Cole (108).

For most of the novel, it has been Barney's sister Tabitha who has taken action. Like a Nancy Drew–type girl detective, she has tried to find out things in order to act. To a certain extent, she has succeeded in converting the uncanny into the familiar, confiding in one of the uncanny Scholar relatives Great-Uncle Guy, for instance, which leads him in turn to come and see the whole Palmer family and quickly become another member of the extended family in both senses of belonging. Troy, in comparison, the "dead opposite" (99) of Tabitha, has denied even hearing the footsteps of Barney's haunting, and has claimed not to believe a word of Tabitha's story. Unlike the outgoing Tabitha, she has barely even left her room, and seems imprisoned even in her own body: "her pale face looking out of its cloud of dark hair like a ghost glimpsed at a top window of a dark tower" (78). But it is Troy who needs to confront Cole, and she can do so because she too contains the uncanny.

I called Tabitha self-possessed, and so she is, but it is about Troy you would use the phrase "uncannily self-possessed." She is, as the description of her suggests, "self-contained," to such an extent that even her own siblings find her, and her tidy bedroom, "eerie and astonishing" (78). It turns out that Cole has simply been haunting the wrong Palmer child, and that while Barney resembles him physically, Troy actually shares his uncanny gift for magic. Curiously, an Internet search of the phrase "uncannily self-possessed" reveals it to be frequently coupled with the phrase "baby-faced" or some other phrase denoting an unnatural youthfulness.[5] This is usually to express a *contrast* between the babyish features of the person discussed and their uncanny self-possession. Troy herself stresses the maturity that distinguishes herself from her siblings, with reference to the exams she has to sit. It is Cole who is described as looking "like a grown-up child." Barney recognises in him a "dark childish part" that has never been able to grow up, because, he realises, he has never been able to reveal his hidden powers. Something in him is "clenched," "folded in tight," "stunted" (99). Troy's self-containment, her tidiness, can similarly be seen not as a sign of maturity but as a symptom of a similar stuntedness.

When she reveals her magical powers, she becomes, quite simply, spectacular: "she held out her arms, became a flowering tree, a flying bird, a burning girl, a creature made of stars....She shrank to the size of a seed, grew great and dim like a mist spreading through the room, blazed once more and then became Troy again...Troy in a room full of family" (121).

In the end, the book has raised the spectre of the uncanny only to resolve the complicated plot with a celebration of canniness, and an alignment of canniness with maturity, with growing up. Freud notes that just as the word heimlich contains such a spectrum of meanings that it "finally coincides with its opposite, *unheimlich*" (1985: 347), so does the word canny include as one of its possible meanings, possessed with magical powers, the ability to perform unnatural feats. This is what Troy finally reveals: a canniness so far at the edge of canniness as to border on the uncanny. Canniness allows for effective action to be taken in the face of the uncanny, because of its location in a powerful sense of self. Great-Granny claims it is quite possible to suppress the uncanny through "unselfishness" (Mahy 1982: 122) but while she has resisted using her uncanny powers, she comes across quite clearly as an uncanny figure in the book: she is described as resembling "a doll brought out of a glass case at a museum" (19). Canniness, however, is not so much a form of selfishness, as a kind of self-possession that also involves self-sharing. Troy makes the same sort of connection with Great-Uncle Cole that Tabitha has made with Great-Uncle Guy, making a role for him within the Palmer family, so that, as Tabitha puts it, he can learn to be "more of an uncle and less of a magician" (129). And Troy's good intentions by the end of the novel extend beyond the family: she plans to work with Cole to "change the world...make it better in some way." ("Better for everyone or better for you?" Barney asks [131]—"suspiciously" is the adverb offered in the text but "cannily" would fit nicely too.) The canny, by the end of *The Haunting*, has come to possess the uncanny.

The Time of the Ghost by Diana Wynne Jones ends, as *The Haunting* does, with the uncanny situation it sets up resolved, and the heroine of the novel possessed of a new canniness, a new sense of self which enables her to take effective action. Yet *The Time of the Ghost* begins, rather than ends, with the heroine of the novel lacking, like Troy, the usual "boundaries with the rest of the world" (Mahy 1982: 121). Lacking, too, Troy's control over this permeability of the self, she experiences this condition as absolutely uncanny. There are even more twists in the plot of *The Time of the Ghost* than there are in *The Haunting*, with the very first twist to tell the story of a haunting from the point of view of the ghost itself.

Where in other ghost stories the appearance of a ghost transforms what might otherwise be a familiar, domestic or school setting into the unheimlich, for the point of view of the character in *The Time of the Ghost*, the very familiarity, or heimlichness, of the scene in which she finds herself is unsettling from the start. Unable to locate the feeling of uncanniness in her surroundings—it being "broad daylight" and "summer, just as it should be" (Jones 1981: 7)—she eventually comes to realise she herself, or rather, her own lack of a locatable self, is what is so uncanny. Trying to identify herself by what she is wearing, she looks down, only to find there is nothing to look down at, and the panic which overtakes her at this point threatens not only her own dissolution, but the dissolution of the whole scene around her, as if it might just "shake itself right away from her, and she would be left with utter nothing" (9).

Even before the ghost herself is aware of her own uncanniness, however, the reader senses an uncanny quality to the narrative, and the ghost's own stated sense of the uncanny is the least of it. In the very first paragraph, we are told "she raised herself to look over the hedge," and the oddness of this movement, as well as the rather odd perspective on the "sleepy grey-green fields" that follows, are not likely to be consciously noted on a first reading (7). When, a couple of paragraphs further on, however, her discomfort with her unusual perspective, looking down over the fields, makes her decide to "[subside] to her usual height," the reader is likely to realise, before the ghost herself does, that something is not quite right (8).

The reader, in fact, shares with the ghostly narrator a perspective remarkably like that of Gothic cinema, as Misha Kavka describes it in her chapter "The Gothic on Screen" in *The Cambridge Companion to Gothic Fiction* (2002). Kavka argues that Gothic film has its own contribution to make to the Gothic genre, as it "reveals and recon-stitutes an underlying link between fear and the manipulation of space around a human body" (210). A similar connection is made in *The Time of the Ghost*, with the hedge operating at the beginning of the novel as the "threshold" which Kavka suggests is so impor-tant to Gothic cinema, representing, as it does, "the liminal" that in turn represents unstable subjectivity, the blurring of boundaries, and a tension between the representable and the unrepresentable. But where in Gothic cinema, the frame of the screen offers "cut-off points of visibility," emphasising the limits of the audience's vision, the hedge represents a threshold that ought to limit visibility yet fails to. Instead it is the ghost's own body that not only can't be seen, but can't even quite be seen to not be seen.

> She only had to look down. But first she seemed to have forgotten how to do that. Then when she did—
>
> Panic spread roaring, to its fullest size. She was swept away with it, as if it were truly a huge balloon, tumbling, rolling, bobbing, mindless. (Jones 1981: 8)

With the uncanny located in the heroine's own lack of a locatable self, issues of identity and self-possession are very clearly fore-grounded right from the start of *The Time of the Ghost*. Even more so since, even as the ghost finds herself able to identify people and locations as she meets them (her intelligence is described as limited to what she encounters like "a narrow torch beam" (8)—or, perhaps, a Gothic camera angle), at the beginning of the novel she is not at all sure which of the sisters in her family she might be the ghost of. Although she does fairly quickly settle on an identity, the reader may be less sure than she is that she has settled on the right one, and later on in the novel she herself comes to question her identity again. Indeed, with the question of her identity taking the place of the question of the identity of a murderer, the genre of the detective novel is suggested almost as much as the Gothic genre. In fact, the detective novel is parodied early on as the ghost believes she has indeed been murdered by her sisters (a belief that a canny reader is not likely to share), and only her lack of corporeality prevents her from rifling very satisfactorily through their drawers for clues. The reader, on the other hand, can look for clues to the ghost's identity very much as a reader in a detective novel looks for clues to the murderer's identity.

Most evidently evoked and parodied is, of course, the Gothic genre, although with the Gothic an element of parody is intrinsic to the genre itself. Part of what works so well in this novel is the way Gothic elements are employed in the service of domestic realism. The ghost's sisters play along throughout the novel with such Gothic conventions as the séance, the exorcism, the calling up of spirits, the worship of inanimate figures, in a way which is perfectly consistent with their very convincing characterisation. When the other sisters ask Imogen why she talks like a book all the time, the sort of book they are referring to is Gothic melodrama, not a book like *The Time of the Ghost* at all. "I'd rather play a xylophone compounded of dead men's bones!" Imogen complains, unhappy with the quality of the piano provided for her, and it is clear to the reader that she is being absolutely *Imogen* at this point (24).

The uncanniness of the situation for the ghost's sisters, in so far as any of them admit to a sense of the uncanny, arises from the way events seem to support beliefs they are only playing at holding. They play at exorcising a ghost they are only playing at believing in, Fenella arguing that the exorcism can't work anyway without a priest present, and Cart compensating for this by putting on a "pompous priestly voice" (96). The word "play" comes up again and again in the séance scene, as Cart, for instance, dismisses Imogen's anxiety about "playing with something nobody understands" as just part of a pattern of Imogen "not play-ying" (67). Even their Worship of Monigan, which, it turns out, has led to the accident that sends the ghost back in time from her hospital bed to haunt her own family, is undertaken only as a game Cart invents to amuse her sisters. When the ghost finds herself haunting a Worship of Monigan scene, her overwhelming feeling is of boredom and remembered boredom: "She knew she had thought it was pretty boring when Cart first invented the Worship of Monigan a year ago" (22). Yet she also remembers the game did begin to make them feel uncomfortable, and Cart claiming that the game was coming true: "At that time, the ghost remembered wondering if Cart was just saying that to keep them all believing even though Cart was tired of the game" (106), which may indeed have been the case, even though, as it turns out, Cart was quite right about the game coming true.

This fits with Alice Mills' reading of Freud's concept of the uncanny, when she argues that to experience a sense of the uncanny depends on "an almost complete disbelief in the numinous" (1999: 7). Yet apart from this feeling of discomfort about their Worship of Monigan, which may or may not have been a cover for boredom, on the whole the sisters performing the various Gothic rites in the novel are not the ones who are really finding them at all uncanny. Fenella's insistence, as the séance breaks up, that there really was a ghost present, is a characteristic act of self-*assertion* on her part. Imogen's claim to be scared of the ghost when the behaviour of the dog leads them to believe, or pretend to believe, in the presence of the ghost also comes across more as a self-indulgent act of attention-seeking, rather like her customary "grieving," than a genuine acknowledgement of the uncanny, while Cart tends to be matter-of-fact about these Gothic motifs in their lives, alternatively arguing logically against the supernatural or finding practical, if not really believed in, strategies for dealing with them.

It is rather the ghost who truly experiences the uncanny, even though she tries to reassure herself at one point that "*Ghosts aren't scared of ghosts!*" (Jones 1981: 98). Most uncanny of all is her own status as a ghost, and the eerie simultaneity of familiarity and unfamiliarity, heimlich and unheimlich, in almost every impression she has of what used to be her home. She herself makes a connection between the two issues, of identity and of the troubling relationship between the familiar and the unfamiliar, finding herself again and again "startled by something she should have known as well as the back of her hand. *Perhaps it is because I haven't got a back of my hand at the moment,* she thought, trying to make a joke out of it" (38). But it is the ghost, too, for whom these conventional trappings of the Gothic novel, the séance, the invocations, the exorcism, are felt as truly uncanny, while the ghost's own actions work to dispel the uncanny. It is the actions of the other characters which are unsettling—literally unsettling to the ghost, with the exorcism spinning her into the kind of disembodied panic her own ghostliness drove her into at the start of the novel.

A large part of the uncanniness of these rituals comes from the participants' own lack of belief in what they are doing. Imogen is the only sister who is really concerned about their dabbling in "something nobody understands" (66) and even she continues to participate. The others are all quite reckless in their readiness to act. In this, they are more like Tabitha, in *The Haunting,* than Barney, perhaps because they do not really experience the uncanny. In *The Haunting,* though, any action is seen as a positive counter to the uncanny, even if it isn't always very effective. In *The Time of the Ghost,* almost every action the sisters take provokes dread on the part of the ghost and also the reader. As Imogen recognises, their lack of knowledge about what they are doing is dangerous, a lack of knowledge the reader is acutely aware of, following everything from the perspective of a ghost the other characters can't even perceive. The sisters, in no position to act cannily, constantly open the narrative to the uncanny, while being neither uncanny nor really aware of the uncanny themselves.

One of the reasons for thinking that these hauntings in adolescent fiction are more about intellectual uncertainty and the establishment of an identity than about repression and the return of the repressed is the way the main characters seem to be affected more by what *other* characters have repressed than by what they have repressed themselves. This is a distinction that is made unusually explicitly of course in Mahy's *The Haunting*, as the psychological reasons why Barney might be troubled, or "haunted," are put forward only to be shown inadequate as explanations for what is really going on. As we will see, Charlotte in *Charlotte Sometimes* (Farmer 1967) is similarly disturbed not by her own repressed past but by the ways in which the family she is billeted with is haunted by the past.

In *The Time of the Ghost*, however, a similar kind of displacement happens with the uncanniness that stems from intellectual uncertainty, or, rather, less uncertainty than simple ignorance. But even the displacement of intellectual uncertainty in *The Time of the Ghost* can in fact be understood again in terms of displaced repression, once the reversal that the book is structured on, of taking the ghost's point of view, is taken into account. Because it is of course the sisters of the ghost who are in the position of Charlotte in *Charlotte Sometimes* or Barney in *The Haunting*: the intellectual uncertainty is displaced on to them because they are the ones who are in the position of being affected by someone else's repression—the ghost's. The ghost is haunting them, and they are haunted not by their own past, but by the ghost's need to return to her own past. They are haunted, weirdly, by the future: haunted by a future self of the ghost who needs to recover her past, but in doing so, haunts not her former self (she does come to do that but her former self doesn't notice), but her sisters.

If canniness depends on a sense of identity, so that it can be understood as a kind of self-possession, identity in turn is shown to depend very much on other people, and their recognition. This accounts for the significance of siblings in all these stories. In *The Time of the Ghost*, it is important that the sisters, as well as the ghost, come to understand her predicament, that she has, as Sally, bonded herself to Monigan as part of their childhood game or religion (or some combination of the two). The sisters, in the past, or in the time of the ghost, must give up some plan for the future, or sense of themselves, as compensation for the release of Sally. But in order for one of the sisters, Imogen, to join in, she has to be persuaded by the sisters in the future. And for this to happen, the ghost first has to solve the question of her identity, since she first of all settled on Imogen as the sister she herself must have been.

It is interesting that Imogen is the sister she initially identifies with, since Imogen is the most Gothic of the sisters, with her melodramatic diction, her ethereal, blonde beauty and her characteristic "grieving." It is this "grieving" that the ghost recognises in the later, grown-up

Imogen, though she doesn't at first identify it with Imogen, thinking she is recognising Sally: "Sister Sally was familiar, and her discontent was the most familiar thing of all" (Jones 1981: 115). Ironically, she has had no sense of the familiar in her encounters of the real Sally. Her actual physical self in the present frightens her, with her leg in plaster looking to her like a rotting mummy that she first identifies as Monigan (109–110). She has no sense of familiarity when she haunts Sally in the past, either, even when she haunts her supposing that she is herself: "She had no sense of identity with her. She had no idea what this Sally thought or felt" (103). And yet the familiarity to the ghost of "Sister Sally" is doubly ironic, in that the discontent that seems so familiar to her in Imogen is familiar because it is a discontent she shares. Imogen's appearance seems to point to her as a grown-up Sally, because her drab, washed-out appearance is what might be expected of Sally after years of discontent.

Imogen and Sally have grown up alike, it turns out, in their discontent, and alike, also, in that neither of them has established an effective sense of identity. Imogen's "grieving," which had characterised her so distinctively in the scenes set in the ghost's past, serves only, in the present, to suggest that she must be the grown-up Sally. And the grown-up Sally's self-doubt is, she realises, "as well known in her as grieving was in Imogen" (220) and clearly very boring for her sisters. While Cart and Fenella have both changed dramatically, Sally and Imogen have kept the same markers of identity that distinguished them as children, and this is shown to both diminish and blur identity. Imogen's development has been furthered restricted by her insistence on pursuing a piano career, despite a lack of talent or enjoyment for the piano, fulfilling rather a childhood ambition based on what her mother has identified as her talent, while Sally of course has been bonded to Monigan, as well as to an unhealthy relationship with the boy she developed a crush on as an adolescent. As Sally comes to realise, "Both of them had wanted something to cling to, and they had both clung to something that was no good to them" (220). Despite the uncanny being located, at the start of the novel, in the ghost's lack of anything to cling to, the novel ends, as does *The Haunting*, with the uncanny overcome through a new self-possession that is represented as a release from a more limited sense of identity.

The third novel I want to look at, Penelope Farmer's *Charlotte Sometimes*, is the closest of the three novels to a conventional school story. The boarding school setting allows Charlotte's own uncertain identity to be accounted for both in terms of the lack of recognition she would normally have in her own family, and in terms of an intellectual uncertainty that comes from being not at home, not on familiar territory. The word "unfamiliar" is used several times by Penelope Farmer to describe Charlotte's displacement: "Her bed was uncomfortable in an unfamiliar way....All the sounds around her were unfamiliar" (1967: 4). This unfamiliarity, though there is not yet anything uncanny about it, is already enough to make Charlotte unable to function effectively: the unfamiliarity of the bed makes her unable to get to sleep, and unable, even, to cry. Instead, she thinks of her younger sister, Emily, suggesting the etymological link between familiarity and family. In contrast to Charlotte, another new girl Susannah not only cries readily at bedtime, but before bedtime has chattered and giggled, even in response to jokes Charlotte is sure she could not have heard. In particular, she has talked about "her family, her father and mother and brother and sister" until "Susannah's family seemed more real to Charlotte than the school yet seemed," and more real, she goes on to feel, than her own self (9).

Described by one reviewer as the most "haunting" children's novel published that year (back cover), *Charlotte Sometimes* introduces an uncanny element to Charlotte's displacement in the boarding school setting, and so moves away from the genre of the school story, when Charlotte finds herself on alternate days swapping places in time with another child Clare, taking Clare's place at the same school forty years earlier, while Clare substitutes for her in the present day. *Charlotte Sometimes* could in fact be said to have the most conventional ghost of the three novels, since the schoolgirl Clare is both from the past and is in fact dead at the time of her appearance in the present day, unlike either Sally or Great-Uncle Cole. And yet because they are continually swapping places with each other, Charlotte and Clare never actually directly encounter each other, and so Clare never appears in the novel, making it, in a sense, a ghost story without the ghost. Instead, the story focuses on the uncanny situation Charlotte is in, not only when she visits the past, but equally when she takes her own place in the present day only to find herself expected to be the same child as a child she has never even met.

While the opening of the novel frames the theme of identity in relation to the unfamiliarity of the boarding school environment, and while Charlotte's sense of the unfamiliar is connected to the inability to act that is associated with the uncanny in both the other novels, the emphasis soon shifts to considering the issue of identity in relation to the expectations of other people, and what it means to be recognised or misrecognised by others. Charlotte is even more unable to act assertively in this new uncanny situation she finds herself in, unsure of what is expected of her either as Charlotte or as Clare. What was an ordinary shyness becomes an abnormal reticence. She realises that she herself has become uncanny, in her effects on others, especially Emily, Clare's sister, who supposes her to be Clare: "It would be frightening for Emily, Charlotte thought, quite uncanny and odd" (46). The word "odd" has been used earlier in the novel, along with the words "disconcerting" and "strange" but it is only in this consideration of Emily's perspective that the word "uncanny" is used. As in the other novels, the uncanny in *Charlotte Sometimes* is associated not just with a loss of identity, but with the misrecognition of identity, particularly within the family.

Charlotte does eventually let Emily in on the fact that she is not Clare. Once Emily knows this, she is able to observe that in fact Charlotte does not look exactly like Clare, only similar, and yet no one either in the present day or in the past seems to notice. Charlotte finds herself covering up for the gaps in her knowledge of Clare's life while in the past, and covering up in the present for everything she has missed on the days Clare was taking her place. It is explained that at first "she must have been quite numbed by the strangeness to have behaved as she did, so normally, though in another time" (25). But she continues the pretence, covering up an "intellectual uncertainty" that becomes less about the unfamiliarity of the place she is in than about her unfamiliarity with who she has been, or what she is supposed to have said and done, in the times when Clare has been substituting for her: "Often she did not know what had happened, what was going on, and she was afraid of showing it, of saying things that might make everyone suspicious. It seemed safer usually not to speak at all" (41–42). She is more "herself" in the past, when substituting for Clare, than she is in the present, substituting, it begins to seem, for Clare's substitution of herself. In the past, one girl at least knows her as herself.

Charlotte's attempt to imitate an imitation of herself, that she herself hasn't been present to observe, is a wonderfully apt symbol for the struggle to establish an identity in adolescence. It is almost too obvious a symbol to analyse, and works too directly to require the full resources of the Gothic mode, which really come into play in Part Two of the novel when the girls leave the school and are billeted in the haunted Chisel Brown household. But it is with the séance, the Gothic occasion at the centre of Part Two of the novel, that Charlotte finds herself quite immobilised by the uncanny: "by now she did not feel she could be sure of anything. The séance seemed the more dangerous, because so unknown and unknowable; and yet eventually, almost inevitably, she let Emily persuade her to hide in the window bay. She could not help herself any longer" (145). In the first part of the novel, her withdrawal from action is an attempt to hide the uncanny, which makes her powerless to act to establish her identity; here, hiding her own self, she puts herself into a still further uncanny situation. At the very centre of the novel is this moment of helpless immobility.

Charlotte Sometimes is unusual in its three-part structure, with the most obviously Gothic elements contained in the strange middle section set outside the school. The billeting of the girls in the Chisel Brown household does have some significance in terms of the plot, in that it introduces a new problem to be solved, the problem of how Charlotte will return to her own time now that she and Clare are no longer sharing, across time, the bed which in some uncanny way has effected their transitions. Charlotte does in fact attempt to resolve the situation with a midnight break-in to the school dormitory, but inside the school she ends up once again in hiding, immobilised by terror, afraid not so much of the uncanny as of the uncanny effect her story would have on anyone who discovered her. In any case, it turns out there is nothing Charlotte can do since the bed is already occupied by another girl. In the end the girls simply end up eventually returning to school as boarders again, and Charlotte and Clare are able to trade places once again and return to their own times. The plot, then, is resolved in a way that requires no real agency on the part of the girls, and the whole of Part Two comes to seem little more than an extended intermission.

Yet the girls do seem implicated in the haunting of the Chisel Brown household, not directly, through cause and effect, but through an uncanny mirroring and doubling of details and identities. This is a household haunted by the death of the heroic soldier son Arthur, and his sister Agnes's forbidden knowledge of his cowardice. Charlotte finds herself repeating, without knowing it, many of the situations Agnes recalls Arthur in, such as the time Charlotte finds herself immobilised with terror in the monkey puzzle tree. Emily, on the other hand, seems haunted by her missing sister, and finds strange echoes of her earlier life with Clare. For instance, the toys that Agnes brings out for the girls (the doll and the tin soldiers) remind Emily of the doll and soldiers just like them she and Clare used to own. These toys in turn had their own histories, Clare's doll being the only thing left of their dead mother's possessions, and the soldiers being handed on to Emily by their father because "he'd really wanted me to be a boy" (94). Emily's identity, it seems, is complicated by her relationship with Clare and the distinctions between them that other people have determined for them, and this in turn complicates her relationship with Charlotte as Clare's stand-in. Charlotte meanwhile begins to dream about Arthur and Agnes, until she suspects she may have gone back briefly in time as Agnes in the same way she switched places with Clare. This is when Charlotte's identity really does begin to seem as permeable as Barney's, or as diffuse as the ghost's in *The Time of the Ghost,* and it is under the spell of this new fear that she might be becoming Agnes that she feels she "could not help herself any longer" and gives in to Emily's insistence that she hide in the window bay to partake in the séance.

Yet it is also in the strange intermission of Part Two that Charlotte, completely displaced now from her own identity as Charlotte and living as Emily's sister Clare, begins to assert herself as a schoolgirl, not inauthentically like her classmate Susannah in the present time, but as a result of genuine feeling for the other characters. Despite the fear of heights that overcame her in the monkey puzzle tree, she finds herself scrambling over an outdoor ledge outside a school window to help another, still more frightened girl. She speaks out again and again in defence of shy classmates, the cowed Agnes, and even the memory of Arthur, insisting "I don't *believe* he wasn't brave!" (154). In particular, her relationship with Emily develops from the role-playing it begins as into a real and powerful relationship with its own distinctive dynamics. When Charlotte first found herself in the past, the difference between herself and Clare was something at first felt by Emily only as an uncanny unease, not something she could define. This is her explanation for her slowness in noticing what had happened: "I don't suppose I ever looked at you properly—or Clare. I mean, I knew you—her—too well, at least I thought I did, perhaps that's why I never noticed you were different" (73). This seems quite a different idea about how recognition works, and the importance of family in forming identity, than is given in the other novels. But, in fact, both Barney and Troy have felt overlooked or misrecognised even by those family members closest to them, and Sally too, and her sisters, have been misrecognised through being cast into roles so that much of their potential is overlooked. Emily's growing awareness of Charlotte's difference from Clare suggests her relationship with Charlotte may be helping her define her knowledge of Clare as well as her knowledge of Charlotte.

Part Three of the novel, the shortest part, is set back in the boarding school, with Charlotte back in her own time. She is helped in establishing her identity as Charlotte by the fact that one of the other girls, Elizabeth, has been let in to the secret by Clare, with whom she made close friends during the period of substitution. Elizabeth recognises that Charlotte has once again replaced Clare (none of the other girls notice), and so Charlotte can ask her about the similarities and differences between her and Clare. She asks insistently, needing "to define herself, Charlotte, as much as Clare," but able to do this through the recognition of her by someone else (184).

Charlotte Sometimes is unlike the other two novels in having the middle section, the section in which a family's pattern of repression most clearly haunts the main character, quite separate structurally and in terms of cause and effect from the primary plot and its concern with the definition of identity. There does still seem to be some need for a subplot to do with repression, and its displaced effects, even when the connection between this issue and the theme of identity definition doesn't seem at all clear. In *The Haunting*, Barney's crisis is caused by his haunting by the family member Cole, and the revelation of family secrets solves Troy's own difficulties in establishing her adolescent identity. In *The Time of the Ghost*, Sally's own unfamiliarity with her past and her presence in the past as a ghost is what produces the uncanny for her sisters, as well as being uncanny for herself. And just as the displaced effects of repression cause the crisis in each of these novels, a canny sense of self-possession is necessary to solve the crisis, solving a crisis in identity in a way which also involves the revelation of secrets. In both novels, it is not only the main character who needs to be self-possessed, but the siblings as well. In *Charlotte Sometimes*, the self-possession of Emily and Elizabeth is important for Charlotte's definition of self. But the uncanny situation Charlotte and Clare find themselves in, while it causes Charlotte's crisis of identity, is not solved by Charlotte's canniness, but simply resolves itself.

What the unusual structure of *Charlotte Sometimes* makes clear is the importance of Charlotte's self-possession on its own terms. Charlotte's self-possession is not a solution to the uncanny in terms of plot, but it is the only solution to *facing* the uncanny, including the uncanniness of other people and their hidden anxieties and desires. It is also, as the boarding school setting emphasises, the solution to dealing with the "new and unfamiliar," that situation or setting in which you are not at home, not at ease. In fact, this is true for the characters in the other novels too. *The Haunting* ends with the focus not on Troy and her vague plans to "change the world," but back on Barney, now looking forward to the birth of his baby sister, with a new sense of confidence about his own abilities and the role he might play in the family. *The Time of the Ghost* ends with Sally not only comfortably surrounded by her family and friends, but with a new sense of her abilities too, and a new sense of purpose, "so excited at the thought of all she could paint, that a sort of flush ran through her, bringing a kind of easiness with it" (Jones 1981: 220). She is at ease with her own canniness, at home with her own self.

ENDNOTES

1. *Harry Potter and the Sorcerer's Stone*, Christopher Columbus (director), Los Angeles: Warner Bros., 2001.
2. *Buffy the Vampire Slayer*, Joss Whedon (writer & director), Los Angeles: Mutant Enemy Productions, 1997–2003.
3. In particular, J. K. Rowling's Harry Potter series has been criticized as formulaic in its use of the traditional school story genre, most notably by A. S. Byatt (*New York Times*, 11 July 2003). Academic criticism of her use of the school story genre includes "From Elfland to Hogwarts, or the Aesthetic Trouble with Harry Potter," J. Pennington, *The Lion and the Unicorn*, January 2002 ("essentially a realistic description of common British schooling practices with the magic an awkward touch sprinkled in" pp. 79–80) and "Morality and Midnight Feasts: Imperialism and the British School Story," Laura Channing, *Kidz Books*, August 2005; "The Rise and Rise of Harry Potter," Nicholas Tucker, *Children's Literature in Education*, December 1999; David Steege, "Harry Potter, Tom Brown, and the British School Story: Lost in Transit?" in *The Ivory Tower and Harry Potter: Perspectives on a Literary Phenomenon*. Edited with an Introduction by Lana A. Whited. Columbia: University of Missouri Press, 2002. Rowling's use of the school genre is also commonly mentioned in book reviews, and interviews, including "Harry, Jessie and Me," Simon Hattenstone, *The Guardian*, 8 July 2000; and the review of Harry Potter by Danny Yee on his site http://dannyreviews.com/ (2000).
4. The article by Ernst Jentsch to which Freud refers can be read in *Angelaki* (translated by Forbes Morlock, 1996).
5. For instance, Scarlett Johansen is described as self-possessed and baby-faced in a review of her performance in *Lost in Translation* (http://www.slatetv.com/id/2088215/); Truman Capote is another who is described as both baby-faced and uncannily self-possessed (http://www.sdreader.com/published/2004-11-18/reading.html).

REFERENCES

Farmer, P. [1967] (2002). *Charlotte Sometimes*. London: Red Fox.

French, S. [1981] (2003). *Cannily, Cannily*. Camberwell, Australia: Penguin.

Freud, S. (1985). The uncanny. In J. Strachey (Ed.), *Sigmund Freud, Volume 14, Art and Literature*. London: Pelican.

Jentsch, E. [1906] (1996). The uncanny. F. Morlock (Trans.). *Angelaki, 2* (1), 7–16.

Jones, D. W. [1981] (2001). *The Time of the Ghost*. London: HarperCollins.

Kavka, M. (2002). The Gothic on screen. In J. E. Hogle (Ed.), *The Cambridge Companion to Gothic Fiction*. Cambridge: Cambridge University Press.

Mahy, M. [1982] (1992). *The Haunting.* London: Puffin.
Mills, A. (1999). *Seriously Weird: Papers on the Grotesque.* New York: Peter Lang.
Whedon, J., Writer/director (1997–2003) *Buffy the Vampire Slayer.* Mutant Enemy Productions.

10

HERMIONE IN THE BATHROOM: THE GOTHIC, MENARCHE, AND FEMALE DEVELOPMENT IN THE HARRY POTTER SERIES

June Cummins

Anyone teaching, as well as many people reading, the Harry Potter series is aware that J. K. Rowling borrows from, or blends in, a number of literary genres while writing her books. A learned, sophisticated reader could rattle off the names of particular genres, such as school stories, the *Bildungsroman*, high fantasy, epic, medieval legend, and so on; while even a relatively untutored or inexperienced reader can sense the connections between Harry Potter and well-known stories such as *Star Wars* or famous fairytales like Cinderella. Yet despite the classic "trappings" of a Gothic novel, including "castles, ghosts, corrupt clergy, and so on," as described by Donna Heiland in *Gothic and Gender* (2004: 4), not much mention of the Gothic has been made in the critical discourse of the Harry Potter novels. For example, as of June 2006, a search on the terms "Harry Potter" and "gothic" through the MLA bibliography database yielded zero hits. On the first page of her article "Generic Fusion and the Mosaic of *Harry Potter*," Anne Hiebert Alton lists "gothic" as one of the genres within the series, along with "pulp fiction, mystery...horror stories, detective fiction, the school story and the closely related sports story, and series books" (2003: 141), but does not go on to explore the Gothic elements of the books. This lack of attention is understandable for the very reason addressed in Alton's article title: "Generic Fusion." The Gothic elements merge so smoothly into so many other genres within the Harry Potter series and are so natural to its setting that they are almost invisible or at least so normalized that it appears as if they do not merit attention.[1]

Yet Rowling's use of Gothic elements or conventions goes beyond the architecture of Hogwarts or the inclusion of classic haunted characters such as ghosts and werewolves throughout the series. Significantly, Gothic elements of the novels rise to the surface of the stories when the topic under consideration or at least narrative exposition is that of female development. At crucial junctures, the Gothic is blended with elements of Horror or the Grotesque in a swirl of allusions that evoke age-old narrative traditions surrounding female development. Specifically, Hermione, a most decidedly *un*-Gothic heroine for the vast majority of the Harry Potter series, slips into a Gothic mode at a moment of important psychical and perhaps physical transformation. Another character, however, Moaning Myrtle, very much a Gothic, as well as comic, character shows up in and remains in a Gothic mode throughout the series. As I elucidate the Gothic elements of her work, I hope to demonstrate how J. K. Rowling pushes hard on these elements when she needs to tell the story of female development.

Gender has long been a primary concern of critics who examine Gothic literature, and it has been consistently present in the discourse even as other issues become primary to critical attention, such as race, class, national identity, and other aspects of sexual identity. The popularity of Gothic novels and the continual regeneration of the genre through various revivals and revisions attest to its durability and relevance. That as recently as 2004, Donna Heiland could publish a book called *Gothic and Gender: An Introduction* demonstrates that gender remains a fresh and primary concern of Gothic criticism even though it was first addressed more than thirty years ago by Ellen Moers in *Literary Women* (1976). Over the years, critics have ranged from seeing Gothic narratives as repressive of female characters to arguing that they are subversive and empowering.[2] Rowling's use of Gothic conventions in the context of gender issues allows us to examine the significance of both her deviances from and conservations of such use, especially in terms of what they tell us about the construction of female gender in the series.

I believe the Gothic elements of the Harry Potter series are made suddenly visible in a pivotal scene occurring in the first book, *Harry Potter and the Sorcerer's Stone* (1997), which is titled *Harry Potter and the Philosopher's Stone* in the United Kingdom. Rowling calls attention to this scene on her website, in a section of it called "Characters." If one clicks on "Hermione," one discovers this text:

When we were editing 'Philosopher's Stone' my editor wanted me to cut the scene in which Harry, Ron and Hermione fight the troll. Although I had accepted most of the smaller cuts he wanted me to make I argued hard for this one. Hermione, bless her, is so very annoying in the early part of 'Philosopher's Stone' that I really felt it needed something (literally) huge to bring her together with Harry and Ron.

(http://www.jkrowling.com/accessible/en/)

Although J. K. Rowling's Harry Potter books are mostly about a boy, Harry Potter, much significant action occurs in the girls' bathroom. Moaning Myrtle, the girl trapped in the restroom for 50 years, becomes a crucially important character in *Harry Potter and the Chamber of Secrets* (1999) when she shows Harry and Ron the way to the Chamber, through the sink in her bathroom. Moaning Myrtle, with her tears, sighs, pimples, and suicidal tendencies, is, among other things, a parody of a teenage girl. Part of that parody is her residence in the girls' bathroom and her intimate familiarity with sinks, pipes, and toilets. With Myrtle, Rowling simultaneously makes fun of and points out the important status of the girls' bathroom in the lives of (pre)teenage girls. But Myrtle is not the only character to perform a significant function in the girls' bathroom. In the first book of the series, another critical event occurs in this valuable space. Harry and Ron lock a troll in one, forgetting that Hermione is crying in a stall within. When they suddenly realize that she is trapped with the troll, Harry and Ron storm the bathroom, slay the troll, and make Hermione a woman. 7

This scene is Gothic for several reasons. First, it includes the classic Gothic paradigm of a woman threatened by a man, usually in a castle or other very large and old abode, and then rescued by another man. According to Heiland, a "typical gothic heroine" is one who is "fairly passive, finding her way out of one disastrous situation after another only because someone comes along to rescue her" (2004: 28–29).³ Similarly, the scene takes place in a classic Gothic space: an interior, hidden room or chamber. Claire Kahane explains:

Following clues that pull her onward and inward—bloodstains, mysterious sounds—she penetrates the obscure recesses of a vast labyrinthean [sic] space and discovers a secret room sealed off by its association with death. In this dark, secret center of the Gothic structure, the boundaries of life and death themselves seem confused. Who died? Has there been a murder? Or merely a disappearance? (1985: 334)

At this point in the series, the toilet stall hidden deep within the girls' bathroom (and in turn deep within Hogwarts) is not yet associated with death, but it will be when it becomes evident that Myrtle, a ghost, is its resident.

Second, the intrusion of the troll, a giant and a kind of monster, launches *Harry Potter and the Sorcerer's Stone* into the realm of the British nineteenth-century Gothic novel.[4] Judith Halberstam, in *Skin Shows: Gothic Horror and the Technology of Monsters* (1995) examines the function of monsters in several famous British Gothic novels that include monstrous characters and argues that these monsters are used in order for humans to define themselves against. "Within the nineteenth-century Gothic, authors mixed and matched a wide variety of signifiers of difference to fabricate the deviant body—Dracula, Jekyll/ Hyde, and even Frankenstein's monster before them are lumpen bodies, bodies pieced together out of the fabric of race, class, gender, and sexuality" (1995: 3). As will become clear in my analysis of Hermione in the bathroom, the troll serves not only to horrify and threaten Hermione but also to assist her in *not* becoming monstrous herself. A monster acting in this capacity made certain novels Gothic, Halberstam claims. "The emergence of the monster within Gothic fictions marks a peculiarly modern emphasis upon the horror of particular kinds of bodies" (3). At stake in the Hogwarts girls' restroom is in fact Hermione's body and the relationship between it and horror. Although Rowling does not make it explicit, a subtext of blood courses underneath this bathroom scene, and it is this implied emphasis on blood that makes it a specific kind of Gothic, the Gothic horror story. Halberstam clarifies: "monsters not only reveal certain material conditions of the production of horror, but they also make strange the categories of beauty, humanity, and identity that we still cling to" (6). This subtext of horror, and with it, the grotesque, is the third layer of Gothicism in this episode.

Where is the blood in the bathroom scene? Although Rowling never mentions menstruation in these books, many female readers intuitively associate the girls' bathroom with menstruation and specifically with menarche, the first period. In their book *Blood Stories: Menarche and the Politics of the Female Body in Contemporary U.S. Society* (1996), researchers Janet Lee and Jennifer Sasser-Coen relate several stories that involve girls getting their first period in the quasi-public space of the girls' bathroom. More than one anecdote entails a girl crying in the bathroom when she realizes she has begun to menstruate, and this scenario—a girl getting her period in a public bathroom and starting to cry—is famously described in the classic text of menarche, *Are You There God? It's Me Margaret* (Blume 1970). Margaret's friend Nancy

Wheeler, normally very composed and in charge of everyone including herself, loses it when she realizes she has begun to menstruate while sitting on a toilet in the public restroom of a restaurant. Margaret, in the next stall, explains:

> Just as I was finishing up, I heard Nancy moan.
>
> "Oh no—oh no—"
>
> "What is it, Nancy?" I asked.
>
> "Oh please—oh no—
>
> "Are you okay?" I banged on the wall separating us.
>
> "Get my mother—quick!" she whispered....
>
> Nancy started to cry. "Please get my mother." (105–106)

Margaret runs back to the dining room and tells Nancy's mother, "Nancy's sick. She's in the bathroom crying and she wants you" (106). By the time Margaret and Mrs. Wheeler get to the stall, Margaret "could hear Nancy sobbing." Margaret crawls under the stall wall to unlock the door for Mrs. Wheeler and finds Nancy with her "face...buried in her hands" (106). For the rest of the scene, as Nancy and her mother take care of Nancy's period behind the closed stall door and Margaret waits and listens, Nancy cries so hard that her mother says, "Nancy, calm down...I can't help you if you don't stop crying" (107).

Lee and Sasser-Coen recount similar anecdotes: One woman, remembering when she discovers her first period and her mother tells her she's a "little lady now," says "I began bawling; I sat on the toilet and I just cried because I didn't want to have my period" (1996: 107). Another recounts being the new girl at school and unprepared for menarche: "And then, because there is nothing else I can do, I sit down on the toilet and weep" (3). Nancy Wheeler is almost inconsolable, and she's a girl who *wanted* to get her period. Lee and Sasser-Coen relate such crying to the trauma many girls experience when they first start menstruating: "Contemporary research from a variety of different perspectives...suggests that girls' experiences of menarche are characterized by ambivalence and even trauma" (33).

When Hermione runs off to the bathroom to cry—because she overheard Ron call her a "nightmare"—her pleas to be left alone and her refusal to come out could easily remind some readers of themselves or other girls who rushed off to the girls' bathroom because of the sudden or unexpected arrival of their periods. But even if this association does not readily come to mind, and even though Rowling does not refer directly to menstruation, Hermione's removal to the bathroom and emergence from it as a changed person follow a pattern vividly demonstrated through *Blood Stories*. For Hermione's embarrassed and ashamed retreat to the girls' bathroom is simultaneously a retreat from the bossy, unliked girl she had been. Her emergence from the bathroom is simultaneously an entry into friendship with Ron and Harry and a new image of herself as likable—in other words, as feminine ("But from that moment on, Hermione Granger became their friend. There are some things you can't share without ending up liking each other, and knocking out a twelve-foot mountain troll is one of them" [1997: 179]). Hermione's transformation enacts Lee and Sasser-Coen's description of menarche as an event whereby "individual girls produce themselves as women and gender relations are perpetuated" (1996: 36). Arguing that "it is through the body that women are integrated into the social and sexual order, and it is in part through the discourses and practices of menarche that heterosexuality and 'hetero-reality'...are constructed in everyday life" (86), these researchers help us see that menarche is construed as marking girls' entry into a sexualized and subordinated womanhood. While Hermione can be seen as a feminist heroine, her experience in the girls' bathroom, and its aftermath, follows the pattern that Lee and Sasser-Coen describe over and over again: the transformation girls undergo—the losses they experience—when they begin to have their periods.

Hermione is an unattractive and undesirable character for two thirds of *Harry Potter and the Sorcerer's Stone*. She is described as having bushy hair and big teeth and as being bossy (Rowling 1997: 105). Ron is appalled with Hermione immediately and grows to dislike her more and more as she demonstrates an aggressive intelligence and annoying insistence on following the rules. Her eagerness not only to study but also to wave her outstretched hand furiously in class repels him and the other children. Hermione does not seem to care that her actions and interests bother them until she overhears Ron's insult. Later in the books, as Rowling develops a subtle sexual tension and attraction between Ron and Hermione, Hermione's unexpected response to Ron's comment makes sense in hindsight. She had cared what he thought because she was moving from girlhood into "sexualized" womanhood.

Menarche, Lee and Sasser-Coen explain, is a process "whereby a female body is transformed into a feminine one" (1996: 38). But this process requires abjection and disguise. Menstruation, throughout much of history and in many cultures, is typically construed as disgusting and shameful. Menstrual blood is viewed as filthy, odiferous, and gross. Adrienne Rich claims that men have traditionally viewed "the female body [as] impure, corrupt, the site of discharges, bleedings, dangerous to masculinity, a source of moral and physical contamination" (quoted in Lee & Sasser-Coen 1996: 13). More recent theorists have extended observations like Rich's to the notion of the female grotesque.

Mary Russo, in *The Female Grotesque* (1994), explains that the term "grotesque" (with its root in "grotto") is naturally aligned with the female body, which is always positioned as abnormal. "As bodily metaphor, the grotesque cave tends to look like...the cavernous anatomical female body....Blood, tears, vomit, excrement—all the detritus of the body that is separated out and placed with terror and revulsion.... on the side of the feminine—are down there in that cave of abjection" (1994: 1–2). Russo believes that even when grotesque characters in literature and film are posited as male, they represent femininity and need to be abjected (13). I am arguing that the disgusting, secreting troll that lumbers into the girls' bathroom represents the grotesque aspects of femininity and particularly of Hermione's menarche and the "mess" she may be dealing with in the locked stall. Harry and Ron are overwhelmed by the "foul stench" of the troll and disgusted by "lumpy gray glue" that coats Harry's wand when he pulls it from the troll's nose. This odor and excrement can be seen as stand-ins for menstrual blood itself. When Harry and Ron knock out the troll, they are slaying the grotesque—abnormal—aspects of Hermione's menarche, if not of her very personality.

The emergence of the grotesque in this scene links it not only to Gothicism, in general, which often relies on disgusting and gross imagery, commonly involving mutilated or desecrated human bodies, but specifically to a branch of the genre called the Southern Gothic. While Rowling is not of course a writer of the American South, her writing in this scene implicitly displays an intertextual link to a Southern Gothic literary tradition. Moers believes that "the savagery of girlhood accounts in part for the persistence of the Gothic mode into our own time" (1976: 107) and points to the American writer Carson McCullers's use of freaks in her work: "McCullers cloaks with humorous tenderness her unsentimental perception of the freakish self as originating in female adolescence" (109). Elaine Showalter brings Moers's point even closer to Rowlings's use of the grotesque, in the form of the troll, in *Harry Potter and the Sorcerer's Stone* (1997). "Moers suggested that the keynote of the modern, post-war American Female Gothic was its obsessions with freaks. She pointed to Southern Gothic writers such as Flannery O'Connor, Katherine Anne Porter, and Carson McCullers, whose adolescent heroines see the discomforting changes in their bodies mirrored in grotesques and freaks" (1991: 135). Showalter's gloss of

Moers helps us see the same operations at work in this scene in *Harry Potter*. Claire Kahane also sees the Southern Gothic, and modern Gothic in general, as grotesque: "Repeatedly, as so much of what we call modern Gothic illustrates, when the unseen is given visual form, when we lose the obscurity of the Gothic darkness, the Gothic focuses on distorted body images and turns into the grotesque" (1985: 343).

Of course another intertextual device linking the scene to the Gothic is that of the damsel in distress, a character stereotype totally opposite to Hermione's character in all other dangerous scenes that include her in the series. During this critical scene, Hermione becomes a traditional ingénue character—the princess who needs rescuing by her prince(s). Suddenly without her quick answers and beloved rules and completely terrified, Hermione can only "shrink" and "s[i]nk to the floor in fright (Rowling 1997: 176)," inactions that are a far cry from the long paragraphs she usually utters (all in one breath) and from standing up in class to wave her hand even higher. Now she is immobile and mute: "But she couldn't move, she was still flat against the wall, her mouth open with terror" (1997: 175). Meanwhile, Ron and Harry are brave and powerful. Thinking quickly and using their strength, Ron throws a pipe at the troll and Harry jumps onto his back; they attack the troll until they succeed in knocking him out.

Their heroic actions have a definite effect on Hermione. When the adults are about to punish the boys, Hermione lies about why they were in the bathroom—getting herself into trouble and saving their skins. In doing so, she blames her own intelligently inquisitive nature for her supposed mistake. "'I went looking for the troll because I—I thought I could deal with it on my own—you know, because I've read all about them.' Ron dropped his wand. Hermione Granger, telling a downright lie to a teacher?" (177). It is this noble lie that endears Hermione to the boys and that marks the change from a female body to a feminine body. Mary Pipher, in *Reviving Ophelia*, notes the consistence and persistence of this transformation. In their preteen years, she explains, "girls are expected to sacrifice the parts of themselves that our culture considers masculine on the altar of social acceptability and to shrink their souls down to a petite size....The rules remain the same: be attractive, be a lady, be unselfish and of service, make relationships work....This is when girls learn to be nice rather than honest" (1994: 39). Hermione, suddenly helplessly feminine, serves the boys by lying for them. Her intelligence, loud mouth, and self-confidence all disappear during this episode. When the adults arrive and hear Hermione's story, Professor McGonagall calls Hermione "you foolish girl" (Rowling 1997: 178).

Critic Linda Phelps sees this sort of self-estrangement as a form of "alienation," a way that women experience a sense of split self as they begin to realize how society defines them sexually. "We are…alienated because we are separated from our own experience by the prevailing male cultural definition of sex—the male fantasy of active man and passive woman. From an early age, our sexual impulses are turned back upon ourselves in the narcissistic counterpart of the male fantasy world. In social relations with men, we are alienated from ourselves as initiating, self-directed persons" (quoted in Lee & Sasser-Coen 1996: 91). Thus, Hermione becomes alienated from the strong, controlling person she had been as she serves in a traditionally passive female role during a rescue scene. The troll then represents not only the grotesque but also the part of her that has become alien—the powerful girl she had been—both must be abjected.

Russo, the author of *The Female Grotesque*, sees two primary approaches to the understanding of the grotesque in modern culture, one that she calls the "carnivalesque" and that connects a grotesque body to society and people, what we might term a sociocultural perspective. The second approach relates the grotesque "most strongly to the psychic register and to the bodily as cultural projection of an inner state" (1994: 9). Not surprisingly, this second approach is rooted in psychoanalysis and was taken up by Julia Kristeva, who devoted a book-length essay, *Powers of Horror: An Essay on Abjection* (1980), to the subject of abjection.

Current theorists of horror movies who are interested in the abject turn to Kristeva's definition of it: "the jettisoned object…radically excluded" (2) and "what disturbs identity, system, order. What does not respect border, positions, rules" (4). Barbara Creed, looking closely at horror movies that clearly and graphically invoke menstruation, namely *The Exorcist* and *Carrie*, views abjection as that which is

placed on the side of the feminine [and] exists in opposition to the paternal symbolic, which is governed by rules and laws.... Analysis of the abject centres on ways in which the "clean and proper self" [Kristeva's term] is constructed. The abject is that which must be expelled or excluded in the construction of that self. In order to enter the symbolic order, the subject must reject or repress all forms of behaviour, speech, and modes of being regarded as unacceptable, improper or unclean....All signs of bodily excretions—bile, urine, shit, mucus, spittle, blood—must be treated as abject, cleaned up and removed from sight. It is this aspect of abjection which is central to *The Exorcist*, its graphic display of bodily excretions." (1993: 37–38)

Creed interprets both *The Exorcist* and *Carrie* as depicting menstruation, if not menarche. Of *Carrie* she writes, "Significantly, Carrie
only develops the powers of telekinesis when she first bleeds; the suggestion is that her blood is both powerful and magical. Ultimately,
woman's blood is represented in the film as an abject substance and
helps to construct Carrie as monstrous" (1993: 81). Carrie is abject
and at the end of the film abjected; her world cannot contain her
monstrosity.

Kristeva's definition of the abject is helpful not just in the psychic
mode, the understanding of the individual psyche as described by
Russo, but also in what Russo calls the "social body," the sociocultural
mode. Creed claims that "Kristeva is attempting to explore the different ways in which abjection works within human societies, as a means
of separating out the human from the non-human and the fully constituted subject from the partially formed subject" (1993: 8), a process
that ably describes Hermione in the bathroom and the abjecting of
the non-human troll in the service of the constitution of her subjectivity. Thus John Stephens, examining teen movies such as *Scream II*,
I Know What You Did Last Summer, and *The Opposite of Sex*, sees abjection at work in ways that maintain social rules and roles. He writes,
"The abject becomes abjected, cast out, in a move which reaffirms and
upholds consensual forms of identity and social organization" (2003:
125). Stephens is especially concerned with gender roles and sees representations of the monstrous as coding for them, not unlike the way I see
the monstrous playing out when Hermione is in the bathroom. Writes
Stephens, "In teen films which thematize abjection, across a spectrum
from horror to carnivalesque realism, the monstrous (or an equivalent
deviancy) occupies the border between normal and supernatural or
between the performance of proper and improper gender roles" (126).
Ultimately, after examining several teen movies and television shows,
Stephens concludes that these movies "acknowledge the development
from abjection to agency as pivotal for the human transition from teen
to agential adult" (135). This view aligns him with Russo, who sees
potential for political change in the acknowledgement and celebration
of the female grotesque. Explains Russo:

> The images of the grotesque body are precisely those which are
> abjected from the bodily canons of classical aesthetics. The classical
> body is transcendent and monumental, closed, static, self-contained,
> symmetrical, and sleek; it is identified with the "high" or official cul-
> ture of the Renaissance and later, with the rationalism, individualism,
> and normalizing aspirations of the bourgeoisie. The grotesque body

is open, protruding, irregular, secreting, multiple, and changing; it is identified with non-official "low" culture or the carnivalesque, and with social transformation. (1994: 8)

Similar to the way Russo provides two different options for the employment of the grotesque in culture and literature, theorists of the Gothic also offer various ways to look at the genre, both positive and negative. Some critics divided Gothic novels into two groups, the "feminine gothic" of female writers such as Anne Radcliffe, and the "masculine gothic" of male writers such as M. G. Lewis.[5] Heiland arranges Gothic novels according to their treatment of patriarchy. She believes that "early gothic novels make absolutely clear the genre's concern with exploring, defining, and ultimately defending patriarchy" (2004: 8). Analyzing the way different authors either establish, uphold, or attempt to critique patriarchy, Heiland does not see true subversion of this defining aspect of Gothic literature until "feminist, postmodern, postcolonial" writers such as Margaret Atwood and Ann-Marie Macdonald "envision a world in which differences—of gender, of race, of nationality—are eventually embraced rather than eradicated" (67).

Where does Hermione fit in this spectrum of views regarding the grotesque, as posited by Russo, horror, as viewed by Stephens, and Gothic novels, as examined by Heiland and others? Is Hermione an "agential" adult who opens the way for social transformation and a postmodern heroine who subverts patriarchy and other forms of oppression? It's true that we later will see Hermione developing a social consciousness and activism when she protests the treatment of and organizes the house elves. Even at the end of *Harry Potter and the Sorcerer's Stone*, we see her acting bravely, intelligently, and heroically, not at all passively, when she figures out the logic puzzle of poisons that brings Harry to the final confrontation (an important scene that Chris Columbus eliminates from the film version of the book). Perhaps we can argue that Rowling needs a Gothic mode only momentarily, because she knows that "the problematics of femininity [will be] thus reduced to the problematics of the female body, perceived as antagonistic to the sense of self, as therefore freakish" (Kahane 1985: 343) at the very moment of menarche and of becoming Ron and Harry's friend. But once she gets past this scene, she no longer needs to position Hermione as a Gothic character or her story as in the Gothic mode. We can argue that she moves beyond it and in doing so repudiates it. Hermione emerges triumphant, not as a passive, immobile victim.

But even though Hermione leaves the bathroom, someone else remains. It's not Hermione but Moaning Myrtle—a carnivalesque, grotesque joke of a girl—who stays in the bathroom, endlessly examining her pimples and incessantly getting her period. Myrtle, as a ghost, is the bodiless embodiment of the abject of female adolescence. She *lives* in a toilet and is continually associated with toilet water. When Hermione first describes Myrtle to an appalled and incredulous Ron and Harry in *Harry Potter and the Chamber of Secrets*, she uses scatological language not normally found in the Harry Potter series. "'She haunts one of the toilets in the girls' bathroom on the first floor,' said Hermione.... It's been out-of-order all year because she keeps having tantrums and flooding the place. I never went in there anyway if I could avoid it; it's awful trying to have a pee with her wailing at you—'" (Rowling 1999: 132–133).

Hermione does not maintain a connection to the scatological and after the bathroom scene is no longer seen as gross, but Myrtle continues to be associated with offal and filth. She is fully aware that she is a reject, and those around her are quick to connect her rejected status to what is disgusting. When Hermione and the boys run into Myrtle at the Deathday Party, Hermione tries to compliment Myrtle, but Myrtle won't accept it.

> "Don't lie to me," Myrtle gasped, tears now flooding down her face, while Peeves chuckled happily over her shoulder. "D'you think I don't know what people call me behind my back? Fat Myrtle! Ugly Myrtle! Miserable, moaning, moping Myrtle!"
>
> "You've forgotten pimply," Peeves hissed in her ear.
>
> Moaning Myrtle burst into anguished sobs and fled from the dungeon. Peeves shot after her, pelting her with moldy peanuts, yelling *"Pimply! Pimply!"*. (135)

By implication, Myrtle is associated with things even more disgusting than pimples; Harry and Ron watch "with their mouths open" when she gives "a tragic sob, [rises] up in the air, turn[s] over and dive[s] headfirst into the toilet, splashing water all over them and vanishing from sight, although from the direction of her muffled sobs, she had come to rest somewhere in the U-bend" (157). In a sense, Myrtle *is* pee and shit, or at least lives intimately with them.

In addition to always representing, by actually becoming, the abject, Myrtle is a ghost. As such, she hovers between life and death, between having a physical body and not being visible. Judith Wilt finds this ghostly state inherently Gothic: "The Gothic always blurs or even dissolves the boundary between life and death....The special contribution of the Gothic to this enterprise, as a stable genre of its own, is the creative domain of the undead, the should-be-dead-but-isn't, the never-was-alive-but-is, the looks-alive-but-isn't" (2003: 41). Wilt finds this ghostly space as creative; can we apply that term to Myrtle?

Myrtle is not an author or artist; we don't see her making anything other than a watery mess. But she does play an important role as a resident of the toilet. Twice in *Chamber of Secrets* and once, much later, in *Goblet of Fire*, Myrtle gives the "main" characters crucial information at critical times. In *Chamber*, it is she who points the Riddle diary out to Harry and Ron (Rowling 1999: 230), and later, it is she who vaguely gestures the way to the chamber of secrets, through the sink across from her toilet stall (300). Both of these acts lead to Harry saving Ginny's life.[6] In *Goblet of Fire*, she shows up when Harry is in a different bathroom, trying to figure out the secret of the Golden Egg, which he needs to know to compete in the Triwizard Tournament. This time, Myrtle actively helps Harry, telling him exactly what to do: "I'd try putting it *in* the water, if I were you" (2000: 461). And when Harry isn't quite successful, she further instructs him: "You need to put your head under too" (462). These acts may not be creative, but they are helpful and necessary—*to Harry*. Thus any agency that Myrtle exhibits during the course of the books serves not in her development but in Harry's.

In the bathroom scene in *Goblet of Fire*, sexuality starts bubbling under the surface of the bath Harry is in. For the first time, a side of bathrooms other than merely the place of dirt and filth is revealed. Bathrooms can also be a place where people first discover their own sensual nature, or share sexual play with another person. Rowling sets the scene: "When the deep pool was full of hot water, foam, and bubbles …Harry turned off all the taps, pulled off his pajamas, slippers, and dressing gown, and slid into the water….Highly enjoyable….it was to swim in hot and foamy water with clouds of different-colored steam wafting all around him" (460). Into this luxuriously sensual scene, Myrtle suddenly appears. Harry is outraged. "Myrtle!…I'm—I'm not wearing anything!" (461). Myrtle assures him she hasn't seen anything and adds, "You haven't been to see me for *ages*," words that pick up on and work the sexual tension introduced when Harry realizes Myrtle is in the room (461). The two then have a conversation in which it becomes increasingly clear that Myrtle has something of a crush on Harry[7] and that she has a sexual curiosity natural in someone of her age. When Harry demands to know if she sneaks up to this bathroom to watch the prefects take baths, she "rather slyly" answers "Sometimes…but I've never come out to speak to anyone before" (462). When Harry prepares to leave, Myrtle asks him, "Will you come and visit me in my bathroom again sometime?" (466), adding to the parody behind her character (here, she references Mae West, although most young readers would not catch it). Myrtle clearly desires Harry romantically, driving home the point that "the 'body' that emerges from female gothic textuality is a highly gendered one" (Hoeveler 1998: 18).

But Harry does not return the interest, a point Rowling makes rather harshly. He answers her plea hesitantly: "'Er...I'll try,' Harry said, though privately thinking the only way he'd be visiting Myrtle's bathroom again was if every other toilet in the castle got blocked" (Rowling 2000: 466). While Myrtle may see herself as a sexually developing young woman, eager to spy on naked prefects, Harry cannot see her as anything but abject, as always part of the toilet. Just a few moments earlier, he tried hard *not* to think of "Moaning Myrtle zooming down a pipe to the lake with the contents of a toilet" (464). Of course his attempt resulted only in further consideration of all that is disgusting about Myrtle. Hence, Myrtle's future does not exist. Even if she feels she is growing, everyone around her will forever see her as fixed, static, infinitely stuck in the bathroom.

Recent critics see ghostly presences in literature as disruptive and thus subversive. Claims Jeffrey Weinstock, "Neither living nor dead, present nor absent, the ghost functions as the paradigmatic deconstructive gesture, the 'shadowy third' or trace of an absence that undermines the fixedness of...binary oppositions" (2004: 4). It is tempting to see Myrtle in that light, as disrupting gender binaries and opening up the possibilities for new and different avenues for female development. But she does not. Instead, she remains what Kahane calls "a ghost signifying the problematics of femininity" (1985: 336). While Hermione can exit the Gothic mode, Myrtle does not. She remains a Gothic character, and she stays in the toilet forever.

Hermione's story slips into a Gothic mode when she reaches puberty/becomes a woman, but she then exits that mode to go on to become a much more dynamic and genre-busting character. Moaning Myrtle, however, is *stuck* in the bathroom, which is the very site of female development, and is *stuck* in a Gothic mode as a permanent ghost. We can argue that Myrtle is sacrificed to the Gothic plot. While there are parodic and comedic elements to her, and we laugh at her character, her tears are actually quite symbolic of the sadness behind the way girls still get arrested—stuck—in certain patterns of behavior and expectations, even today, in our supposedly post-feminist world. Myrtle, then, is a kind of heroine in her own right, as she serves as a reminder of a path many girls take, while Hermione represents the potential alternative.

Rowling, in her attempts to create an "ungirly," strong female heroine (one modeled on her own childhood self), develops Hermione and gives her mobility. But she leaves behind another girl, Myrtle, a sacrificial heroine who, like the troll, is used to produce normalcy. Halberstam is again useful here: "Gothic fiction is a technology of subjectivity, one which produces the deviant subjectivities opposite which the normal, the healthy, the pure can be known" (1995: 2). Hermione and her friends continue to develop into healthy and well-adjusted adults. Moaning Myrtle will remain locked in her stall, always crying and moping, and forever reminding us of the Gothic horror of the real girls who get stuck in the limiting space of female adolescence.

ENDNOTES

1. Lisa Hopkins, in *Screening the Gothic* (2005), does discuss *Harry Potter and the Sorcerer's Stone* in this context, but she sees the film as much more Gothic than the book: "The film is clearly Gothic. Obviously, this element is already strongly present in the book, but it is considerably more developed in the film, for the book is also interested in other things.... The film thus omits or minimizes the non-Gothic elements and replaces them with Gothic ones" (131). Hopkins lists the Gothic elements of the film, most of which are visual, such as lightning flashes. She believes that the film is Gothicized because it deals with issues of identity while the book does not. As this article will make clear, I believe the book is very much about identity, particularly female identity construction, and that this issue comes to light through Gothic elements in the book that Hopkins does not address.

2. Diane Long Hoeveler (1998) separates herself from critic Kate Ferguson Ellis (1989) through the understanding of the Gothic as "subversive," claiming Ellis sees it as such while she, Hoevelever, believes "the female gothic [is] more problematic, as both subverting and at the same time reifying postures of complaisance and acquiescence on the part of women" (1998: xv–xvi).

3. Kate Ferguson Ellis also sees "aristocratic villains, haunted castles, and beleaguered heroines" (1989: xii) as hallmarks of the Gothic novel, all of which apply to this scene, with the exception of the adjective "aristocratic."

4. Moers explains the effect of the troll being a giant monster: "What are monsters? Creatures who scare because they look different, wrong, non-human. Distortion of scale was the first visual effect employed by Gothic novelists in creating monsters, particularly gigantism" (1976: 101).

5. See Kate Ferguson Ellis, introduction to *The Contested Castle: Gothic Novels and the Subversion of Domestic Ideology* (1989). In a disavowal, Eve Kosofsky Sedgwick claims that "in a text like *Frankenstein*, as arguably in most Gothic novels, the male paranoid plot is not separate

from the maternal or monstrous plot" (1980: ix), revealing that she is arguing against other critics who did divide Gothic plots in this way. Helene Meyers, in *Femidical Fears: Narratives of the Female Gothic Experience*, sees that feminist critics divide themselves between "power feminism" and "victim feminism" (2001: 6).

6. Ginny is another female character who temporarily enters a Gothic mode while she is pubescent. When Harry finds her in the deeply buried chamber of secrets, another manifestation of Kahane's "secret room sealed off by its association with death" (1985: 334), she is lying "facedown...a small, black-robed figure with flaming-red hair" (Rowling 1999: 307). It is in this scene where the muffled blood of the bathroom scene finally appears. When Harry and Ginny emerge from the chamber, they are "covered in muck and slime and (in Harry's case) blood" (327). After considering the troll scene as one marking a girl's entry into puberty, through menarche, it's a short step to seeing Ginny as undergoing a similar rite in a Gothic tableau. That Harry is also covered with abjected blood and muck at the end of this scene hints at a future important connection between him and Ginny.

7. This crush actually first revealed itself earlier, at the end of *Chamber of Secrets*, when Myrtle realizes Harry has survived his ordeal: "'Oh, well...I'd just been thinking...if you had died, you'd have been welcome to share my toilet,' said Myrtle, blushing silver" (326).

REFERENCES

Alton, A. H. (2003). Generic fusion and the mosaic of *Harry Potter*. In E. Heilman (Ed.), *Harry Potter's World: Multidisciplinary Critical Perspectives* (pp. 141–162). New York: RoutledgeFalmer.

Blume, J. [1970] (1991). *Are You There, God? It's Me, Margaret*. New York: Bantam Doubleday Dell.

Creed, B. (1993). *The Monstrous-Feminine: Film, Feminism, Psychoanalysis*. London; New York: Routledge.

Ellis, K. F. (1989). *The Contested Castle: Gothic Novels and the Subversion of Domestic Ideology*. Urbana; Chicago: University of Illinois Press.

Halberstam, J. (1995). *Skin Shows: Gothic Horror and the Technology of Monsters*. Durham, NC; London: Duke University Press.

Heiland, D. (2004). *Gothic and Gender: An Introduction*. Malden, MA; Oxford, UK; Carlton, Victoria, Australia: Blackwell Publishing.

Hoeveler, D. L. (1998). *Gothic Feminism: The Professionalization of Gender from Charlotte Smith to the Brontës*. University Park: Pennsylvania Sate University Press.

Hopkins, L. (2005). *Screening the Gothic*. Austin: University of Texas Press.

Kahane, C. (1985). The gothic mirror. In S. N. Garner, C. Kahane, & M. Sprengnether (Eds.), *The (M)other Tongue: Essays in Feminist Psychoanalytic Interpretation*. Ithaca, NY; London: Cornell University Press.

Kristeva, J. [1980] (1982). *Powers of Horror: An Essay on Abjection*. Leon S. Roudiez (Trans.). New York: Columbia University Press.

Lee, J. & Sasser-Coen, J. (1996). *Blood Stories: Menarche and the Politics of the Female Body in Contemporary U.S. Society*. New York; London: Routledge.

Meyers, H. (2001). *Femicidal Fears: Narratives of the Female Gothic Experience*. Albany: State University of New York.

Moers, E. (1976). *Literary Women: The Great Writers*. Garden City, NY: Doubleday and Co.

Pipher, M. B. (1994). *Reviving Ophelia: Saving the Selves of Adolescent Girls*. New York: Putnam.

Rowling, J. K. (1997). *Harry Potter and the Sorcerer's Stone*. New York: Scholastic.

_____. (1999). *Harry Potter and the Chamber of Secrets*. New York: Scholastic.

_____. (2000). *Harry Potter and the Goblet of Fire*. New York: Scholastic.

Russo, M. (1994). *The Female Grotesque: Risk, Excess, and Modernity*. New York; London: Routledge.

Sedgwick, E. K. [1980] (1986). *The Coherence of Gothic Conventions*. New York: Methuen.

Showalter, E. (1991). *Sister's Choice: Tradition and Change in American Women's Writing*. Oxford: Clarendon Press.

Stephens, J. (2003). "I'll never be the same after that summer": From abjection to subjective agency in teen films. In K. Mallan & S. Pearce (Eds.), *Youth Cultures: Texts, Images, and Identities*. Westport, CT: Praeger Publishers.

Weinstock, J. A. (2004). The spectral turn; Introduction. In J. Weinstock (Ed.), *Spectral America: Phantoms and the National Imagination* (pp. 3–17). Madison: The University of Wisconsin Press.

Wilt, J. (2003). "And still insists he sees the ghosts": Defining the gothic. In. D. L. Hoeveler & T. Heller (Eds.), *Approaches to Teaching Gothic Fiction: The British and American Traditions* (pp. 39–45). New York: Modern Language Association of American.

11

MAKING NIGHTMARES INTO NEW FAIRYTALES: GOTH COMICS AS CHILDREN'S LITERATURE

Laurie N. Taylor

Traditionally, comics have been dominated by hypermasculine values and male characters. As Bradford W. Wright's *Comic Book Nation,* Charles Hatfield's *Alternative Comics,* and Geoff Klock's *How to Read Superhero Comics and Why* all show, from the mainstream superheroes and superhero teams to even the subversive tradition of the Undergrounds, the more prominent comics' characters and values are masculine. In *Reading Comics* Mila Bongco goes further, explaining that women in comics were not afforded as prominent a place as either heroines or villains, and instead were delegated to the positions of superhero girlfriends or damsels in distress (108–111). Even when the characters are younger adults and teens, and even when the characters are women, the masculine values come across through the visual portrayal of hypermuscular or hypersexualized bodies as well as masculine narratives. However, because comics are a full medium, the values and norms presented vary greatly. Yet, comics overall have presented masculine values and male characters. Many comics deviate from this norm, including Adrian Tomine's *Summer Blonde,* the *Action Girl* comics, and the Underground *Wimmin's Comix.* Each of these represents an individual exception to the larger hypermasculine tradition, rather than a larger shifting of focus for comics as a whole or for any particular comic's genre. While many comics do feature women and children as characters, these characters are most often othered within a comic's tradition that focuses more heavily on adult male characters. Goth comics more often subvert typical comic art styles and worldviews by focusing most often on child characters, and child characters who are more mature and reliable than their parental counterparts. In doing so, Gothic comics present a rupture in the traditional history of comics, a rupture which allows for a new space for children, girls, and women in comics.

Goth comics follow in a tradition of subversive tales like Christina Rossetti's "The Goblin Market." These works, largely by female writers and often written for children, challenged patriarchal values by giving metaphorical expression to the extent of female confinement and oppression, as well as by revising tales to reflect more feminine values. Indeed, critics like Ellen Moers have noted that the female Gothic tradition arose as protest to patriarchal oppression. In *Literary Women*, Moers coined the term "Female Gothic" to refer to the manner in which Gothic literature expressed the problematic position of women within with patriarchal society. Later critical texts like Kate Ferguson Ellis's *The Contested Castle*, Maggie Kilgour's *The Rise of the Gothic Novel*, David Punter's *The Literature of Terror*, and Fred Botting's *Gothic* all studied the Gothic and the possibilities opened and closed by the concept of the Female Gothic. Within these and other analyses, the female Gothic has differentiated into the domestic Gothic, the lesbian Gothic, and other forms. Goth comics work from the concept of the female Gothic to create tales that subvert the normal patriarchal system present in comics by using tropes from the Gothic and the female Gothic. Likewise, Goth comics frequently rely on revisionist tales, like the *Nightmares and Fairy Tales* series, and on conventions from the Gothic in order to present subversive stories that empower child characters and readers. These stories problematize children's issues, the concept of childhood, and children's literature in an effort to reshape power dynamics that have traditionally placed children in a disempowered, vulnerable position. Furthermore, the creators of Goth comics alter typical distribution methods, artistic styles, and narrative conventions in order to present gothically inflected stories that empower child characters and explore the position of childhood in society. All of these alterations begin with a change in the context of Goth comics.

The change in context comes from alterations based on conventions transferred from the Gothic. The Gothic traditionally subverts normative values by presenting large family histories (often personified in aging mansions and castles) and then showing those family structures to be corrupt or failing, often through clandestine marriages, incest, and orphaned children. As Anne Williams argues in establishing a poetics of the Gothic, the Gothic itself has often been used to subvert social structures like patriarchy and to argue against gender and class based oppression (1995). Goth comics likewise present distorted worlds to argue against normative social structures, especially as those structures relate to the idea of the child and childhood. The context and world settings for most Goth comics are a darker version of the real world. In these darker worlds, children are often left alone and ignored, school is a terrifying place, parents are often negligent or abusive, and monsters abound. Following Roni Natov's description of the antipastoral, Goth comics' worlds reject the possibility of the pastoral in the same manner, but they do so using Gothic conventions. Natov explains that the antipastoral is "defensive—sometimes an exploration of the denial of childhood fear [. . .] It is about the dislocation of childhood [. . .] It is an imaginative disconnection, a landscape of isolation" (2003: 159). Goth comics, like the antipastoral, rely on this landscape of isolation to explore issues of childhood fear and their function and they do so by using Gothic themes. Goth comics also explore the fears of childhood and the dislocation of childhood when children are isolated and when the world of childhood is disjointed.

While creating these worlds of isolation, the Gothic provides direct social commentary because in the Gothic audience and thematic approaches are often conjoined, as Maggie Kilgour argues in *The Rise of the Gothic Novel*:

> Gothic readers are also often described, if not by the authors then by critics, as children or at best teenagers; Addison said that ghost stories appeal because they remind us of childhood—although Edith Birkhead thought that fairy tales were best for small children and gothic novels should be the next stage in our development as adolescents. (1995: 33)

As Goth comics rely more heavily on the Gothic's subversive tradition, they problematize issues of audience and theme, which in turn problematizes the place of children reading comics and in comics in both their visual and narrative representations. By presenting dark, dystopian worlds from the perspectives of the children main characters, Goth comics argue against the structures that children most often confront: parents and family, school, neighborhood, and other children. These contexts give rise to typical stories relating to teen and pre-teen angst—frustration with school, siblings, parents, and with social interaction in general; however, the altered contexts invert typical value systems. For instance, while the stories generally afford clear divisions of good and evil, good and evil are defined differently in much the same way that the Gothic presents inverted or subversive world structures. In Goth comics, monsters are likely to be considered good because they are friendly and helpful, parents and schools are normally bad because they are ineffectual or malevolent. These clear yet inverted divisions facilitate the fairytale-esque nature of Goth comic stories and situate Goth comics as material that problematizes children and childhood through the place of children in comics.

Goth comics often set stories in which children are safe with certain monsters but tormented by school, their parents, and other traditionally safe areas. *Courtney Crumrin, Squee, Makingfiends.com, Gloomcookie* and other Goth comics all deal with this to some degree. For instance in *Squee*, Squee's parents are abusive, Squee's schoolteacher is neglectful, and the Prince of Darkness—one of Squee's classmates—actually turns out to be Squee's friend and protector. In a slightly less extreme example, in *Nightmares and Fairytales* Gwen is a young girl who's just moved to a new home with her parents. Her parents are abusive and neglectful, and lock Gwen in a closet after she tells her parents about the monsters in that closet. The next day, the police remove her from the closet after the monsters have killed her parents and Gwen happily leaves to live with a kind old woman neighbor (2004). In both of these cases, the power dynamics are inverted and call into question the concept of safe spaces of childhood by presenting parents as unsafe and monsters as friendly.

The stories in Goth comics use Gothic settings, are frequently targeted at young adult readers, and often feature children as the main characters. Goth comics—including works like *Johnny the Homicidal Maniac, Squee, Courtney Crumrin*, and the majority of comics published by Slave Labor Graphics[1]—feature castles, dark towers, Victorian houses, graveyards, and other typical Gothic settings. Revisioning typical Gothic settings, Goth comics also include modern day versions of such settings with dilapidated buildings as ruins and suburban homes as castles. Similarly, Goth comics rely on Gothic storylines, from evil monsters to twisted family trees, to present stories about children in these worlds.[2] *Courtney Crumrin* takes place in her uncle Aloysius' home, where her parents move the family after amassing a great deal of credit card debt. The home itself is a mansion located in a wealthy area. However, this home is "the most talked about house in the whole neighborhood" because "it is well known that terrible things happen there, and that old man Crumrin is madder than a Victorian hatmaker" (2002: 7). Visually, the house is drawn as a decaying Victorian mansion with multiple floors and hidden recesses. The house itself serves as a backdrop for different storylines with hidden books and monsters lurking in the dark corners. Similarly, one story in *Nightmares and Fairytales* takes place in an oceanside, hilltop mansion where a man's wife is deathly ill. After she dies, the man marries his wife's nurse, to his young daughter Betty's great dismay, and the new couple are soon haunted by the dead woman. The mansion and prior marriage serve to set up the later events, which include a stormy overcast day and Betty's evening drowning in the waters beside the house. In both of these instances, the revisionist Gothic settings and family trees facilitate the overall narratives in such a way as to question the family relationships and the place of children within the family.

The narratives of Goth comics often focus on seemingly simplistic stories—like the fear of dust mites—within complex emotional studies, like childhood fear in the lack of parental attention and love (*Squee*). In addition to the focus on emotionally complex issues like parental love, Goth comics present different conceptions of beauty and human appearance, using the manga-style large heads and eyes with small bodies. Goth comics also rely more heavily on character discussion than on action than most comics do. This is in part because many of the main characters in Goth comics are physically weak, like the children Squee and Courtney Crumrin, and because the completely unworldly events are often set in normal or realistic worlds, just normal worlds gone mad. For instance, *Squee* has to fight the dust mite because his parents refuse to care for him. In doing so, he mainly argues with the dust mite before the dust mite dies from Squee previously—and off page—increasing the cold air flow from the air conditioning to kill the mites, as he learned from the Discovery Channel. In this combination of physical weakness with witty dialogue, altered standards of beauty, and an emphasis on marginal cultures, Goth comics present a changed view of children and women in comics.

The Gothic, in its inverted structures, often allows for alternate presentations of women and of sexuality. Using the Gothic and an altered art style, Goth comics break with the traditional presentations of women and children in comics in order to present children characters that are not stereotyped and to present children outside of the overly constraining context of comics' sexuality. As a visual form, mainstream comics tend to present characters in visually stereotyped, reductive manners. In *From Girls to Grrlz*, Trina Robbins chronicles comics made for girls, beginning with the early *Archie* series as specifically marketed to girls (1999: 9). While *Archie* was atypical in its lack of superheroes, *Archie* still presented idealistic versions of the female form. The comics for girls that followed *Archie* also presented ideal versions of women and girls and the requirement for stereotypically attractive characters remains a constant for mainstream comics.[3] In presenting both women and men[4] as hypersexualized, even children in comics are often drawn in a hypersexualized or hyperidealized manner. With the majority of characters presented inside such a totalizing framework, comics are often trapped in a system that only allows characters to be visually represented as hypersexualized, regardless of the stories and themes of the comics or the ages of the characters.

Goth comic conventions allow for all characters to be presented in an atypical fashion. Goth comics succeed in presenting characters that cannot easily be classed as attractive or unattractive, and even in presenting characters who are nonsexualized. This presentation is particularly important for children and women because, as Christine Wilkie-Stibbs, argues, the feminine subject allows for "an exploration of an alternative aesthetics for children's literature that gives voice to some latent silences and apparent absences in a body of children's literature texts, and in the critical discourse about children's literature" (2002: 1). This feminine subject is precisely what is foregrounded in Goth comics with their frequent use of children and women main characters, their Gothic narrative structures, and their alteration of typical visual representations. Wilkie-Stibbs continues on that the feminine acts as an alternate language system that is particularly relevant to children's literature, "because children, like women, have been excluded and silenced in language except to speak in the language of the Father's law [. . .] this is relatively untheorized in the field of children's literature studies" (43). In traditional comics and children's literature, the silencing of women and children comes from both the language and the visual rhetoric of the texts.

Goth comics, in contrast, open a discussion of children and women in their textual and visual representations because they are unlike most typical comics in both their depiction of women and in their creation by women. In typical comics "women superheroes are not real women, nor are they made by women" (Bukatman 2003: 65–6). Many Goth comics are written by women, including Amy Winfrey's *Making Fiends* and Serena Valentino's *Gloomcookie,* and many others focus on realistic female or child main characters, including *Courtney Crumrin, Lenore, Johnny the Homicidal Maniac,* and *Squee.* While many other Goth comics are not written by women, they still decenter traditional comics' structures both thematically and visually in order to create an alternate space for women, and subsequently children, in comics.

In order to explore both children and women characters in a manner that does not stereotype either group, Goth comics often rely on the narrative conventions of the Gothic and of Victorian myth. Nina Auerbach (1982) explains that Victorian myth often presents women as either angel or demon, but Auerbach argues that women in these myths are actually two sides of the same powerful figure. Goth comics, like the Victorian myth on which they draw, recombine the angel and the demon in a manner that respects the otherness of the children and women characters, while also allowing them to be powerful and primary characters. In doing so, these comics open new options for the representations of children and women in comics and for children and women reading comics that have implications for forms of children's literature.

Goth comics revise typical comics' stories, the themes of those stories, and the presentation of those stories to create a narrative space that exists outside of the traditional boundaries of comics and children's literature. For this, Victorian myth and fairy tales serve as the basis for many Goth comic narratives, but these myths and tales are revised in much the same way that feminist fairy tale revisions operate. Jack Zipes (1987) notes that feminist fairy tale revisions speak with voices that are normally silenced and they focus on changed world views. Like feminist fairy tales, Goth comic stories work from these voices and world views to highlight "the illusions of the traditional fairy tales by demonstrating that they have been structured according to the subordination of women, and in speaking out for women the feminist fairy tale also speaks out for other oppressed groups" (xi). For their narratives, Goth comics often draw on fairy tales because they allow for the fusion of reality and monstrosity within a revisionist framework. Similarly, Zipes argues that discussions of fairy tales and feminism require discussions on "power, violence, alienation, social conditions, child-rearing and sex roles. It is no longer possible to ignore the connection between the aesthetic components of fairy tales [. . .] and their historical function within a socialisation process which forms taste, mores, values, and habits" (2). To include these complex issues within comics, the comics have to draw on a revision that would allow for visual imagery that does not immediately place women and children as sexualized or as immediately categorized based on their appearances. In order to do so, the visual style of the comics must be altered, as well as the themes in the comics, so that children and women characters could carry with them the social commentary of the revisionist fairy tales without having it subsumed under the weight of sexuality and the history of children and women in comics. Goth comics rely on a different visual style and they draw more heavily on a tradition of Victorian myth than a comics' tradition, like superheroes or crime stories, for their narratives. For their use of Victorian myth, Nina Auerbach notes that, "As all clean-minded Victorians knew, a normal, and thus a good woman, was an angel, submerging herself in family, existing only as daughter, wife, and mother"

(1982: 4). Auerbach goes on to argue that this angel is also a demon, and a figure of feminist empowerment through the radically other nature of womanhood. Like the radically other form of the demon or angel, Goth comics present children, also often held as angels or demons, within a framework that allows children to be both angel and demon, complete with its radical possibilities.

Courtney Crumrin offers a powerful example of this duality. Courtney, the main character, exists in an inbetween stage because she is placed outside of her immediate family and is closer to her uncle Aloysius, who happens to be a Warlock, or male Witch. Courtney's parents move with her into her uncle's mansion, complete with its Gothically antique furniture, long windows, and seemingly always dark skies. In this mansion-castle setting, Courtney's parents neglect her or are cruel, and she is firmly situated as an outsider in her dealings with her schoolmates, her teachers, and even the monsters around her uncle's home to a degree. Courtney even has to defeat her doppelgänger angel who, like Virginia Woolf's angel, behaves perfectly in school and at home. Courtney's angel appeases the very people and customs that Courtney despises. Courtney's angel is the perfectly typical all-American girl who enjoys shopping, wears heart-shaped barrettes, gets along well with her parents, and displays enthusiasm in organized activities like school and sports. In arguing with her angel, the angel says that she's better at being Courtney than Courtney and that even their parents prefer the angel version. The real Courtney yells, "My mom would kiss a diseased mollusk if it could get her into a cocktail party. They're both selfish morons" (2002: 20). Courtney's retort situates her as having different values from her parents and different values from society at large. This, combined with the art style that shows the prettiness of the angel to be out of place in Courtney's messier world, shows one of the manners that Goth comics portray the complexity of children and childhood.

In another retelling of Victorian myth, this time specifically a retelling of Christina Rossetti's "The Goblin Market," Courtney journeys to the Goblin Market to try and save the real baby she was to babysit for, instead of the changeling that occupies its crib (2002: Vol. 1.3). The entire tale is Gothically illustrated, beginning in the mansion home of the Finches family and then being populated with monsters that lead Courtney to the market. The tale is also a tale of entrapment: Courtney never agreed to babysit; her parents made an agreement with the Finches and forced Courtney to do so in hopes of improving their own social standing by aiding the wealthier Finches.

The Finches agreed to have Courtney as the babysitter not because they wanted her—especially given her elementary school age—but because they believed she was too much of an outcast to hold a party or otherwise damage their home. In the market, Courtney takes a drink offered to her by the changeling and is caged. Thus, her foray into the market tells a story of entrapment through her parents, her social obligations passed from her parents, and even through her attempt to act in a moral manner by trying to save the real baby. Eventually Courtney is saved by her uncle and, importantly, neither the Goblins nor the uncle is shown to be evil while Courtney's parents and the parents of the baby-sat child are shown as impotent to help or even realize the dilemma. As Sandra M. Gilbert and Susan Gubar note, Christina Rossetti's works often depict multiple subversive possibilities for women "Like *Maude*, 'Goblin Market' (1859) depicts multiple heroines, each representing alternative possibilities of self-hood for women" (2000: 564). *Courtney Crumrin*'s revisioning of one of Rossetti's tales to empower a young girl and to critique the world in which the girl lives harnesses the subversive power of Rossetti's story for a modern day mass-audience.

Like *Courtney Crumrin, Gloomcookie* by Serena Valentino focuses on a main female character named Alexandria, or Lex. In one story arc of *Gloomcookie,* the main character is Alexandria as a fairy Princess who travels to distant lands. She travels by flying; then, her wings are cut and she is trapped in the evil lands of the Gargoyle Queen and cannot escape. The comic then moves to a more usual real-life situation with the same girl as a young adult in the Goth subculture. The girl is shown as trapped by her situation in clubs and everyday life with people that are a burden. As such, the comic connects her trapped life as a fairy with broken wings to her life as a young adult woman, with the castles of the fairy tale connected to the clubs and stores of a fantastically inflected real world. This story thus parallels Victorian narratives of entrapment that gave voice to the predicament of women, as well as the contemporary confining nature of comics' conventions for comics' art styles and the confining nature of the concept of childhood for children.

Nightmares and Fairytales, also by Serena Valentino, presents many separate tales of young girls who are oppressed in some way. Some of the tales are retellings of *Cinderella* and *Snow White,* retellings where those oppressing the title characters are killed or forced into marital relations with demons for their misdeeds. Other stories focus on young girls in various worlds where the girls are mistreated and the monsters come to protect the girls.

In the fifth issue of *Nightmares and Fairytales*, a young girl named Gwen has just moved into a new home with her negligent and abusive parents. The new home is both gothically described and illustrated to be like that of a haunted mansion or castle with tall windows, odd spires, and the promise of supernatural happenings. In the story, Gwen tries to be a good child to appease her parents, but nothing she does manages to mitigate their cruelty. One of the main factors that angers Gwen's parents is Gwen's fear of monsters and of her new home. While her parents lock her in a closet to keep her from complaining about the monsters, Gwen finds solace with her next door neighbor, a kind old woman named Beatrice who gives Gwen the magical doll Annabelle. Annabelle and Beatrice know that the monsters in the home are actually Gwen's friends and the real monsters are Gwen's parents. Beatrice even tells Annabelle to, "Kill those monsters," when referring to Gwen's parents (2004 Vol. 1.5: 20). Annabelle and the literal monsters do so and the story ends with Gwen leaving to live happily with Beatrice, or Aunt Bea by the end of the story. This is far from a typical fairy tale where a young girl is rescued by handsome price. Unlike most fairy tales, this tale puts Gwen in a modern day setting with the oppression not of patriarchy, but of her parents. Gwen must not escape into a marriage, but into a new family. The new family is not the perfect new union promised in most fairy tales, but an atypical family of a grandmother figure and helpful monsters that look after the child.

Taking a more humorous look at the same issues is the *Making Fiends* Flash-animated strip by Amy Winfrey. *Making Fiends* focuses on two elementary-age female characters; Vendetta who is evil, and Charlotte who is nice. As the theme song states, "Vendetta's always making fiends while Charlotte makes friends." In each episode, Vendetta makes monsters that attack everyone and all fear her, except for Charlotte who obliviously befriends the monsters. Vendetta and the other children are unhappy for some reason, generally at being forced to be near each other, and Charlotte exists outside of any knowledge of unhappiness. Even in this humorous format, the school and parents are powerless to help or change the situation. Only Charlotte's uncontrollable positivity has any impact on Vendetta's powers, which once again empowers children in worlds that are out of control and filled with monsters.[5] *Making Fiends* utilizes a Goth comics' art style with simple lines and colors augmented by oddly ornate twists and other Gothic flourishes.

In each of these comics, the main characters are female and either young adult or children characters. This is striking given the fact that each of these comics addresses some level of entrapment and disappointment with that entrapment—either in the confines of family, society, school, or personal expression.

The representation of children and women in Goth comics shows children in comics in a new light for a mainstream audience. Most comics, particularly superhero and cartoon character comics to which children readers have access, present children as innocent blank slates. Goth comics allow children to be villains and, more importantly, they show children to be complex characters within complex worlds where morality is often unclear. The Gothic serves as the narrative and stylistic grounding for these representations, allowing the art and narrative of Goth comics to break from the bounds of traditional mainstream comics. As Nina Auerbach demonstrates, "The myth of womanhood flourishes [. . .] in the vibrant half-life of popular literature and art, forms which may distill the essence of a culture though they are rarely granted Culture's weight imprimatur" (1982: 10). Goth comics counter the typical notion of children and women found in other popular literature and art. Importantly, Goth comics counter the typical notions by rewriting fairy tales and nightmares in both their image and textual representations.

While many comics feature women and children characters, these characters are most often othered within a comics' tradition that focuses more heavily on adult male characters. Goth comics more often subvert typical comic art styles and worldviews by focusing most often on child characters, but child characters that are more mature and reliable than their parental counterparts. In a male-dominated genre, as Alan Moore notes in *Alan Moore's Yuggoth Cultures and Other Growths,* women in comics are almost always in a precarious place because of the art style and history of comics. Goth comics, however, represent a new turn in comics development and a new turn in children's literature; largely by and about women, they challenge patriarchal patterns of representation in much the same way as did their Gothic forebears in Victorian litera-ture. Goth comics have created their new space by drawing on themes of children's narratives, like fairy tales, and then inverting them stylis-tically and thematically.

Goth comics' relationship to Victorian myth and the power of both are perhaps never clearer than in the wish for freedom and escape as expressed through a wish for wings. Charlotte Bronte's letter to a friend expresses the desire to be free as visualized through wings: "Such a strong wish for wings - wings such as wealth can furnish - such an urgent thirst to see - to know - to learn - something internal seemed to expand unexercised" (qtd. in Auerbach 1982: 112). The wish for wings is clear in Goth comics, with Courtney Crumrin playing with magic to escape her dreary life at school and her inadequate parents, Squee's wish for escape, the *Gloomcookie* story of a girl trapped by her broken wings, and the many stories in *Nightmares and Fairytales* where girls and children wish to fly away to escape their circumstances. As if these connections are not direct enough, Hot Topic, a young adult retail clothing store that often sells Goth comics, also sells costume wings for regular wear. The wish for freedom and for escape—from the confines of traditional society, family, and gender norms—fill the pages of Goth comics, making Goth comics a subversive genre for all marginalized creatures, especially the children and women in comics.

ENDNOTES

1. For a list of Goth comics, their writers, and publishers, see *Goth.net*'s links for Goth comics, (1 May 2005. 1 Dec. 2002) http://www.goth.net/links/comics.html. For a list of the most prominent Goth comics and short descriptions, see Sequential Tart's "Recommended Reading List: Goth" (1 May 2005. 1 Jan. 2002) http://read.sequentialtart.com/rrl_goth.pdf.

2. *The Sandman*'s Death character is typically described as a Goth character, but *The Sandman* comics and the later spin-offs like the *Death* comics are horror or fantasy comics instead of Goth comics. The storylines, themes, world settings, and art styles are vastly different from what are typically referred to as Goth comics.

3. Underground comics and non-mainstream comics have explored alternative depictions of women, but these still placed female characters within the dominant framework, and these most often did not reach a mainstream audience, see Trina Robbins, *From Girls to Grrlz: a History of Women's Comics from Teens to Zines* (San Francisco: Chronicle Books, 1999) pages 85–114.

4. While men in comics are often presented as hypersexualized, many leading superhero males are not. For instance, the Hulk, the Beast, and Wolverine are closer to animal-creatures than direct masculinity. Women characters, on the other hand, are rarely represented as anything less than idealized female sexuality.

5. Similar to *Making Fiends* is the animated television show *Invader Zim*. *Invader Zim* focuses on one young boy, who happens to be an alien trying to overtake the Earth. Instead, he suffers through school, incompetent adults, and the horrors of fast food. Most of the other children ignore Zim, except for his arch-nemesis Dib. The other primary, and most powerful character, in Zim's everyday life is Gaz, Dib's cruel, strong, and brilliant sister. In *Invader Zim*, most of the children have no parents or the parents are never around. One episode focuses on the yearly dinner with Dib, Gaz, and their father. Their mother is notably absent, as are Zim's parents.

REFERENCES

Atchison, L. (Mar 2000). "The Goth Genre and Slave Labor Graphics." *Sequential Tart*. Retrieved 1 May 2005. from http://www.sequentialtart. com/archive/mar00/art_0300_10.shtml.

Auerbach, N. (1982). *Woman and the Demon: The Life of the Victorian Myth*. Cambridge: Harvard UP.

Bassette, A. (Dec 2003). "Take a Walk on the Dark Side of Comics." *Yo! Youth Outlook* Retrieved 1 May 2005 from http://www.youthoutlook.org/news/ view_article.html?article_id=765397992556e3eee3bdb39b0d075626.

Bukatman, S. (2003). *Matters of Gravity: Special Effects and Supermen in the 20th Century*. Durham, NC: Duke UP.

Friedman, E G. and M Fuchs. (1989). *Breaking the Sequence: Women's Experimental Fiction*. Princeton, NJ: Princeton UP.

Gilbert, S. M. and S. Gubar. (2000). *The Madwoman in the Attic: The Woman Writer and the Nineteenth-Century Imagination, 2nd Edition*. New Haven: Yale UP.

Gravett, P. (2004). *Manga: Sixty Years of Japanese Comics*. New York: Harper Design.

Kilgour, M. (1995). *The Rise of the Gothic Novel*. New York: Routledge.

Moore, A. (Nov 2003). *Alan Moore's Yuggoth Cultures and Other Growths*. Issue 3. Urbana, IL: Avatar Press.

Naifeh, T. (2002). *Courtney Crumrin and the Night Things* (Vol. 1). Portland, OR: Oni Press.

_____. (2003) *Courtney Crumrin and the Coven of Mystics* (Vol. 2). Portland, OR: Oni Press.

_____. (2004) *Courtney Crumrin in the Twilight Kingdom* (Vol. 3). Portland, OR: Oni Press.

_____. (1 July 2004). "Latest News." *Courtney Crumrin* Website. Retrieved 1 May 2005 from http://www.thenightthings.com/night_things/Court-ney_news.htm.

Natov, R. (2003). *The Poetics of Childhood*. New York: Routledge.

Robbins, T. (1999). *From Girls to Grrlz: a History of Women's Comics from Teens to Zines*. San Francisco: Chronicle Books.

Valentino, S., Gebba, J., and C. McFri. (2002). *Gloomcookie*. (Vol. 2; Graphic Novel Collection of Issues 7–12). San Jose, CA: Slave Labor Graphics.

Valentino, S., FSc, and J. Archer. (2004). *Nightmares and Fairytales Volume One: Once Upon a Time...* (Graphic Novel Collection of Issues 1–6). San Jose, CA: Slave Labor Graphics.

Vasquez, J. (1997). *Z? JTHM: the Director's Cut*. (Graphic Novel Collection of *Johnny the Homicidal Maniac* Issues 1–7). San Jose, CA: Slave Labor Graphics.

_____. (1998). *Squee's Wonderful Big Giant Book of Unspeakable Horrors*. (Graphic Novel). San Jose, CA: Slave Labor Graphics.

Williams, A. (1995). *Art of Darkness: A Poetics of Gothic*. Chicago: University of Chicago Press.

Wilkie-Stibbs, C. (2002). *The Feminine Subject in Children's Literature*. New York: Routledge.

Winfrey, A. (21 Jan 2005) *Making Fiends*. Retrieved 15 June 2005 from http://www.makingfiends.com.

Zipes, Jack. (Ed.) (1987). *Don't Bet on the Prince: Contemporary Feminist Fairy Tales in North America and England*. New York: Routledge.

12

FANTASTIC BOOKS: THE GOTHIC ARCHITECTURE OF CHILDREN'S BOOKS

Rebecca-Anne C. Do Rozario

The words shone momentarily on the page and they too sank without trace. Then, at last, something happened. Oozing back out of the page, in his very own ink, came words Harry had never written. (J. K. Rowling, *Harry Potter and the Chamber of Secrets*)

Back to his own world, created from paper, printer's ink and an old man's words. (Cornelia Funke, *Inkspell*)

There is a Gothic architecture of books, both as objects of and within children's literature: books filled with secrets and potentially dangerous passages, the narratives as labyrinthine as any castle interior or ruins, the dust jackets as intimidating as any fortress walls. Entering such a book is, potentially, as perilous to the reader as to the characters within the story. These are children's books of a Gothic persuasion; they include ever-more peculiar books that are magic or that have magical potential, that are devious and complex. The books comprise a fascinating Gothic library marketed to children, through which their fictional counterparts conspire and scheme to counter the intertext of Gothic ruins and enigmas which hem them in and threaten them with intertextuality itself. Deidre Lynch notes the Gothic tradition's literary impulse, arguing that early Gothic authors "are remarkable [...] for the density of their intertextual allusions" (2001: 31). In making these allusions, authors create characters who are, as Lynch indicates, "surrounded by books, ink, and paper" (29). In regard to children's books, material rather allusive intertextuality—the book, ink, and paper—becomes the Gothic manifestation.

This shift, essentially from allusion to materialisation, is a response to the more commonplace intertextuality of children's literature itself. John Stephens argues that children's literature is "radically intertextual because it has no special discourse of its own," occupying, as it were, "the intersection of a number of other discourses" (1992: 86). Responding to the "ordinariness" of intertextuality in the genre, these particular children's books reinvest it with significance by actualising it as Gothic peril. They subsequently realise absence in the dearth of a founding discourse, alongside the profusion of discourses that are fragmented, alternated and hidden so as to re-emerge mysterious. The discourses become the stuff of the bibliophilia of children's literature, its compilation and rewriting of myth, fairy, folk, and other tales. As Lynch suggests, bibliophilia infuses Gothic novels, but in children's books, it also destabilises the fundamental ontological distinctions between text and lived experience. Bibliophilia, manifested in its intertextual excesses, becomes the architecture of the Gothic novel through which the secrets of children's literature can be endlessly whispered and through which the distinctions between reader and text can be repeatedly dispelled.

Intertextuality itself complements the essential Gothic paradox of the quest to discover a secret that is, in fact, itself an explosion of the potential and rival meanings/texts compressed within a dialogue of secrecy. Discourses of identity are often secret, concealed beneath general labels. Thus, in three of the examples in this essay, the origins of a young male protagonist are obscured under the broad designation of "boy." Jonathan Stroud's Nathaniel, protagonist of *The Bartimaeus Trilogy*, is stripped of all identity as a small child, "officially unformed" (2003: 64), his birthname a forbidden utterance when he is made a magician's apprentice. His new master refers to him simply as "boy." Farid in Cornelia Funke's *Ink* trilogy is unnamed in the story from *One Thousand and One Nights* from which he originates and consequently enters *Inkheart* (2003) as "boy."[1] Marcus Sedgwick's Boy in *The Book of Dead Days* (2003) and *The Dark Flight Down* (2004) searches for his origins through the two novels, only to discover that he has only ever been "Boy."

Each boy is, in fact, one of the many possibilities of the written designation, the secrets of their origins located in the indefinitely branching out, semantic family tree. Likewise, each book is itself just one possibility of many, hence most of the books discussed here are parts of series. Even within the books within the series, there is the suggestion of a yet wider proliferation of books. *Ptolemy's Gate* (2005), part of

The Bartimaeus Trilogy, playfully acknowledges other adventures that go unnarrated, but nonetheless have titles pointing to further, unwritten books: "these included the case of the Afrit, the Envelope and the Ambassador's Wife, the affair of the Curiously Heavy Trunk and the messy episode of the Anarchist and the Oyster" (36).[2] Other titles signify the origin or source of the narrative in which they appear, sometimes even doubling as the title of the book about the book of that title, such as *Inkheart*, although the source text only appears as quoted or referenced fragments.

The encounter between books thus preserves the coherency of the unwritten text in the title of the written one and in the act of preservation, leaves that text open to infinite possibility. As Jan B. Gordon argues: "In the attempt to get closer to some source, the language of Gothic narrative often encounters only other language, other texts, which it redeems from oblivion by an act of infinite prolongation much as it, too, might be easily extended by infinite sequels which make the permanent death of the monstrous unlikely" (2004: 68). Thus the preservation of *Inkheart* in Funke's *Inkheart* permits extension that constantly revives the monstrous hidden in the original book and produces narrative alternatives throughout the trilogy, while likewise revealing further narratives, like legends of the White Women and songs of the Motley Folk, that lie behind the source text. Fenoglio, author of the "source" *Inkheart*, acknowledges that he can't tell if he wrote all the tales that exist in that text, responding when his character, Dustfinger, capitalizes upon one such tale: "Perhaps I wrote the sentimental story that gave him the idea myself…I really don't remember, but never mind, there are always gaps" (2005: 644). Further possible, hidden texts are continuously discovered in such gaps. Dustfinger's consequent death is, too, an alternative to the one that Fenoglio wrote for him in *Inkheart*, prompting Farid, who became his friend and apprentice, to seek out yet more textual fragments that can undo his death.

The act of "prolongation," the infinite unfolding of alterity, appears to be an answer to cultural crisis. David Punter and Glennis Byron acknowledge: "The Gothic is frequently considered to be a genre that re-emerges with particular force during times of cultural crisis and which serves to negotiate the anxieties of the age by working through them in a displaced form" (2004: 39). Just as the Gothic experienced a resurgence with the Industrial Revolution, the increasing speed of technological innovation and postmodern anxiety informs the popularity of the consequent development in Gothic literature. Allan Lloyd Smith acknowledges a conjunction between the postmodern and Gothic: "The information revolution, by providing too much information and boundless signs without referents, subjects the protagonist to a sensory disarray comparable to the confusions of a Gothic victim" (1996: 15). Unsurprisingly, children's books have relocated themselves within the Gothic genre as books themselves have been displaced among burgeoning alternatives and myriad, fragmented signifiers. The technological change dislocating narrative from the traditional, concrete materials of the manuscript informs the regeneration of the book itself as a repository to simultaneously organise, classify, and offer up such disarray.

As PlayStations, television, PCs, iPods, and other items jostle for the attention of children, books have reinvented themselves as lost relics, apparitions that exist in ink and paper as the encroaching realm of cyberspace and multimedia reforms narrative into digitalised data and generated image. Books thus become supersignifiers of their own potential as entertainment and adventure, as objects of story in their own right. In *The Princess Bride* (1973), William Goldman's fictional alter ego reflects on his father reading the source book of that name to him: "Me the sports fanatic, me the game freak, me the only ten-year-old in Illinois with a hate on for the alphabet wanted to know *what happened next*" (1973: 9). The 1987 film adaptation likewise introduces the small male reader, preoccupied with his video games and initially disinterested in the bound pages his old-fashioned grandfather reads to him. The boy is the figure of crisis, apparently lost in hyper-reality, until he himself seeks out the unfolding textual. Smith argues that technological change suggests a scenario of "the system running itself, for itself; and hence generates antihumanism, plots beyond comprehension. Either there are plots or, perhaps worse, there are none, an unendurable void of meaning" (1996: 16).

Books which advertise their authors seem to offer an alternative to such paranoia and negation, while simultaneously their plots can appear to propagate independent of human agency, and authors themselves become shadowy identities behind the authorial inscriptions. In Funke's *Inkheart* and *Inkspell* the author Fenoglio's plots seem to become self-determining and the heroine Meggie herself realises: "She had seen only the characters who emerged from the words to meet her, never the writer who had made them up [...] in general one thought of writers as dead or very, very old" (2003: 257). The characters in Fenoglio's *Inkheart* also experience existential angst over the question of his authorship, reflecting contemporary anxieties about the system and disintegration of fixed meanings/origins as embodied in the book's author.

Goldman's Prologue likewise tells the story of Goldman's search for the book, *The Princess Bride*, and his tussle with the original author's plot digressions, even though, of course, that author and his book are fiction themselves.[3] Yet the search for the book is significant: the text can only be revealed when the object of paper and ink is itself sought out.[4] So, too, do various characters throughout the *Ink* trilogy seek out a copy of *Inkheart*. Books are increasingly regarded as archaic, particularly those that are bound and engraved, intimating that they have joined other Gothic props and objects. Technology, in essence, displaced the book into the supernatural. Even the covers of these children's books recreate themselves as ancient relics, covers mimicking leather and stone with old-fashioned calligraphy imprinted upon the binding. The books wear their tactile antiquity on their sleeves.

The book on the shelf is thus an extraordinary representation of itself. The dust jacket may be printed with gold gilding and the appearance of leather. The Gothic lettering of the title may suggest something supernatural and, indeed, bookish. The cover can even be embossed with creatures and objects that appear to be sitting upon or escaping from a book in turn illustrated on the dust jacket, as in the case of first English-language editions of *Inkheart*. This is not simply a bound edition one picks up and opens in the usual manner. It is a book imprinted with the representation of a far more astonishing book.

Many of these books create a resonating signifier from the title, so that the title itself seems to echo down through the depths of the paper and ink. In others, the enigma of a paranormal book resonates, *The Book of Dead Days* about a book apparently without specific title, remaining as secret beneath its general designator as Boy. The title draws upon a distinctly Gothic heritage, Sedgwick's "Author's Note" describing the days between Christmas and New Year as "Dead Days. Days when the doors between our own world and the unseen one that lies just beneath the surface are opened" (2003: v). These are lost days where barriers between life and death are tenuous. The streets in the unnamed city are thus known by names like Dead Duck Lane and The Deadway and most scenes occur in cemeteries, crypts, and catacombs. There is a spareness to the style of narration that mimics the insubstantiality of Gothic phantasm, the fading of distinctiveness that comes with decay and death. As Gordon argues "the archaeology which most nearly approaches the existential environment of Gothic sensibility is the *fragment*: incomplete or unfinished; [...] time reduced the decaying artifact and hence life-in-death" (2004: 59). The central book is also ancient and decaying, ragged, "itself a magical device, and each person who looks into it learns something different" (Sedgwick 2003: 166). A secret object, it in turn yields further secrets: an infinite variety of possible secrets, in fact, thus paradoxically engaged in ceaseless textual composition even as it physically decomposes.

The twenty-first century dust jacket of *The Book of Dead Days* doubles the decomposition of the ancient book. The matte paper of the dust jacket feels thick and textured and the printed design further gives it the illusion of age as browned, torn, and folded. The author's name appears as a calligraphic signature, ink spots even replicated to simulate the act of writing, beneath the quite old-fashioned print of the title. Yet the title and author's name are clearly printed over the aged paper rather than on it, creating an imprint upon something much older. Apart from a small pen and ink illustration, in which Boy's face is half concealed as he moves through snow in a graveyard, the other feature of the front cover is the photographic reproduction of the blue ribbon that actually does mark the pages of the book itself, thus reinforcing the doubling of the image of the book. The whole effect is to produce a visual layering that conceals even as it offers up images.

The sequel, *The Dark Flight Down*, creates a new echo even as the old book is burnt: "finally the ancient, stained, grimy, ink-littered pages began to burn properly" (Sedgwick 2004: 226). Even as Boy orders the book to die, monstrous text reasserts itself, for, as Gordon indicates, final death is not possible. In the sequel, Boy continues to search for his real name and origin, but after the Dead Days, he is now embroiled in a different Gothic landscape of labyrinthine palaces, dungeons, hidden monsters, and mad emperors. Again, names seem vague and unfinished, clues to Boy's identity are simply pieces of histories. A song appears in different fragments throughout the narrative, gradually revealed to be a song composed by Boy's mother, Sophia Beebe, a song that echoes dark secrets of madness and deformity, criminality and revenge. Sophia is a true Gothic heroine, beautiful and virtuous, ravaged by powerful men, and now tragically dead. Yet her song continues to haunt the text, from the blood red title on the dust jacket, which appears to be printed on the stone of the palace itself, to the final words, denying a final ending: "So dance, my dears, dance, Before you take the dark flight down" (2004: 234). As the pages burned, the walls of the palace and its dungeons resonate with textual fragments that allude to the possibility of further secrets.

The act of writing itself may release dangerous secrets. J. K. Rowling's Harry Potter series creates a Gothic parallel to our own "Muggle" world, one in which books can scream, snap, become invisible, put spells upon the reader, or simply yield perfectly horrendous curses.[5] The magic of Rowling's wizarding world infuses its books, creating, across the series, an imagined library of fantastical books to serve the supernatural. The series, however, likewise raises the more personal, ordinary, spontaneous, and contemporaneous kinds of books to Gothic status. The diary, for example, becomes a central text in *Harry Potter and the Chamber of Secrets* (1998). The diary is an everyday repository of deeply personal secrets, but when the ink of those secrets becomes absorbed into the paper of T. M. Riddle's diary, the secrets themselves feed a fragment of soul hidden between the covers. The diary is quite ordinary, purchased rather prosaically from a news agency on Vauxhall Road. Riddle, whom Harry, Ron and Hermione discover is the real name of Lord Voldemort, concealing his origins in an act of anagram, had left an imprint of his schoolboy soul within the diary, one that could only be manifested through the ink invested by a new diarist, in this case Ginny Weasley: "I grew stronger and stronger on a diet of her deepest fears, her darkest secrets" (Rowling 1998: 228).

The ultimate secret of the diary, therefore, can only be manifest by other secrets, hence it is a *very* secret diary, as Chapter 13's title indicates. Yet that deepest secret is itself obsessed by that other Gothic preoccupation: history. Riddle seeks to discover Harry Potter's history, the diary fragment of Riddle having been bound in its own textual temporality and so unaware of Harry's incomplete defeat of his mature self. Even such a textual phantasm is bound to the historical continuum, to a longing and loathing for pastness as it reveals the mystery of his present.[6] Once manifest from the pages, he is defeated when Harry stabs the diary with a poisoned tooth, the ink released in a metaphoric bloodletting. Yet, this was just a fragment of Riddle/Voldemort and as only the second book in a seven-book series, there is no possibility yet of completely vanquishing the fragmented ruin of the evil You-Know-Who.[7]

The Gothic intertext creates an endless possibility for narrative fragments to revolve between the secret and the exposed, always suggesting, but never completely revealing, the whole from which they originate. The origin remains obscured even as the fragmentary textual materialisations multiply. Funke's *Inkheart* opens in a house filled with books. The book is thus filled with, potentially, all books. Funke fixes this in the text by beginning each chapter with a quotation from another book, a fragment of another text intertextually hinting at the chapter's contents. For example, the first chapter opens with a quotation from L. M. Boston's *The Children of Green Knowe* (1975) that describes the noise of a book's turning pages in the night (Funke 2003: 7). Meggie then relates the sound of pages turning to whispers, acknowledging the dialogue with Boston's narrative (8). This opening chapter is a veritable eulogy to the Gothic delights of paper and ink, the whispers and secrets kept under wraps of bound cloth, glue and thread. Her father, Mo, is a bookbinder and prolific reader: "It always took him a few moments to find his way out of that other world, the labyrinth of printed letters" (9).

Meggie and Mo relate to each other through this labyrinth, navigating myriad texts, fragments of books clinging to their lived experience as metaphors. In the absence of an actual castle, books themselves create the architecture, libraries, shelves, boxes, and piles of books configuring paper and ink secret chambers and passages, dungeons, and wild woods.

Funke's book perpetuates this architecture. The cover, with its printed gilded bindings, yields to the chapters, each beginning with those quotations from other books, often indicating yet further books. Focus is, however, maintained upon the relationship of concentricity between worlds prescribed by the two books: the *Inkheart* written by Funke and the *Inkheart* written by Fenoglio. The two worlds are deliberately offset by the two books: Fengolio is the paper and ink creation of Funke just as Fengolio is in turn the creator of the characters in his *Inkheart*.[8] The interweaving intertextuality created by books within books within books is not new, of course. Funke's *Inkheart* has a particularly strong architecture resting upon the Gothic, never fully disclosed, foundation of Fenoglio's *Inkheart*, however. When Meggie discovers Mo attempting to conceal that book from her, she demands: "'What's so special about this one? Will I go blind if I read it? Will it bite my fingers off? What terrible secrets are there in it that I mustn't know?'" (53). Mo conceals the book in a plain cloth binding, removing its title page as though, to remove its title, he removes its identity, but it is a futile gesture since his own adventure necessitates his seeking out the book and that which its text might potentially yield.

Inkheart is the first of a trilogy, all of which will carry "ink" in the title. Distinctions between the reader as character and the read character are blurred by an inky phantasm of corporeal identity, conjured by the act of reading out loud. It takes the act of breath to constitute life from text, mimicking the metaphor of divine animation. Mo, also known as Silvertongue, has the ability to read objects, even people, into and out of books, a kind of "ink-shifting," and *Inkheart*, in particular, holds a terrible secret: when Mo read from its pages, he read Meggie's mother, Resa, into the book along with two cats, Fenoglio's creations of Capricorn, Basta, and Dustfinger in turn appearing in their places. Mo encapsulates the mystery of ink-shifting: "Perhaps there's another, much larger story behind the printed one, a story that changes just as our own world does. And the letters on the page tell us only as much as we'd see peering through a keyhole" (154). The keyhole metaphor reinforces the Gothic derivation of Mo's ability, as one that can only give glimpses of wider mysteries, one he passes on to Meggie along the familial line.

However, while breath may animate, the text is the actual Gothic stuff and without text, Mo and Meggie can't slip objects and people into and out of alternate narratives, creating intertextual disarray.[9] Other forms of text and manuscript to the bound book can be incorporated, however, and Funke permits the author a continuing role in composing Gothic substance. Fenoglio delights in words as the essential Gothic material: "Keepers of secrets, speakers of the truth" (517). He can add to and adapt his book with what tools are available, whether single pieces of paper and pencils or parchment and quills, yet his words frequently provide a 'keyhole' through which further secrets and truths are revealed. The textual fragments written by Fenoglio thus ostensibly fail to coalesce into a single text with beginning and ending. This would seem to be consistent with Gothic behaviour, Gordon arguing: "It rather exists as all 'middle'" (2004: 59). Even Meggie notes in *Inkspell* that Fenoglio's text "seemed to have no beginning and no end" (Funke 2005: 298). Funke, however, disturbs this middle perpetuity of secrecy and possibility in words by challenging it with real ending: death. In Funke's *Inkheart*, words written by Fenoglio on a scrap of paper read by Mo kill Capricorn, bringing that character to an end.

In the sequel, which largely takes place in the Inkworld of Fenoglio's creation, the ink of the printing press or pen becomes an apparition of the human lifeblood, the paper of flesh: "Meggie still sat there looking at the written words on her lap. It seemed to her that they were breathing. Paper made flesh, ink made blood" (2005: 298). In fact, in the original German, the sequel is entitled *Tintenblut* (*Inkblood*).[10] The problematic conjuring of flesh and blood from paper and ink has consequences for Mo in terms of the ink-shifting of his own identity. Fenoglio, himself read into his own Inkworld, has used Mo as the model for a character in his ballads, the Bluejay, and when Mo enters the Inkworld, his dark hair and the scar on his arm effectively write him into the story *as* the Bluejay.[11] What was meant to be simply song becomes flesh and blood, beyond the control of its author. In order to regain control of his story, Fenoglio attempts to bring the fallen Prince Cosimo back to life. As Punter writes, "power *is* a process of writing, of inscription" (2000: 17), suggesting that it is Fenoglio's writing that produces power. Power is not embodied in Fenoglio, but in his composition and consequent characters. He qualifies that simply bringing a person back to life would "lead to hopeless confusion; it would wreck the suspense!" (Funke 2005: 263). The integrity of the process must be maintained to be powerful. Nonetheless, his facsimile of Cosimo further fragments the authenticity not only of his text, but of the status of character. The Cosimo facsimile is an empty character, in a sense the effigy of a now empty crypt, and not all Fenoglio's stories can fill in his blank memory. In fact, these new stories distort the Prince's history, leading him to seek military glory to fulfil the stories told about him. He is consequently killed on the battlefield, his reinscription unable to "cheat" his death.[12]

Fenoglio is not a benevolent presence, being more proficient at writing villains and tragic endings. When actually confronted by his text, therefore, he experiences not the sense of the immortality of authorship, but the constant threat of mortality. He even comes to deny his authorship of *Inkheart*: "No, the author is Death, the Grim Reaper, the Cold Man [...] never mind what I write he'll take my words and make them serve him!" (2005: 644). The permanence of text nevertheless permits substitutions and variations, as Dustfinger shows in creating his own alternate death by drawing on a story Fenoglio himself is challenged to recall. Likewise, Farid intends to use text written by Fenoglio's new apprentice to bring Dustfinger back to life. The power of writing has an uneasy relationship to death, attempts to revive what derives from the textual thwarted and complicated by the myriad possibilities of words. The final words of *Inkspell* thus deny conclusion and suggest a different ending even as the words "the end" are inscribed below them, Farid telling Meggie, "This story will have a happy ending. I swear!" (2005: 675). Yet this inscription itself will inevitably be undone by the next book and the search for the happy ending will, potentially indefinitely, be prolonged.[13]

Gordon addresses the presence of multiple texts within the Gothic genre: "While attempting to set up a world of texts within texts which establish some order in a succession of literary priority and hence authority, what the Gothic mode actually achieves is a constant questioning of the respective legitimacies and status of competing texts by narrowing the difference between them" (2004: 57). As character becomes text and text becomes character, the legitimacy of humanity itself is interrogated. Although not strictly Gothic, Jostein Gaarder's *Sophie's World* (1991) adopts this mode to demonstrate the particular history of philosophy, while breaking down barriers of distinction between the layers of story and thus existence, ultimately denying the difference between "human" and "character," "flesh and blood," and "paper and ink." The book begins with a teenage girl called Sophie, who receives a letter reading, "*Who are you?*" (4). From the basic existential questions posed by pen and paper, leading to theories of the mysteries of life and the universe, the narrative unfolds to reveal that Sophie is a fictional construct through which, along with her teacher, Alberto, Albert Knag is instructing his daughter, Hilde, in philosophical concepts, just as Albert is in turn Gaarder's fictional construct and counterpart. Thus in Gaarder's book, Albert ostensibly writes *Sophie's World* even as *Sophie's World* is experienced by Sophie. Sophie and Alberto seek to escape the constraints of their author, however, who in turn becomes more and more tangible within the book as he is forced to assert his authority over characters he has written. By actually concealing their actions within excessive, unruly, disturbing fragments of text, Sophie and Alberto ostensibly move beyond their author's control.[14] Such "ink-shifting" destabilises the reader's own reality as reader of the book, just as Sophie's reality is ultimately overturned by the discovery that she is "made up," making the book itself a catalyst of the uncanny.

Gothic tropes and motifs often move into and inhabit the architecture of books, as in Jonathan Stroud's *The Bartimaeus Trilogy* in which the djinni, Bartimaeus, periodically assumes the role of author, even adding his own humorous footnotes to pass on esoteric background. Stroud's series roughly coincides with the adult fiction bestseller, *Jonathan Strange and Mr Norrell* (2004) by Susanna Clarke.[15] Both authors recreate a London in which magicians, in league with otherworldly creatures, meddle in imperial politics and the authors add to the Gothic architecture of the books themselves by generating footnotes that act as textual "secret antechambers," divided off from narrative to provide hints and clues to other secrets. Clarke's footnotes provide a scholarly atmosphere for her architecture, imparting historical facts and citing further books, such as William Pantler's *Three Perfectible States of Being*, with full bibliographic detail (2004: 166). Although all such footnotes are clearly an invention of the author herself, the very nature of their textual form lends them authenticity and once again provides the impression that Clarke's book derives from a wider literary legacy from which further secrets may be mined.[16] Stroud's use of footnotes serves the excess and unmanageability of the supernatural. The *Bartimaeus Trilogy* is split between first- and third-person narrative and the footnotes appear in those chapters narrated by the supernatural itself, namely Bartimaeus. The djinni is a being of no discernable form forced into an effigy of confinement/enslavement by the summoning of a magician: by words. It is an effigy that can be altered at will, but which nonetheless makes the djinni *"alone and vulnerable in a world of vicious definition"* where in his natural state, he merges with *"fluidity"* itself (2005: 412). The footnotes in Bartimaeus's narrative permit his narrative voice to fragment textual integrity, the literary equivalent of clever, witty, often libellous asides, which also reproduce his own resistance to the fixity of form.[17]

The switches between Bartimaeus's narration and the third person narratives, which are typically split between Nathaniel, the teenage magician who has enslaved Bartimaeus, and Kitty, the adolescent revolutionary planning to bring down the government of magicians, likewise disrupt, interrupt, and fragment authorial authority, opening the account of Bartimaeus' adventures to alternative versions. Bartimaeus at times himself narrates third person, distinguishing between the fluidity of his thoughts and the physical actions of his form: "The buffalo studied a hoof with feigned indifference" (Stroud 2004: 117). Essentially, he reinforces the differences of spirit and guise, the narrational switches indicating his own authorial authority over his form's appearance.[18] He also directly alludes to outside forces upon the way in which the narrative is written, explaining the presence of asterisks in a footnote: "These polite asterisks replace a short, censored episode characterised by bad language and some sadly necessary violence. When we pick up the story again, everything is as before, except that I am perspiring slightly and the contrite imp is the model of co-operation" (Stroud 2003: 168). Bartimaeus' direct intervention, at times playfully betraying his own vanity while simultaneously pricking the vanity of others, in telling the story ultimately unfolds the wider historical continuum. Nathaniel and Kitty are exempt from participation in writing the story, and chapters that are written from their perspectives are confined to the present or the brief past of their own lives. Bartimaeus' very personification within the text insinuates remnants of pastness into the book, for Bartimaeus' history stretches back, ruins exposed in his self-proclaimed epitaphs: "I have rebuilt the walls of Uruk, Karnak and Prague" (17).

Bartimaeus essentially conjures himself from the first words of the trilogy as a Gothic emblem, manifesting as "a yellow, choking cloud of brimstone, in which indistinct black shadows writhed and roiled" (15). That trace of brimstone leaves more than an unpleasant scent upon the book. Gordon proposes that "Gothic traces [...] become emblems of absence, of some secret contained within the historical, a hidden lineage of the past" (Gordon 2004: 71). It is not until the final volume of the series, *Ptolemy's Gate* (Stroud 2005), that the relevant hidden lineage is fully exposed. The djinni can appear in any form, suggesting that he has no ultimate form. He is simply a constant shifting and duplication of form and every time he is revealed, he is likewise concealed within the chosen guise. Bartimaeus' favourite form throughout has been that of a young Egyptian boy. It is this trace of the past that leads Kitty through a textual labyrinth, searching for the identity of that facsimile in books of all languages in libraries and magicians' houses, following the clues provided by the djinni's multiple names. Ironically, it is a footnote itself that reveals both Bartimaeus' identity and that of the boy whose form he most frequently emulates: "A footnote indeed!" (212).

The Egyptian boy was one of Bartimaeus' past masters, Ptolemy or Ptolemaeus. Ptolemy was the one magician to travel to the "Other Place," a place of essence where the spirits originate, and he leaves the story of his journey in a book. And so another text interposes with Stroud's, Ptolemaeus's *Apocrypha*.[19] Appropriately, the title itself indicates the dubious authenticity and origin of the text and Nathaniel himself calls it "a work of fiction" (364). Bartimaeus advises Kitty against seeking to emulate Ptolemy with a clear Gothic-inspired admonition: "Ptolemy's long gone, and the modern world is dark and complicated. You can't make a difference" (222). However, the *denouement* of Gothic is the vanishing of difference. Kitty's plan for the final revolution is to emulate Ptolemy's act herself and create cooperation between corporeal human and noncorporeal spirit, but there are barriers and Ptolemy's Gate forms the only known doorway for a human to pass through into the Other Place.

This is the difference that seems insurmountable, but as Gordon argues: "If the Gothic novel depends for its efficacy upon a structure of progressive impediments or successively graded *difference* which lures even as it impedes, a *difference* which narrative method, dwellings, and setting all seem to share, the heart of Gothic terror, the awful secret which lies behind the façades, is not differences, but its opposite, the disappearance of all differences" (2004: 62). Once Kitty has the key to the Greek text, she is able to utilise the secret formula, even though the meaning of the words themselves remains secret. In the Other Place, she becomes part of an essence where she has "no singularity to call her own" (Stroud 2005: 388). The "awful secret" is indeed the "disappearance of all differences," but this disappearance is also a suicidal act. Kitty survives passing through Ptolemy's Gate—just. She has, however, aged terribly on her return. Ptolemy and Nathaniel each, having transgressed the impediments to erase difference and combine their physical forms with Bartimaeus' spirit, dismiss Bartimaeus at the moment of corporeal death. Yet, even these suicidal acts fail to create closure.

The textual *denouement* remains unwritten. In the moment of Nathaniel's sacrifice, Bartimaeus failed "to get a word in edgeways" (515) and what he thinks of Nathaniel is never articulated in the concluding words, but 'inferred' by that erasure as "we were, to all intents and purposes, one and the same, I rather think he knew anyway" (515). However, Bartimaeus is potentially able to perpetuate the image of Nathaniel. Nathaniel is not destroyed, but becomes himself a fragment of Bartimaeus' memory, particularly evident in their also having inhabited the same corporeal form. Nathaniel will possibly "return" as one of Bartimaeus' many forms, eternally reproduced by spirit and text.

Children's literature is increasingly inhabited by such books, descendents of Romanticism that have re-imagined themselves the objects of romance and terror, repositories of the esoteric and sites of "ink-shifting" between the reader and the read. They are relics of the past duplicity of text and bound book in an Information Age of anxiety and disarray, offering myriad possibilities while simultaneously erasing difference.

ENDNOTES

1. For clarity and convenience, the trilogy is referred to as the *Ink* trilogy in this essay.
2. The adventures are named by Bartimaeus in a footnote.
3. Goldman ostensibly presents his *The Princess Bride* as an abridgement of Morgenstern's *The Princess Bride*, treating the invented nation of Florin and its famous author as real and even claiming it in his own heritage.
4. Of course, with e-books and hypertext, more and more books reveal their texts online, but the tradition of searching for a lost book retains its validity. As Walter Benjamin wrote in an essay on collecting books: "*Habent sua fata libelli*: these words may have been intended as a general statement about books. So books like *The Divine Comedy*, Spinoza's *Ethics*, and *The Origin of Species* have their fates. A collector, however, interprets this Latin saying differently. For him, not only books but also copies of books have their fates" (1968: 61). This analogy itself suggests the Gothic potential of books by the invocation of "fates." Benjamin goes on to compare the collection of books to a child's ability to "accomplish the renewal of existence in a hundred unfailing ways" (61), likewise reflecting that the actual attainment of a book lends to its prolongation and unfolding possibilities.
5. Ron gives a rundown of some of the more perilous books in *Harry Potter and the Chamber of Secrets*, including: "And some old witch in Bath had a book that you could *never stop reading*! You just had to wander around with your nose in it, trying to do everything one-handed" (1998: 172). This takes the interminability of text, perhaps, to the extreme.
6. Fred Botting writes, "Gothic atmospheres—gloomy and mysterious— have repeatedly signalled the disturbing return of pasts upon presents" (1996: 1). The majority of Rowling's books are set at Hogwarts, a school that was attended by Voldemort and later by Harry's own parents. When Harry comes to Hogwarts, the past is regularly conjured up to explain and impinge upon Harry's present, frequently troubling and even alarming.
7. Wizards and witches are generally afraid to speak Voldemort's name and resort to "You-Know-Who," again conspiring to conceal horror beneath an undistinguishable signifier.
8. To follow back the patrimony of the title even further, Capricorn is the villain after whom, presumably, the book is named because, in the words of Fenoglio, his "wicked heart is black as ink" (2003: 342). Fenoglio

displays affection for his "monstrous" creation, one itself steeped in Gothic criminality.

9. When the Inkworld's glass men are read into Mo's world, they shatter at the vibrations of lorries, a threat that didn't exist in the world in which they had been created, indicating that intertextuality is overtly treacherous if rendered corporeal (2003: 151). Thus Funke suggests the belief that people and objects are not necessarily better off in a text in which they don't belong, questioning the outcomes of intertextuality itself.

10. The English editions are entitled *Inkspell*, shifting the meaning towards the magic conjured from ink, rather than the more substantial embodiment of ink itself.

11. Funke herself engages in a form of ink-shifting, since, as Fenoglio models the Bluejay on Mo, Funke models Mo on the Hollywood actor, Brendan Fraser (see dedication of *Inkspell*).

12. With Fenoglio's words, too, Mo is able to bind a book of blank pages that makes another prince, the Adderhead, immortal once his name is inscribed therein. Continuing the analogy between words and life and death, the Adderhead remains immortal unless three specific words are likewise inscribed on the blank pages. The process of inscription is thus empowered to extend or end life within the text.

13. Goldman plays this sleight-of-ink with *The Princess Bride*, revealing that while his father always stopped reading from Morgenstern's source text with a happy ending, Goldman discovers that the source text continues, describing the characters being chased as they make their getaway, the text ending with the indefinite prolongation of inscribing "…", while Goldman's commentary provides simply one possibility of what happens next (1973: 317).

14. Of course, Gaarder himself remains, presumably, in control of his characters, but it is worth noting that when Sophie and Alberto break away from Albert Knag, they encounter the characters of other stories, stories not written by Gaarder.

15. Clarke's novel also exhibits "ink-shifting"; in this case, a famous book written by the Raven King has been consumed by a man, the man's son becoming the living embodiment of the book, gloriously tattooed with its words. The ink itself invades the corporeal flesh, establishing a textual patrimony in flesh and blood.

16. Gordon argues that the provision of "textual patrimony is practically an obsession of the Gothic mode" (2004: 60).

17. Goldman achieves a corresponding effect in *The Princess Bride*, by breaking into his abridgment with authorial commentary, often indicating the fragmentary nature of the text itself, as in his interruption of *Buttercup's Baby* in the anniversary edition: "*Guess what? It stops there. Bang, the little riff on happiness, end of section. I call this the 'Unexplained Inigo Fragment.'*" (1973: 365)

18. In *Ptolemy's Gate* (2005), even Bartimaeus' authority is challenged when he is summoned by Kitty and appears as a horned demon. Kitty's remarks on his "knobbly warts" and lack of clothing diminish the authorial terror of his form: "the towering demon shrank" textually (195).

19. The copy in *Ptolemy's Gate* is bound by Mr Hyrnek, whose son, Jakob, was Kitty's childhood friend and involved in the devastating incident that turned Kitty to rebellion. The background presence of Hyrnek's printing firm (Mr Hyrnek particularly noted for his exquisite binding of magic books) like Funke's ascription of the trade of book binder to Mo, remind the reader of the physical qualities of books as objects and the history of the craft of making books, even as books themselves become Gothic relics and communicators of the uncanny.

REFERENCES

Benjamin, W. (1968). Unpacking my library: A talk about book collecting. In Hannah Arendt (Ed.) & Harry Zohn (Trans.), *Illuminations* (pp. 59–67). New York: Schocken Books.

Botting, F. (1996). *Gothic*. London; New York: Routledge.

Clarke, S. (2004). *Jonathan Strange and Mr Norrell*. London: Bloomsbury.

Funke, C. (2003). *Inkheart*. Anthea Bell (Trans.). Frome, Somerset: The Chicken House.

———. (2005). *Inkspell*. Anthea Bell (Trans.). Frome, Somerset: The Chicken House.

Gaarder, J. [1991] (1996). *Sophie's World: A Novel about the History of Philosophy*. Paulette Møller (Trans.). London: Phoenix.

Goldman, W. [1973] (1999). *The Princess Bride*, 25th anniversary ed. London: Bloomsbury.

Gordon, J. B. (2004). *Narrative Enclosure as Textual Ruin: An Archaeology of Gothic Consciousness*. F. Botting & D. Townshend (Eds.), *Gothic: Critical Concepts in Literary and Cultural Studies (Vol 1)* (pp. 55–82). London; New York: Routledge.

Lynch, D. (2001). Gothic libraries and national subjects. *Studies in Romanticism, 40* (1), 29–48.

The Princess Bride. (1987). R. Reiner (Director). Los Angeles: MGM.

Punter, D. (2000). *Postcolonial Imaginings: Fictions of a New World Order*. Edinburgh: Edinburgh University Press.

Punter, D. & Byron, G. (2004). *The Gothic*. London: Blackwell Publishing.

Rowling, J. K. (1998). *Harry Potter and the Chamber of Secrets*. London: Bloomsbury.

Sedgwick, M. (2003). *The Book of Dead Days*. London: Orion.

———. (2004). *The Dark Flight Down*. London: Orion.

Smith, A. L. (1996). Postmodernism/Gothicism. In V. Sage & A. L. Smith (Eds.), *Modern Gothic: A Reader* (pp. 6–19). Manchester; New York: Manchester University Press.

Stephens, J. (1992). *Language and Ideology in Children's Fiction*. London; New York: Longman.

Stroud, J. (2003). *The Amulet of Samarkand: The Bartimaeus Trilogy*. London: Corgi Books.

———. (2004). *The Golem's Eye: The Bartimaeus Trilogy*. London: Doubleday.

———. (2005). *Ptolemy's Gate: The Bartimaeus Trilogy*. London: Doubleday.

13

THE NIGHT SIDE OF NATURE: GOTHIC SPACES, FEARFUL TIMES

Roderick McGillis

My interest here is in the Gothic as a form that pervades youth culture. But rather than list the many instances of the Gothic in works for the young—from picture books dealing with the Golem or with gargoyles or ghosts to YA books that mine the horror genre to films and video games that turn on our fears of things lurking in the dark—I am more interested in asking why a form that we might think inappropriate for young readers is so pervasive in the various forms of textuality produced for them. When I say "we might think," I must quickly add that I do not think the Gothic is inappropriate. However, it does deal with the lurid and the taboo. It unearths skeletons from the past and it raises fears for the future. It presents its reader with images and characters and themes we might think are too raw, too disturbing for young readers. Its themes include algolagnia, incest, desecration, blasphemy, and sado-masochism. Its two great themes, according to Patrick McGrath, are transgression and decay (1997: 154), and we might think of children's literature as a literature that promotes positive social behaviour and growth, rather than describing transgression and decay. Fragmentation and dissolution characterize the Gothic. This is a genre that seeks to disorient us.

In the Gothic, children may die and innocence may fall, tainted by infection growing from a bad seed. The Gothic is not, at least traditionally, a cheery genre. Human failure is possible in the Gothic. The Gothic world is decidedly not a pleasant place; it is ambiguous at best. It is not safe. The Gothic is the opposite of the pastoral. It thrives on darkness, deep forests, and dank city streets. It moves into ramshackle buildings, the older and bigger the better. Murkiness is the state of the Gothic. So much fog makes clear vision well nigh impossible in the Gothic world. In short, we might conclude that as a form of narrative that deals with questions of right and wrong, the Gothic teeters in the direction of wrong—even when the good guys win. Van Helsing may stake the Count in Bram Stoker's famous novel, *Dracula* (1896), but he does so only after Mina has tasted the blood of the vampire, and we have many retellings of the story that remind us just how piquant that taste is. The vampire has its attractive side, as Buffy well learned, and the monster always has its sympathetic side. Anne Rice has given us vampires who are more urbane, more sensitive, and more worthy of admiration than the rest of us shabby mortals.

Populating the Gothic are various monsters; the genre is something of a teratology, examining freakishness, otherness, abnormality, and deviance. Indeed, the Gothic gave us the post-human before we ever thought of genomes and cloning and other forms of altering the human form. Late eighteenth- and early nineteenth-century Gothic fiction gave us humans as automatons, as composite creatures, vampires, and werewolves. These various forms of "othered" humanity, of post-human being, continue to fascinate. The Gothic hero-villain is, by definition, both attractive and repulsive—a monster even as he exudes charisma. Characters in the Gothic must make hasty choices that turn out, more often than not, to be unwise choices. For example, when chased by a demon vehicle, a character chooses to run down the center of the road; or frightened by shadows and creaks in a cottage by the woods, a character will flee into the forest right into the clutches of the waiting monster; or hearing eerie sounds from a dank and dark basement, a character will descend into the darkness alone with only a candle's feeble flame or the narrow beam of a flashlight to guide the way.

Unwise choices may explain why the Gothic is a genre suited to stories about children and adolescents. One of the most famous Gothic stories presents us with a grown child, ostracized precisely because he does not conform to standards of beauty adults take for granted and precisely because he takes for granted that the world holds tolerance dear. Frankenstein's creation receives a bad education; he mistakenly thinks humanity has something to do with the concept "humane"; he naively chooses to trust the first people he meets; and he suffers accordingly. Another monster, the vampire, turns up in Gothic stories with great regularity, and he or she often serves an allegorical function, representing a rapaciousness worthy of late capitalist desire for production and consumption. We might recall Marx's observation that the "prolongation of the working day beyond the limits of the natural day, into the night…quenches only in a slight degree the vampire thirst for the living blood of labour" (1867: 185).

AN INTERROGATION OF THE GOTHIC NOW

Why are this form and this sensibility with us so insistently now? My answer is that we live in fearful times and the Gothic reflects fear and maybe even combats this fear in some strange way (see Edmundson 1997; Grunenberg 1997). The not-so-long ago fin de siecle was quickly followed by terrorism of an unprecedented kind that has spawned more horrific acts, so that knowing whom to trust has become a major difficulty for many of us. The electronic panopticon, the all-seeing technological eye, allows the private at any moment to become public. We are under scrutiny constantly. Paranoia pervades our culture (Grunenberg 1997: 168). Just about everything has become a potential danger, from insect bites to sunshine to the air we breathe to luggage left near a park bench. Even our chickens may threaten us. Our schools too have become scary places. Perhaps not every school sits atop the Hellmouth, but schools at every level have their bullies, their gangs, and students who wield their weapons of choice. The schoolyards, the streets, parks, and playgrounds of contemporary urban spaces are dangerous. They understandably may generate fear among the young. Even the space we think of as home may hold its dangers. We are in extreme times—triple XXX times. Paul Virilio sees this age of extremity and most notably of "extreme sciences" (especially in genetic research) as without value. He writes: "Thanks to the decryption of the map of the human genome, geneticists are now using cloning in the quest for the *chimera*, the hybridization of man and animal" (2000: 51). He sees on the horizon a monster, "born of the labour of a science deliberately deprived of a conscience" (50). The parcels of human flesh painted with ghoulish relish by Francis Bacon are perhaps as good a metonymy for what Virilio calls the "denatured" living being, as well as for what some of the extreme sciences can leave behind. The more recent work of Paul Thek, with its "assemblages of bloody chunks of meat in glass and steel cubes" (Grunenberg 1997: 167) carries similar import.

In other words, we live in a scary world. The blood-dimmed tide moves toward the shore, and the ceremony of innocence is drowned. We fear the rough beast. Of course human beings have always feared the rough beast and always lived in a scary world, but at certain times things get just a bit scarier: at the end of centuries, in times of war, in times of revolution, in times of rapid change. In such times, the Gothic finds purchase. It expresses fear even as it accepts fear as inevitable. The Gothic may express our helplessness in the face of global forces set on controlling the way we live. Or it may work to inure us to terrible things, to numb our reactions so that we take the daily tide of turmoil as natural. This aspect of Gothicism Mark Edmundson describes as "cynicism, timidity, fear of life" (1997: 67). But, as Edmundson also argues, the Gothic can have a "regenerative" function (6). Our obsession with things that go bump in the night need not result in what Virilio describes as "a pitiless art" (27) or in a silencing of the voices of silence (71). The art of the Gothic haunts us in order to elicit not only the scream or the gasp—sounds that signal a closing of reflection in the instant of fear—but also to elicit the shock that prompts desire for change. Like all fantasy, the Gothic is a manifestation of desire, only it demonstrates that our desire for what Lacan designates the "real" may be a desire that leads to disintegration. We need to look carefully at our fantasies; we need to consider carefully the world we want. At the very least, the Gothic confronts us with humanity's desire and this desire reflects thanatos as often as it reflects eros. McGrath argues that in the Gothic "a sort of death wish" is "implicit" (1997: 154). To tip the balance in favour of eros, the Gothic must find a way, as Edmundson has it, to have "the Gothic and the visionary or renewing drives confront each other directly" (1997: 6). Such direct confrontation occurs when the Gothic challenges our accepted orthodoxies, when the haunting works to revision our sense of things.

We can see a renovating Gothic in those works that situate the Gothic chronotope in sublime settings. The Alps where Frankenstein and his monster wander and the wind-swept northern icescape in the same novel, the estranging Borgo Pass and Carpathian Mountains that are home to Dracula, the labyrinthine ancient streets of decaying European cities, the haunting woods where Young Goodman Brown sees his townsfolk in a new light, even the long New Zealand beaches that Rose Lovell-Smith writes about elsewhere in this volume—all these are sublime expressions of Gothic's uncanny force. The sublime combines terror, pain, and power. It reminds us of the Real in its fearsome yet coherent unspeakability. The sublime allows for an articulate silence. It is humbling, and therefore expressive of what is human. When the sublime and the Gothic meet, the result is a landscape of extremes and a time that is revelatory. Reason cannot match the imaginative power of the sublime; reason can only fail to grasp desire's reach as expressed by Gothic's fantasy. We see how small we are. Grunenberg has it that "the Gothic sublime today reflects a hesitant and apprehensive state of mind obscured by deep fear of the unfamiliar future" (1997: 160), but I think it serves children's literature more positively. In this literature, the Gothic and its attendant images of the sublime may serve to dislocate the reader in ways that just might be formative rather than deformative.

Gothic appeals to the young for the same reason it appeals to the less young: it delivers characters who transgress. The Gothic hero is most often a villain who runs roughshod over conventions of piety and civilized restraint. This character has charisma. Gothic hero-villains impress us with their willingness to burn like hard gemlike flames. They burn right to the socket. They display their darkness without reserve; they wear their outlandishness on their sleeves. They invite our gaze while staring unblinkingly back at us. They unsettle us with their returned gaze. They position us to see the world awry. They remind us that freakishness just may be the human norm. Gothic hero-villains are us in our most unrepressed moments. They perform the polymorphous perverse we have necessarily repressed. They either clarify the need for control or satisfy vicariously desire's reach. Whatever other cultural service they render, Gothic fictions keep reminding us that we are haunted beings, plagued by frightening forces both inside our psyches and in the world out there where we play out our social selves. And our haunted condition need not render us helpless, running into the dark forests of the night or down dark highways.

Adolescents are, perhaps, as intensely haunted or even more haunted than the rest of us. Their bodies as well as their social milieu are in flux, changing as they—both body and social group—morph (or should I say grow?) into maturity. The pressures both within and without on the early adolescent bring trepidation and confusion. The body begins to manifest its thirst for satisfaction in ways that test social decorum, and the social group likewise begins to manifest its thirst for pleasure and control. Peer pressure and biological urgency haunt the growing person, even in the light of common day.

POPULAR GOTHIC AND M. T. ANDERSON'S *THIRSTY*

Mark Edmundson contends that popular Gothic today "breeds fear and anger, shuts down the power to make humane distinctions, eclipses thought" (1997: 61). Edmundson sees the culture of Gothic in which we live as largely complicit with the forces of dullness. He goes so far as to connect the culture of Gothic today with the failure of "benevolent religion" to convince us "to believe in God's presence" (67). Instead, Edmundson believes, many people have "turned from hope in benevolent religion to fascination with the Gothic" (67). He seems to take for granted that the Gothic presents a world "infested with evil," a world in which "all power is corrupt, all humanity debased, and that there is nothing we can do about it" (67–68). For Edmundson, the Gothic presents us with justification for paralysis, for political inertia. The world is a cesspool, and so we had best get used to it. Without a Higher Power to which we can look for guidance, we are left with "Gothic despair for life's meaning" (68).

In his sweeping look at the contemporary culture of films and talk shows and high profile trials and news media interested in sensation, Edmundson makes a compelling case. However, aside from his interest in Wes Craven's *Nightmare on Elm Street* films, he does not take much time to look at youth culture. Had he looked at the Gothic in books and films for the young, he might have come to rather different conclusions than the ones I highlight. If I take here just one example, the TV programme *Buffy the Vampire Slayer* (1997–2003), what we have is a vision of high school that is as fresh as anything Edmundson could wish for. Buffy and her friends triumph because they do care, and they do believe in forging a human community. At the end of the series Sunnydale may disappear into an apocalyptic hole in the ground, but most of the main characters are set to begin new lives, more hopeful lives. Sunnydale was never that sunny anyway. More recently, the British film, *Shaun of the Dead* (2004) makes a similar gesture to the one we had in *Buffy*. The monsters turn out to be precisely those people we thought were paragons of normalcy, and the geeks and freaks and blondes and ditzy ones are the concerned, so concerned, in *Buffy* at least, that they will turn to research to save the world from Armageddon. In the Gothic we are in the territory of teratology, and today's Gothic just may suggest that we find the real monsters in positions of influence and power. And it may also suggest that we are not helpless in the face of such influence and power. The Gothic presents its characters with choice—the choice between right and wrong.

In my argument for the Gothic's strengths as a challenge to homogeneity and to the horrors we face daily, I focus not on *Buffy* or on *Shaun*, but on the novel *Thirsty* (1997) by M. T. Anderson. As the book cover notes, all the main character, Chris, wants is to be normal, but for some strange reason, he seems to be turning into a vampire. How does he deal with this transformation into a predator? How does he accommodate his increasing "thirst"? And just what is this "thirst" that holds him in sway? Obviously, Anderson makes a direct correlation between Chris's emerging vampirism and the changes that take place in puberty. (A similar Gothicizing of puberty takes place in the Canadian film *Ginger Snaps*, 2000.) He finds himself changing, and he struggles to understand and control these changes. One of the clever moments in a book filled with clever moments combines Chris masturbatory activity with the vampire's penchant for algolagnia. It is 3:52 A.M., and Chris is awake, hot and thirsty. He goes to the bathroom, and there he takes a long look at his forearm. Here is his reaction to this tasty bit of flesh:

> At the sight of my smooth white skin, fine as cream, I start to salivate. I trace the little blue veins from the wrist up to the plumper muscle.
>
> I lower my mouth. My open lips just nuzzle my forearm.
>
> The points of my canines touch the bare skin. My canines seem larger than usual. My saliva is thick.
>
> Helplessly, I pierce the skin; and helplessly, I start drawing and sucking as ferociously as I can, yanking blood up into my mouth. The pain jolts my elbow up and down, while I feel the blessed blood murmuring over my lips, my chin, down—in the most tantalizing trickle—my throat, a few drops, a spot, more; and I tear at my arm and slash downward with the teeth, rutting up little tracks of meat while the thick, sour tang of my own gore sweetly fills my mouth and cheeks, puffing them out. It hurts like the devil, and I'm moaning, lost in pain and wonder, but now I hack a little more at my arm with the same pleasure I'd peel a scab, so the pain is bigger, harder, cleaner, more burning, more scathing, more cleansing. (Anderson 1997: 136)

This passage is grisly. And funny. Vampire onanism is not something we contemplate every day. When we recall that young Chris wears orthodontic braces and that his enlarged canines bend and dislocate these braces, we are reminded that this young boy is frantic to satisfy his raging hormones. An hour after the moment described in the passage, Chris lays drowsily in bed, his pajamas "twisted all around me" and his braces "just one big loopy tangle" (137). For this boy, puberty comes in with a bang rather than a whimper.

And so humour is one of the ingredients of a Gothic that typifies young adult and children's fiction. Anderson's book has a style and distance from its material that draws attention to form. Form serves to set the Gothic trappings in tension with an imaginative energy that posits the narrative itself as a more productive ritual than the rituals we may find enacted in Gothic plots. In *Thirsty*, the Sad Festival of Vampires and the ritual of interruption that the vampires intend to perform are reminders of a carnival that does not so much level and liberate as it uncovers. What the carnival associated with the Sad Festival of Vampires uncovers is the idiocy of rituals implicated in a capitalist environment (one of the traditional sites for the ritual enacted during the Sad Festival now has a White Hen Pantry and a Texaco station standing where the ritual takes place). It also uncovers the bestial behaviour of human beings. Chris and his friend Rebecca run through the Festival crowds, and Chris notes:

> People are wolfing down fried dough. People are prowling in packs. A child is screaming by the moon-walk, "My arm is broke! My arm is broke!" People are shoving and grabbing
>
> Lights spin over us. There's screaming all round. And above it all, voices booming out over the gruesome disco from the merry-go-round, "We damn him in his thought. We damn him in his speech. We damn him in his being. Our hate is ranged against him."
>
> The crowds push; people sing; someone barfs behind a tent. His back heaves again and again, as if it's being wrung.
>
> "A hot dog! A hot dog! I wanna hot dog!" yowls a child dragging a bear by the ear, but her parents are lost in the crowd. (211–212)

As often in the Gothic, human crowds that jostle and tussle are unpleasant reminders of the madness of crowd activity. References to wolves and packs and yowling and anger remind us that vampires are not the only predators in the world this novel depicts. Further, the regular lynching of vampires cannot but remind us of the history of vigilante style executions dating at least from the seventeenth-century witch trials to more recent racially motivated hangings.

What I am describing is heady stuff for a humorous adolescent novel. But the humour is crucial. It makes tolerable the ugly implications of what goes on in Chris's world, and it reminds us of the space between the narrator, Chris, and an implied author who masters these revels. The opening paragraph nicely opens a space between narrator and implied author.

> In the spring, there are vampires in the wind. People see them scuffling along by the side of country roads. At night they move through the empty forests. They do not wear black, of course, but things they have taken off bodies or bought on sale. The news says that they are mostly in the western part of the state, where it is lonely and rural. My father claims that we have them this year because it was a mild winter, but he may be thinking of tent caterpillars. (8)

The voice here is ostensibly that of a young male; we know this because he speaks of his father in something of a dismissive tone. We learn later that he is a pubescent male. He is also an articulate young person. The phrase "in the wind" echoes both the Bible and Browning (1 Kings 19:11; "The Last Ride Together, stanza 4),[1] and it balances the opening "In the spring," effectively forming a frame for "there are vampires." The word "scuffling" evokes leaves or perhaps shambling and broken persons. The connection between nature and vampires is clear, and it is again when the narrator says his father may be thinking of tent caterpillars. Vampires come in with the wind, like insects. The tent caterpillars bring a note of levity that we see a bit earlier when the narrator notes that, contrary to common knowledge, vampires do not wear black; they wear hand-me-downs or they buy their cheap duds on sale. Vampires are not middle class. The ironic nod to the reader's knowledge of vampire tradition, and the tweaking of this tradition opens the space between narrative voice and another wry voice I here identify as the implied author.

The wry tone, or what I will call the ironic tone, stays with us throughout the novel. The Gothic is an ironic form in the sense that it delivers a brazen world, a world haunted by misdeeds, unconventional desire, overreaching, and just plain nastiness. In this world, clouds cover the moon, and when they break shadows keep us guessing. In *Thirsty*, we have a character who stage-manages the guessing. The same character is this book's Gothic hero-villain, the laconic Celestial Being who calls himself Chet because his actual name is "nonverbal," a mere "pattern of thought" (50). K. A. Nuzum calls Chet a "secondary character" who takes on the "role of elder, a common figure in rites of passage in traditional societies" (2004: 215). Okay, but Chet, it turns out, is not interested in guiding a neophyte to a mature understanding. Chris may gain understanding in the novel, but his gaining of understanding is not Chet's motivation for acting as he acts. He acts for purely selfish motives. And from the point of view of Gothicism, he is hardly a "secondary character."

Chet is insouciance personified. He arrives to solicit Chris's help in defeating the Vampire Lord, Tch'muchgar. He convinces Chris to accept a mission impossible, to take something called the Arm of Moriator into Tch'muchgar's world and thereby either keep the Vampire Lord imprisoned in that world or terminate him. Chet is a good talker, a natural salesman; he tells Chris that he will cure the growing boy's vampirism if he accepts the mission Chet has for him. Chris believes that this Celestial Being is "an avatar of the Forces of Light" and together he and Chris can defeat the Forces of Darkness (Anderson 1997: 42).

Near the end of the book, once Chris has accomplished his quest and taken the Arm of Moriator to Tch'muchgar's dimension, Chris returns to his own world to find Chet "tapping on his knees" what sounds distinctly like: "I've got rhythm, I've got music, I've got my girl, who could ask for anything more?" (228). Chris is, for a moment, relieved, "more relieved than a very relieved thing from Planet Phew" (229). However, his relief is short-lived.

Chris soon learns that Chet is not quite trustworthy; he is other than he says he is. He does not work for the Forces of Light; he works for the Forces of Darkness, only "on a freelance basis" (230). He is a "double agent"; he might even be, as he says, "a triple agent" (229). In other words, he works for himself. His only interest is in his own well being. He is a murky combination of Mephistopheles and a used-car salesman. He has duped poor Chris, whom he refers to as "an incompetent: self-pitying; self-absorbed; self-centered. The perfect teen" (236). Chris is, Chet says, "a complete peckerhead" (236). When Chris naively asks why Chet has lied, Chet responds: "I'm *supposed* to lie. I lie, cheat, kill, make people unhappy, and draw an enormous wage" (232). Chris clearly has not learned the Gothic conventions, and the result is, as Chet says, in his inimitable way: "'You know what, Christopher? You're screwed. Well, I'm going now'" (234). And so Chet, the Celestial Being, leaves poor Chris to his fate: to grow into a vampire and die young at the hands of his social group who are as friendly as the people in Shirley Jackson's story, "The Lottery," on the day of the lottery.

But remember the ironist tone of this story. Sure Chris is fated to become a vampire, but he is not fated to be a sign of the inevitable victory of what the book terms the Forces of Darkness. Chris hides in his room; he refuses to do what so many adolescents do in fiction: run. Instead, he lurks in his room reflecting on what is in store for him, and concluding that he loves the very human beings that he is now fated to prey on. He loves them "because they are so fragile" and "because I am no longer one of them" (247). Early in the book, Chris's mother remarks that vampires are not "even human," and Chris wonders what "would she do, my mother, if she found out a son of hers was not human" (80). In other words, what would this woman do if she found out her son was not what she expected him to be? (Later in the novel, the connection between vampirism and homosexuality is explicit when one of the vampires asks Chris: "You gonna come out of the coffin?" [202].) Clearly, Chris learns what his mother has not learned; he learns to love the "other," to love that which is other than him. And in learning this difficult lesson, Chris knows that he cannot perform the vampire act. As he says, he realizes "that the decision to be human is not one single instant, but is a thousand choices made every second and requires constant vigilance. We have to fight to remain human" (248). As the narrative closes, Chris huddles behind his bedroom door, feeling the thirst that now consumes him.

One of the clever things in this book is the connection between the vampire's thirst and his lack of reflection. When the thirst is on Chris, he cannot see himself reflected in water or in a mirror or in any reflecting surface. Consequently, he becomes "obsessed with my reflection" (60). He is, he says, "proud of my reflection," that is until he notices that his "hair is lanky and hangs down….My eyes look sunken and dark and my features look haggard and ugly" (61). He has the teenager's concern with appearance, but more than this he has anyone's concern with his very existence. When the thirst is upon him and his reflection disappears, he knows the vampire self is taking hold. He is losing his sense of being a normal human being. He is entering a zone of non-being, of absence, of existence without a sense of otherness. Why this is so scary is simply because without a reflection, we are back before self-consciousness, before our awareness that others exist and that we too are other than what we wish to be. Chris is constantly indulging in fantasies in which he has success with the girl he admires, Rebecca Schwartz. But these fantasies are only possible in a world that has reflection. Without reflection, we are alone and empty. Chris finds himself "all alone." He blames Chet for his situation, a situation in which "I can't speak to anyone, can't tell anyone; and the thing I want to tell them most, the thing I need to say to them, is just that: that I can't speak, and that I'm all alone; and how can you tell people you're all alone when you're all alone?" (153). Like his author, he is empty.

If we read *Thirsty* with religion in mind, and the book draws attention to religion in its use of the abandoned church for the vampire ritual and in its focus on the human's Sad Festival of Vampires, and in the Manichean struggle between Forces of Light and Forces of Dark and so on, then we must conclude that Chris's world is a godless world. Traditionally, or at least in the Bram Stoker brand of vampire story, the battle between vampire and human is a battle for the human soul, and usually the humans manage to stem the tide of vampires lead by an anti-Christ such as Dracula. In *Thirsty*, however, things are confused because the Gothic hero-villain does not side with either the Forces of Light or the Forces of Darkness. He is a lone wolf, so to speak, out for himself. He's a good capitalist looking to sell his services to the highest bidder. He manages to find gainful employment and to ignore the terrible goings-on in the world: "starvation, and fighting in the Middle East, and senators talking about the national debt" and "those other stories about the mobs, the lynchings, all over America" (138). At the end of the book, Chris is left with nothing but his fight to remain connected to humanity.

From a psychoanalytic perspective, the book gives us a character who confronts the Real, that amorphous and threatening and murky pre-reflective condition. Chris faces the agony of discovering that he is that which he wants not to be; he is a non-being in the human community. He is, in other words, a thing that cannot be integrated into common reality. Instead, he experiences Reality, that Lacanian pre-verbal, pre-other state we want to find satisfying but we discover as what Žižek calls "*a nightmarish apparition*" (2002: 19; italics in original). Chris finds himself on the cusp of a new condition, one that is for most human beings a condition of not being, excluded from the human community because his canine teeth are pointy beyond what others deem safe. He is, perhaps, homo sucker, to adapt an expression I find in Žižek's work (83). He is a sucker for believing Chet's spiel about saving the world from Tch'muchgar. He is a sucker for the romantic fantasies his culture had fed him and which fill his personal fantasies. He is a sucker because he is a vampire. He is a sucker because he has no reflection. Having no reflection and desiring to have one, he has one recourse: to focus his fantasies on himself, to find pleasure in himself, to consume himself. He is a self-consuming artefact, left at the book's end crouching behind a door, beseeching a lower case "god," and moaning, "I...am...so...thirsty" (Anderson 1997: 249). These are the final words of the novel, and they leave us with the vision of desire.

Desire remains. It can do nothing else but remain, active, pulsing, infuriating, motivating, and replicating in dreams. And so I return to Mark Edmundson who notes that "Gothic is the art of haunting, and in two senses" (1997: 5). First, the Gothic reminds us that, as Edmundson puts it, life is possessed and "All are guilty" (5). No one escapes unscathed. Second, the Gothic compels its audience to repeat the experience. We read and reread but cannot escape what Chris Baldick describes as "an impression of sickening descent into distintegration" (1993: xix; qtd in Edmundson 5). Disintegration seems to be the way *Thirsty* closes. However, we have seen that Chris resolves to continue "the fight to remain human." We must read this as a fight to remain connected to friends and family even as we know that friends and family are masticating animals: Chris's improved vampire senses allow him to hear his family chewing their evening meal: what he hears he describes as a "factory of noises, the squelching and popping, crunching and scratching" (Anderson 1997: 71). He calls his family's eating "grotesque" (71). Not many pages later, he attends a vampire meeting at which a table is laid for the evening repast. A "middle-aged lady dressed in cornflower blue rayon slacks" invites Chris to take food. "Would you like some of Jennifer or Dave," she asks? "Jennifer Carreiras, fifteen of Haverhill, or Dave Philips, fifty-three of Springfield. Dave has a broccoli garnish, and Jenn has Doris Blum's special cornflakes crust—lots of crunchy bits" (122). Vampires, like humans, dress their food for appearance as well as taste. They are carnivores, but they like a bit of green to set the meal off.

Chris learns he must attempt the impossible: to quell desire. The task is impossible, but unless he confronts the face that is not in the mirror, unless he remembers the good, bad and ugly of human action he is doomed to be like those he comes to revile. What is left once we see humans and vampires as equally rapacious? Well perhaps this is where Jerk comes in. Jerk is one of Chris's two friends. The other one is Tom. Jerk is the hanger-on, the one who has the belittling nickname and who does not seem to understand that it is belittling. Jerk is the reliable one who wants only to hang out with his two friends and get along. He is accommodating, friendly, and a bit dull. At the end of the novel, when Chris finds himself alone and facing a vampire future, Jerk phones and shows his concern for Chris. Chris treats him badly, telling Jerk that, "your only friend is your stupid dog. Your dog is so stupid," and he compares the dog to a girlfriend, although the dog, he says, "will have less chest hair" (244). Jerk hangs up, and Chris realizes just who the real jerk is. The phone call immediately precedes Chris's descent into loneliness and possible disintegration. And we might conclude that Jerk's call and Chris's reaction to it are important in Chris's understanding that the choices we make every second are what matter. Jerk is the unassuming friend, faithful as a dog. Chris learns the value of such a friend.

K. A. Nuzum reads *Thirsty* as an exercise in "mythic" literature. The struggle is between a mythic time that removes one from the flux of history and places one in a liminal space that is outside history. The novel ends, Nuzum points out, with Chris "completely isolated from linear time, from human companionship, from human existence" (2004: 217). True, Chris is alone, isolated, and fearful as the novel comes to a close; however, I am less certain that this condition of loneliness places Chris outside of linear time. The mythic trappings in this novel—Tch'muchgar, the Celestial beings who haunt Chris—are just that: trappings. They deflect us from seeing Chris's real problem as a human problem, and seeing the vampires as aspects of humanity. The book performs a demythicizing of monsters. Chris's trip to Tch'muchgar's dimension with the Arm of Moriator results in the end of Tch'muchgar's existence.

He's dead. The vampires are now Nietzschean creatures, like humans, without their god.

The trauma this book confronts is the trauma of life without direction, only choices every second for which we have no transcendent guidance. This is what Chet has brought the vampires, making them belated creatures, lagging behind humans in their isolation and desire. This vision of a world without end, and without anything but the ongoing working of desire, is not mythic. It is decidedly historic. It is the world we face every day with its mob violence and socially sanctioned killings and predatory activity and senators discussing the national debt. The only difference between humans and vampires is that vampires are perceived by humans to be outside humanity; they are akin to homo sacer, those who are exiled from community, outside the polity and dispensable. Humans can kill vampires with impunity.

This funny book offers a damning picture of humanity. In Chris's world, "everything is falling apart" (160), but unlike the world depicted in Yeats' famous poem, no rough beast slouches towards anywhere to be born. The only rough beast in Chris's world is humanity itself, and its other—the vampires. As in the passage from 1 Kings invoked in the book's first sentence, the Lord is not in the wind or in the earthquake or in the fire. But after fire, a still small voice sounds condemning the recalcitrant and the unbelieving. That voice too is absent from Chris's world, although we have the implied author managing things so that we understand that hope sits huddled in a still small space, a space haunted by desire and just desire.

ENDNOTE

1. The passages from 1 Kings and from Browning are:

> But the Lord was not in the wind: and after the wind an earthquake; but the Lord was not in the earthquake...

(1 Kings 19:11)

My soul

Smoothed itself out, a long-cramped scroll

Freshening and fluttering in the wind.

(Robert Browning 1855)

REFERENCES

Anderson, M. T. (1997). *Thirsty.* Cambridge, MA: Candlewick Press.

Baldick, C. (Ed.). (1993). *The Oxford Book of Gothic Tales.* Oxford: Oxford University Press.

Edmundson, M. (1997). *Nightmare on Main Street: Angels, Sadomasochism and the Culture of Gothic.* Cambridge, MA; London: Harvard University Press.

Grunenberg, C. (Ed.). (1997). *Gothic: Transmutations of Horror in Late Twentieth-Century Art.* Cambridge, MA: MIT Press.

Jackson, S. (1948). The lottery. *New Yorker,* June 28.

Marx, K. [1867] (1970). *Das Capital: a Critique of Political Economy.* F. Engels (Ed.) & condensed by S. L. Levitsky. Chicago: Gateway Editions.

McGrath, P. (1997). Transgression and decay. In C. Grunenberg (Ed.), *Gothic: Transmutations of Horror in Late Twentieth Century Art* (pp. 153–158). Cambridge, MA: MIT Press.

Nuzum, K. A. (2004). The monster's sacrifice—historic time: The uses of mythic and liminal time in monster literature. *Children's Literature Association Quarterly, 29,* 206–227.

Virilio, P. [2000] (2003). *Art and Fear.* London; New York: Continuum.

Žižek, Slavoj. (2002). *Welcome to the Desert of the Real.* London; New York: Verso.

CONTRIBUTORS

Karen Coats is Associate Professor of English at Illinois State University. She is the author of *Looking Glasses and Neverlands: Lacan, Desire, and Subjectivity in Children's Literature* (University of Iowa Press, 2004).

Nadia Crandall holds an MA in English Literature from Oxford University and an MA in Children's Literature from Roehampton University. She has contributed to the OUP Encyclopaedia of Children's Literature; is co-chair of the Children's Book Circle; and has won prizes for her fiction. Publications include work on the illustrations of William Blake and on film adaptations of contemporary fairytales, as well as a series of articles on the children's book business in the United Kingdom. Nadia is developing a PhD proposal which looks at the way new technologies alter our construct of narrative.

Julie Cross is completing her PhD thesis "The Subliminal and the Ridiculous: Children, Humour and Society in 'Funny' Junior Fiction in Britain, 1960 Onwards" at Roehampton University, London. She has published work on didacticism in humorous children's literature, and also gendered forms of humour.

June Cummins is an Associate Professor in the Department of English and Comparative Literature at San Diego State University, where she specializes in children's literature. Her research interests include feminism and female development, ethnic and national identities, and the marketing and commodification of children's literature. Many of these interests play significant roles in the biography she is currently writing of Jewish-American author Sydney Taylor.

Anna Jackson lectures in children's fantasy, contemporary fiction, and the American Gothic at Victoria University of Wellington. Research interests include representations of Sylvia Plath, young adult fantasy fiction, and ghosts in children's literature. Her most recent book of poetry, *The Gas Leak* (Auckland University Press, 2006) includes both Gothic and young adult elements.

Rose Lovell-Smith is a Senior Lecturer in the English Department, University of Auckland, where she teaches a Stage 2 course called Children's Literature: Words and Pictures. Her teaching and research interests include nineteenth-century fiction, feminist writing and women's fiction, oral literature and the fairytale, and women's rewriting of fairytales. She is currently working on a historical study of the illustrated book for older children; and has published recently on Tenniel's illustrations and the natural history connections in Carroll's *Alice* books.

Roderick McGillis is Professor of English at the University of Calgary.

Alice Mills is Associate Professor of literature and children's literature at the University of Ballarat. She has published widely as a critic of fantasy and children's literature. She has edited several anthologies of literature for children and books of essays on the grotesque and the unspeakable. Her most recent book is *Stuckness in the Fiction of Mervyn Peake* (Rodopi, 2005).

Rebecca-Anne C. Do Rozario teaches fantasy and children's literature at Monash University. Her recent publications have concerned children's animation, fairytales, and fantasy.

Karen Sands-O'Connor is Associate Professor and MA coordinator for English at Buffalo State College in New York. She has been widely published on topics ranging from science fiction to Louisa May Alcott, but her most recent works have concerned racial issues in children's literature. Her most recent book is *Soon Come Home This Island: The West Indian in British Children's Literature* (Routledge, 2007).

Anna Smith teaches children's literature, postcolonial writing, and American texts on the supernatural at Canterbury University, New Zealand. Her publications include work on Julia Kristeva, New Zealand women writers and artists, and children's literature. Most recently she has completed a novel, *Politics 101* for Canterbury University Press.

Laurie N. Taylor researches video games and digital media at the University of Florida. Her articles have appeared in *Game Studies*,

Computers and Composition Online, and *Works & Days*. Her current research includes a book-length project on the Gothic in video games.

Dale Townshend is a Lecturer in the Department of English Studies at the University of Stirling, where he teaches on the MLitt in the Gothic Imagination. He is the author of *The Orders of Gothic: Foucault, Lacan, and the Subject of Gothic Writing, 1764–1820* (AMS, 2006); and has co-edited, with Fred Botting, four volumes in the *Gothic: Critical Concepts in Literary and Cultural Studies* series (Routledge, 2004). He is currently co-editing, with John Drakakis, a collection of essays entitled *Gothic Shakespeares* (Routledge, forthcoming).

INDEX